Economic Patriotism in Open Economies

The recent financial crisis has demonstrated more than ever that governments seek to steer their economies rather than surrendering to the free play of market forces. Despite the ambitions of international economic cooperation, such interventionism is decidedly local. Some politicians even proudly evoke "economic patriotism" to justify their choices.

This volume links this phenomenon to a specific set of tensions between economic and political boundaries – the paradox of neo-liberal democracy – and argues that political interventionism in open markets is ubiquitous. The mandate of politicians is to defend the economic interests of their constituents under conditions where large parts of economic governance are no longer exclusively within their control. Economic patriotism is one possible reaction to this tension. As old-style industrial policy and interventionism gained a bad reputation, governments had to become creative to assure traditional economic policy objectives with new means.

However, economic patriotism is more than just a fashionable word or a fig leaf for protectionism. This volume employs the term to signal two distinctions: the diversity of policy content and the multiplicity of territorial units it can refer to. Comparing economic interventionism across countries and sectors, it becomes clear that economic liberalism will always be accompanied by counter-movements that appeal to territorial images.

This book was published as a special issue of the *Journal of European Public Policy.*

Ben Clift is Associate Professor of Political Economy in the Department of Politics and International Studies at the University of Warwick.

Cornelia Woll is Associate Research Professor at Sciences Po and co-directs the Max Planck Sciences Po Center in Paris.

Journal of European Public Policy Series
Series Editor: Jeremy Richardson is a Professor at Nuffield College, Oxford University

This series seeks to bring together some of the finest edited works on European Public Policy. Reprinting from Special Issues of the *Journal of European Public Policy*, the focus is on using a wide range of social sciences approaches, both qualitative and quantitative, to gain a comprehensive and definitive understanding of Public Policy in Europe.

Towards a Federal Europe
Edited by Alexander H. Trechsel

The Disparity of European Integration
Edited by Tanja A. Börzel

Cross-National Policy Convergence:
Causes Concepts and Empirical Findings
Edited by Christoph Knill

Civilian or Military Power?
European Foreign Policy in Perspective
Edited by Helene Sjursen

The European Union and New Trade Politics
Edited by John Peterson and Alasdair R. Young

Comparative Studies of Policy Agendas
Edited by Frank R. Baumgartner, Christoffer Green-Pedersen and Bryan D. Jones

The Constitutionalization of the European Union
Edited by Berthold Rittberger and Frank Schimmelfenig

Empirical and Theoretical Studies in EU Lobbying
Edited by David Coen

Mutual Recognition as a New Mode of Governance
Edited by Susanne K. Schmidt

France and the European Union
Edited by Emiliano Grossman

Immigration and Integration Policy in Europe
Edited by Tim Bale

Reforming the European Commission
Edited by Michael W. Bauer

International Influence Beyond Conditionality
Postcommunist Europe after EU enlargement
Edited by Rachel A. Epstein and Ulrich Sedelmeier

The Role of Political Parties in the European Union
Edited by Björn Lindberg, Anne Rasmussen and Andreas Warntjen

EU External Governance
Projecting EU Rules beyond Membership
Edited by Sandra Lavenex and Frank Schimmelfennig

EMU and Political Science
What Have We Learned?
Edited by Henrik Enderlein and Amy Verdun

Learning and Governance in the EU Policy Making Process
Edited by Anthony R. Zito

Political Representation and EU Governance
Edited by Peter Mair and Jacques Thomassen

Europe and the Management of Globalization
Edited by Wade Jacoby and Sophie Meunier

Negotiation Theory and the EU
The State of the Art
Edited by Andreas Dür, Gemma Mateo and Daniel C. Thomas

The Political Economy of Europe's Incomplete Single Market
Edited by David Howarth and Tal Sadeh

The European Union's Foreign Economic Policies
A Principal-Agent Perspective
Edited by Andreas Dür and Michael Elsig

The Politics of the Lisbon Agenda
Governance Architectures and Domestic Usages of Europe
Edited by Susana Borrás and Claudio M. Radaelli

Agency Governance in the European Union
Edited by Berthold Rittberger and Arndt Wonka

The EU Timescape
Edited by Klaus H. Goetz and Jan-Hinrik Meyer-Sahling

The EU's Common Foreign and Security Policy
Edited by *Helene Sjursen*

Economic Patriotism in Open Economies
Edited by Ben Clift and Cornelia Woll

The Power of the European Court of Justice
Edited by Susanne K. Schmidt and R. Daniel Kelemen

Economic Patriotism in Open Economies

Edited by
Ben Clift and Cornelia Woll

Routledge
Taylor & Francis Group
LONDON AND NEW YORK

First published 2013
by Routledge
2 Park Square, Milton Park, Abingdon, Oxon, OX14 4RN

Simultaneously published in the USA and Canada
by Routledge
711 Third Avenue, New York, NY 10017

Routledge is an imprint of the Taylor & Francis Group, an informa business

This book is a reproduction of *Journal of European Public Policy*, vol. 19, issue 3. The Publisher requests to those authors who may be citing this book to state, also, the bibliographical details of the special issue on which the book was based.

British Library Cataloguing in Publication Data
A catalogue record for this book is available from the British Library

ISBN13: 978-0-415-62474-9

Typeset in Times New Roman
by Taylor & Francis Books

Publisher's Note
The publisher would like to make readers aware that the chapters in this book may be referred to as articles as they are identical to the articles published in the special issue. The publisher accepts responsibility for any inconsistencies that may have arisen in the course of preparing this volume for print.

Contents

Citation Information

The chapters in this book were originally published in the *Journal of European Public Policy*, volume 19, issue 3 (April 2012). When citing this material, please use the original page numbering for each article, as follows:

Chapter 1
Economic patriotism: reinventing control over open markets
Ben Clift and Cornelia Woll
Journal of European Public Policy, volume 19, issue 3 (April 2012) pp. 307-323

Chapter 2
Supranational governance as economic patriotism? The European Union, legitimacy and the reconstruction of state space
Ben Rosamond
Journal of European Public Policy, volume 19, issue 3 (April 2012) pp. 324-341

Chapter 3
From nationalism to European patriotism? Trade unions and the European works council at General Motors
Thomas Fetzer
Journal of European Public Policy, volume 19, issue 3 (April 2012) pp. 342-357

Chapter 4
Homespun capital: economic patriotism and housing finance under stress
Leonard Seabrooke
Journal of European Public Policy, volume 19, issue 3 (April 2012) pp. 358-372

Chapter 5
Supporting the City: economic patriotism in financial markets
Glenn Morgan
Journal of European Public Policy, volume 19, issue 3 (April 2012) pp. 373-387

Chapter 6
The phantom of Palais Brongniart: economic patriotism and the Paris Stock Exchange
Helen Callaghan and Paul Lagneau-Ymonet
Journal of European Public Policy, volume 19, issue 3 (April 2012) pp. 388-404

Chapter 7
Cities as national champions?
Colin Crouch and Patrick Le Galès
Journal of European Public Policy, volume 19, issue 3 (April 2012) pp. 405-419

Chapter 8
Economic patriotism in European agriculture
Wyn Grant
Journal of European Public Policy, volume 19, issue 3 (April 2012) pp. 420-434

Chapter 9
European armament co-operation and the renewal of industrial policy motives
Catherine Hoeffler
Journal of European Public Policy, volume 19, issue 3 (April 2012) pp. 435-451

Economic patriotism: reinventing control over open markets

Ben Clift and Cornelia Woll

ABSTRACT We analyse how tensions between international market integration and spatially limited political mandates have led to the phenomenon of economic patriotism. As discrimination in favour of insiders, economic patriotism goes beyond economic nationalism and can include territorial allegiances at the supranational or the local level. We show how this prism helps to understand the evolution of political intervention in open economies and present the ambition of this collection.

INTRODUCTION

When the financial crisis hit in 2008, the only thing more striking than the vertiginous hikes in public expenditure was the enormous range and scope of new interventionism. After decades of triumphant neo-liberalism, and policy-makers embracing self-regulating markets, suddenly the co-ordinates of economic policy rectitude were thrown into flux. The credit crunch brought the tensions within liberal international economic governance into sharp focus. Long-buried measures reappeared in political toolkits.

Some of this political intervention was entirely novel. Governments were intervening to stimulate consumption, prop up credit markets and prevent the failure of the international financial system, including pursuing unprecedented monetary expansions through untried 'quantitative easing' techniques. States were taking on huge amounts of debt, publicly funding private financial institutions, dictating new rules for executive pay and even nationalizing banks. Very sizable state aid packages supported not only major financial institutions but also struggling major automobile producers. These national rescue packages, bank recapitalizations and selective industry bailouts generate frictions between governments and liberal competition authorities.

What has happened to the long-standing consensus on minimal government intervention and the benefits of liberal markets? In the 1990s, authors from very different backgrounds all pointed out the apparently unstoppable rise of economic imperatives, heralding the demise of politics (e.g., Friedman 2005; Wallach and Sforza 1999; Yergin and Stanislaw 1999). Supranational institutions such as the European competition authorities or the World Trade Organization's (WTO) Dispute Settlement Body seemingly assured the continuous integration of markets. Yet today, the world looks much more fragmented than these accounts predicted. Open markets are constantly challenged, international economic co-operation is faltering and political intervention is decidedly local, not global.

Of course, economic interventionism never ceased completely, even in countries adamantly supporting the liberalization of markets. But the consensus of the 1990s had a lasting effect on how economic policy decisions could be justified. Tellingly, the notion 'industrial policy' almost disappeared from political vocabulary during this time.

In 2005, Dominique de Villepin, then French prime minister, labelled the defence of local prerogatives in integrated markets 'economic patriotism'.[1] Reminiscent of Listian economic nationalism (List [1841] 1974), economic patriotism suggested that economic choices should be linked with concerns for one's homeland. The arrival of this terminology within the political lexicon of policy élites *before* the Great Recession illustrates profound if not self-evident contradictions between international market integration and spatially limited political mandates.

In this collection, we argue that the present crisis may have revealed these contradictions, but the underlying causes have roots that extend far beyond the global financial crisis. In a world characterized by an overlapping network of economic governance regimes, politicians face the 'paradox of neo-liberal democracy' (an idea developed by Colin Crouch [2008]): their political mandate is to pursue the political economic interests of their citizenry under conditions of complex economic, legal and regulatory interdependence where large parts of economic governance are no longer exclusively within their control. Faced with the constraints imposed by international trade regulation or competition authorities which increasingly proscribe traditional industrial policy as analysed by Shonfield (1965), governments had to become creative with policy strategies.

In this collection, we use economic patriotism as a prism to investigate how actors negotiate compromises between abstract economic objectives and territorially bound political obligations. We define economic patriotism as economic choices which seek to discriminate in favour of particular social groups, firms or sectors understood by the decision-makers as insiders because of their territorial status. Economic patriotism entails a form of economic partiality: a desire to shape market outcomes to privilege the position of certain actors. Unlike economic *nation*alism, economic patriotism is agnostic about the precise nature of the unit claimed as *patrie*: it can also refer to supranational or sub-national economic citizenship. Indeed, we argue that transfers between these levels are increasingly common.

We defend two arguments about economic patriotism that diverge from its popular reception. First, economic patriotism, like economic nationalism, needs to be defined by its territorial references and its underlying conception of political economic space, not by its supposed policy content. Although liberals have long used economic patriotism as a term of abuse, equating it with protectionism, this obscures the importance and the multiple facets and forms of the contemporary phenomenon, varying widely across countries and regions. In particular, it does not allow analysing when politicians chose liberal economic policies as a selective strategy to further territorial 'insider' interest (Helleiner 2002; Helleiner and Pickel 2005; Shulman 2000).

Second, although economic nationalism is as old as the nation-states themselves, we are currently observing some novel departures. Present-day economic patriotism is a response to the reconfiguration of economic governance and the interdependence of markets that only fully developed following increasing economic liberalization in the wake of the breakdown of Bretton Woods, the deepening of European integration in the 1980s, and the fall of communism in 1989. The integration of markets and the concurrent weaving together of regulatory frameworks put pressure on national economic intervention to eschew old-style industrial policy. Governments therefore had to become creative to assure traditional economic policy objectives with new means. In particular, they can now transfer economic objectives from the national to the regional level, such as the European Union (EU), which can lead to liberalization within the EU for the sake of protection towards the outside, as in agriculture. The multiple policy instruments in support of local, national or regional economic actors are today more fragmented and less coherent, but no less prevalent.

This collection examines the re-emergence, the evolution and the forms of economic patriotism in the global economy, with particular emphasis on Europe, where the overlap between economic jurisdictions is especially pronounced. We argue that economic patriotism is a universal phenomenon endemic within interdependent markets and economic jurisdictions. Despite using de Villepin's vocabulary, this is not simply a study of French chauvinism. It also seeks to answer why German politicians, despite low levels of patriotism, have treated foreign investors as locusts; why economically liberal British prime ministers proclaim 'British jobs for British workers'; why America, the archetypal liberal market economy, returns to 'buy American'. We attempt to answer these questions by paying attention to the deeper political economic causes to these contemporary phenomena. The taboo-breaking attempts to protect local economies suffering from the global financial crisis are a logical extension of this conundrum: they are remarkable in size, but not in nature.

The remainder of this introduction divides into four parts. A first section situates this study of economic patriotism within the comparative and international political economy literature and cautions against a monolithic conception of economic liberalism. The second section develops economic patriotism as an analytical concept and delimits it from related notions such as economic nationalism. A third section explores different forms of economic patriotism, and provides a typology for mapping the qualitative transformation of economic patriotic political intervention in the economy. In doing so it sets out how political control of the economy is being reinvented. A fourth section maps out the structure of this collection and summarizes its contributions.

VARIETIES OF ECONOMIC LIBERALISM

The apparent struggle between economic liberalism and parochial protectionism has occupied political debates and public discourse. In contrast, academic writing on the consequences of economic globalization is more nuanced and has moved beyond a simple dichotomy between open and closed borders. Scholars interested in the evolution of political economic orders have engaged with the globalization literature to demonstrate that convergence to a unique liberal market model is unlikely (Kitschelt *et al.* 1999). Studies have highlighted the importance of national economic policy styles, neo-corporatist arrangements, the institutional organization of the political economy or production regimes, and a vigorous debate erupted in the 1980s and 1990s to determine how the different capitalist models adapted to the increasing interconnection of markets (Amable 2003; Crouch and Streeck 1997; Hall and Soskice 2001; Perraton and Clift 2004). While some authors insisted on path-dependencies of existing models, others highlighted how firms and individual sectors adjusted differentially (Berger 2005; Piore and Sabel 1984). The varieties of capitalism literature focuses on institutional complementarities within national models and specifies ideal types of national market governance in an open economy (Hall and Soskice 2001; Hall and Thelen 2005; Höpner 2005). In sum, the debates in comparative political economy and industrial sociology pointed to relatively stable sets of institutional arrangements, which characterized socio-economic governance within countries, shaped their adjustment to market opening and conditioned institutional change (Streeck and Thelen 2005). One of the most forceful lessons of this literature is that there is not one ideal type political economy that all countries will emulate, despite undeniable pressures towards liberalization.

We are therefore interested in understanding how the implementation of liberal market policy varies across countries and sectors. Curiously, neither industrial sociology with its focus on firms and sectors, nor the varieties of capitalism literature with its emphasis on institutional stability have much to say about governmental strategies (but see Porter [1990]). Several authors have criticized the silence of the comparative political economy literature about the role of the state (Hancké *et al.* 2007: 4, 14–16; Levy 2006: 22–24; Schmidt 2009). In contrast, our account of economic patriotism entails a more encompassing vision of state action and activism than the governmental defence of institutional comparative advantage suggested, *sotto voce*, in Hall and Soskice (2001). Economic patriotism offers a conception of market relations as always subject to political acts of market-making and market-shaping, and of states as primary authors of interventionism. This is particularly relevant in open economies, where governments and firms are constantly arbitrating about the most adequate level of political and economic authority (Fioretos 2011).

Put differently, within the general move towards market-based solutions and amidst an increasing density of transnational jurisprudence to maintain open markets, the question for governments everywhere is *what kind* of economic liberalism to espouse in order to defend local economic interests in interconnected markets, and what kinds of state action or activism are needed to achieve it. We thus propose a more state-centric account of socio-economic governance. Economic liberalism does not imply the disappearance of the state, as we are frequently reminded (Evans *et al.* 1985; Levy 2006; Schmidt 2009). Analysing comparative capitalisms using economic patriotism avoids two *cul de sacs*: firstly that of viewing socio-economic governance today as a whether-or-not story of market integration (Strange 1997); and secondly assuming the 'co-convergence' on either the liberal or the co-ordinated model (Hall and Soskice 2001; for a critique see Hay [2004]; Crouch 2005). Instead we conceive of the terrain as political choices between a more differentiated range of possible paths of adaptation, each orchestrated to a significant degree by governmental action.

Scholars working from an international political economy (IPE) perspective have theorized who the winners and losers of market integration are in order to determine which policy coalitions should form to support further integration (Gourevitch 1986; Rogowski 1989). Moreover, they draw attention to how market interdependence shifts domestic politics by redistributing power resources among political and economic actors (Gourevitch 1978; Keohane and Milner 1996). According to these studies, pro- or anti-integration political stances are motivated by interest group pressures and class struggle, which in turn is a function of the country's economic endowment (Hiscox 2002).

The IPE literature's focus on 'open economy politics' (Lake 2009) gives us important indications about the coalitions that should be opposed to further integration. Unfortunately, it is not well attuned to studying how such support or opposition affects the multitude of instruments that politicians and economic actors have at their disposal. With its origins in open economy economics analysis of trade and finance, much IPE theorizes in terms of 'open' or 'closed' markets. As the comparative literature has highlighted, these terms are insufficiently nuanced for understanding the present-day economic regulation (Fioretos 2011). We concur, and argue that the IPE literature fails to capture the great variety of instruments and adaptation strategies which emerge from this collection of contributions. As the following contributions demonstrate, regulation of economic activity is today much more internationally intertwined and can no longer be neatly separated into national governance and trade relations. Instead, much regulation has become transnational and the majority of international negotiations today revolve around 'beyond the border' issues (Drezner 2007; Farrell and Newman 2010).

In this context, governments have had to innovate to reinvent their *modus operandi* of economic interventionism, for example by employing urban policy to serve competitiveness objectives (OECD 2006; Crouch and Le Galès 2012). The variegated nature of these policy choices, the state-orchestrated market-shaping and the complexity of the policy terrain of contemporary economic governance are not captured by the dichotomous opposition between open and closed borders which inform traditional IPE approaches. Our analysis more effectively captures the quest for the right kind of regulation: how can policy élites liberalize in a way that benefits mostly its own, how can an industry remain shielded from foreign competition without contravening international liberal market rules? How much regulation is necessary to maintain foreign investment without losing control over crucial companies? With its more fine-grained appreciation of the policy choices, economic patriotism as a conceptual lens helps move beyond the open vs closed borders or liberalization vs protection debates that can stultify studies of economic nationalism.

The fundamental differentiation between our approach and much comparative and international political economy literature is the understanding of the mutual constitution of state and market. The conception of state–market relations underlying this analysis of economic patriotism is informed by Karl Polanyi's work and economic sociology, both insisting on the inescapably embedded nature of market activity (Block 2003; Block and Evans 2005). Polanyi's insight that liberal markets need constant state intervention implies that economic liberalism is *not* a singular, monolithic political economic tradition, but comes in many variants. As Andrew Gamble (1999: 144) put it, 'it may not be possible to live in a world without capitalism, but capitalism need not be a single fate'. Liberal market capitalism rests upon sustained, extensive and politically contested legal and legislative interventionism in economic activity by the 'liberal state' (Polanyi 2001: 79–80, 136–9). Polanyi noted of the 19th-century expansion of *laissez-faire*:

> Laissez-faire itself was enforced by the state. The [eighteen] thirties and forties saw not only an outburst of legislation repealing restrictive regulations, but also an enormous increase in the administrative functions of the state. (Polanyi 2001: 145)

Our approach thus implies an embedded understanding of state–market relations, and highlights the reconfiguration of economic and political space which provides their context. Analysing economic patriotism allows studying the multiplicity of solutions enacted for governing the economy, in particular by focusing on the status of territorial boundaries in political decision-making. Based on these foundations, the third section will set out how to explain and understand patterns of change within economic intervention. Before that, however, we define the concept in more detail to clarify its analytical leverage.

DEFINING ECONOMIC PATRIOTISM

Intuitively, economic patriotism evokes the subordination of economic objectives to the protection of homeland interests. Used as a synonym for economic nationalism, it has been equated with (neo-)mercantilism. Throughout the post-war era, economic nationalism was a common opprobrious term among liberal economists used to discredit policies (see Levi-Faur 1997a). A more recent literature on economic nationalism has argued vigorously, through empirical studies and a re-examination of Friedrich List's 1841 classic *The National System of Political Economy*, that economic nationalism needs to be defined by its nationalist references, not its supposed protectionist policy content (Abdelal 2001; Crane 1998; D'Costa 2009; Helleiner and Pickel 2005; Mayall 1990). List himself, they argue, did not define his argument through policy recommendations (Helleiner 2002; Levi-Faur 1997b). List may be renowned for advocating infant industry protection, but his main contention with economic liberals was a conceptual dispute. Liberalism's 'theory of a cosmopolitan economy' considered policy from the perspective of individuals and aimed to increase prosperity for humanity. This, he pointed out, ignored the importance of nations as intermediaries between individuals and humanity. Rather than developing a 'science that teaches how the entire human race may attain prosperity,' he wanted to limit his 'teaching to the inquiry of how a given nation can obtain ... prosperity, civilisation and power' (List [1841] 1974: book II, ch. XI). The key point, for List, is that political intervention and the shaping of market outcomes in inextricably part of capitalism, even liberal capitalism. That is why, for List, 'free trade' is not really free:

> As long as some nations will persist in regarding their special interests as of greater value to them than the collective interests of humanity, it must be folly to speak of unrestricted competition between individuals of different nations. (List [1841] 1974: 261)

This emphasis on citizens' national identities and their historical and cultural characteristics underpins the difference between economic nationalism and the statist perspective of realism. Economic policy decisions can be rooted in 'representations of economic life as well as socio-cultural memories' and thus be nationalist without being about augmenting power or state-building (Crane 1998: 56; see also Abdelal 2001). Studying the variations and evolution of economic nationalism therefore requires a careful focus on national references rather than policy content, locating analysis historically and culturally within distinctive sets of state–society relations.

One of the most important lessons of this recent literature is the study of 'liberal economic nationalism' (Helleiner and Pickel 2005), wherein nationalist calculations (e.g., a desire for national autonomy, unity or identity) can inform engaging in international economic regimes and liberal commitments. *Dirigiste* France is said to have supported liberal European integration to strengthen its global role, former Soviet countries adopted liberal policies to gain autonomy from Russia and construct independent national identities, and Great Britain and later the United States might have endorsed free trade, not to promote global welfare but to establish a world-wide economic pre-eminence.

Whilst embracing this corrective, we insist that the full complexity of the phenomena which interest us cannot be adequately addressed with the notion 'economic nationalism'. Focusing on economic patriotism rather than economic nationalism frees us from the shackles of methodological and conceptual nationalism. In Europe, insistence on the defence of economic interests increasingly lists European interests alongside national ones. Indeed, economic patriotism can shift scales and espouse a 'fortress Europe' (George 1996) or aim to create 'European champions'. Inversely, it can also shift downward to local interests, even if this implies a disadvantage to other producers in the same country (Goff 2007). For example, the defence of labels of protected origins in the World Trade Organization (WTO) constitutes local economic patriotism – or *Lokalpatriotismus*, which is common in German language. The possibility to shift scales illustrates that the 'paradox of neo-liberal democracy' is not only a problem for policy-makers, it also offers possible solutions by allowing them to shift attention to a different level of political authority.

In defining economic patriotism, it is nonetheless useful to begin with economic nationalism. According to Ernest Gellner (1984: 1), 'nationalism is a political principle, which holds that the political and national unit should be congruent'. The same holds true for patriotism. However, as a theory of political legitimacy, patriotism attributes an intrinsic moral value to the defence of the homeland, even if it does not specify its boundaries. Economic patriotism thus suggests a value ordering where the homeland ranks higher than individual economic interests. As in all studies of motivations, disentangling individual or collective preferences from pure rhetoric can be difficult. However, the moral implications encourage discrimination against outsiders, which is more easily observable. We therefore concentrate on economic discrimination against territorial outsiders.

For lack of space, we are focusing our attention on state-led activity, and supra-national initiatives undertaken by political élites. There are, of course, many other forms of economic partiality rooted in the activities, for example, of consumers, employers, workers or social movements (see Chang 1999; Costa *et al.* 2007; Dubuisson-Quellier 2008; Porter 1990).

FORMS OF ECONOMIC PATRIOTISM

We use the concept of economic patriotism as an umbrella to highlight some fundamental characteristics of economic intervention. Within that, categorizing different forms of economic patriotism is a useful heuristic device, which facilitates the analysis of trends within economic interventionism. In order to specify the distinct forms that economic patriotic activism can take, it is important to distinguish, first, between the discourse and practice of economic patriotism, second, between different types, and third, between the policy content and targets.

The salience of economic patriotism in political discourse is striking, as is the considerable gap that can exist between public declarations and actual intervention. When French president Nicolas Sarkozy urged French automakers to locate their plants at home rather than the Czech Republic in February 2009, many suspected that he counted on European officials, pointing to free movement principles, to make his suggestions inconsequential. Indeed a major reason

Table 1 Forms of economic patriotism

	Liberal economic patriotism	*Conservative economic patriotism*
Supranational economic patriotism	Strategic regional integration	Defensive regionalism
Economic nationalism	Liberal economic nationalism	Classic protectionism
Local economic patriotism	Liberal policies that facilitate the creation of sub-national champions	Defence of local production

for economic co-operation beyond nation-states is to constrain national politicians always under pressure to respond to their electorates. Contributions in this collection interrogate the relationship between political rhetoric and interventionist practice, to evaluate whether economic patriotic discourse amounts to more than 'cheap talk' about parochial intentions in a global era. Analysis of these discursive dimensions unearths that disjunctures between the rhetoric and the reality of economic patriotism can take different forms, including surreptitious partial interventionism in support of the homeland, unadvertized for fear of being accused of economic heresy or xenophobia. Economic patriotism can thus characterize both discourse and practice, and the two might not necessarily coincide.

Second, we can distinguish different forms of economic patriotism, which we separate by their reference points. Patriotic action can appeal to one's nation or some other territorial unit. Along this first dimension, we find: (1) supranational economic patriotism; (2) economic nationalism; and (3) local economic patriotism. Furthermore, economic patriotism can be conservative, i.e., looking to preserve the status quo or 'static efficiency' or offensive, i.e., seeking to enhance 'dynamic efficiency' (Chang 1999) and outward-looking in some innovative way. (4) Conservative economic patriotism refers to the traditional protectionism. Outward looking, or (5) liberal economic patriotism, by contrast, entails selective or strategic liberalization in a way that privileges a particular set of economic actors. Alternatively, it can also aim to support the competitiveness of national firms or citizens operating abroad (see D'Costa 2009). It is possible to cross these two dimensions to get a sense of the possible variation that can exist.

Economic patriotism can aim to shield producers and/or preserve extant comparative advantages at each level, even the supranational one, which the debate about defensive regionalism and 'fortress Europe' has highlighted. In cases where regional markets are not integrated, however, supranational economic patriotism can entail considerable liberalization, even if the political objective is ultimately the creation of a trading block able to defend the regional interests in world markets. Depending on the starting point, the nature of the economic intervention is thus quite different at all three territorial levels.

Table 2 Classifying the policy content of economic patriotism

		Ideological affinity	
		Liberal	*Protectionist*
Policy target	Favouring of insiders	Q1 e.g., selective liberalization in strategic sectors	Q3 e.g., regulation to maintain traditional product and process standards; state subsidies
	Resistance to outsiders	Q2 e.g., risk regulation or competition rules that prohibit standards common abroad	Q4 e.g., classic barriers to trade

At the national level, we find the categories identified by the recent literature on economic nationalism. At the sub-national level, we again distinguish between the defence of existing local production advantages and the creation of local advantages in the process of integrating markets, typically through the creation of sub-national champions. Interestingly, the creation of such champions necessarily implies that the government discriminates in their favour and neglects other sub-national actors, as the contribution by Crouch and Le Galès in this collection shows.

Categorizing different forms of economic patriotism distinguishes the nature of intervention in a very general way. However, to study intervention within one country and over time, it is also necessary to address the policy content and the different instruments which political authorities employ to support the economy. This brings us to our third distinction between policy content and policy targets. Again, we begin by acknowledging that interventions exhibit different degrees of compatibility with market objectives: we posit a continuum from relatively liberal to protectionist economic policies. Conflict over policies often revolves around the fluid boundary between favouring territorial insiders and resisting outsiders. Some policies are designed to support insiders without in principle excluding outsiders, but still in effect strengthen the position of national or regional target groups. Other policies are explicitly designed to block outsiders from participating on an equal footing with insiders, but they can do so with distinctly national criteria or with reference to characteristics that are not territorially bound in principle, although they might be in practice. If we cross these two dimensions, we obtain the Table 2.

In the left-hand column we see policies aiming to liberalize a given sector, but doing so either by concentrating on an industry where the government sees a strategic advantage and hopes to dominate in the integrated market (Q1) or by liberalizing in a way that entails regulation which targets the practices of foreign competitors (Q2). On the right-hand side, we find policies seeking to preserve the status quo, either by maintaining traditional product or process regulation beneficial to insider companies (Q3) or using classic trade barriers (Q4).

Our argument is that the integration of markets and international jurisprudence put pressure on the instruments available to governments. Where economic regimes are multi-layered and contain legal enforcement rights, the political control over the economy therefore had to be reinvented. As Jonah Levy (2006: 2) puts it, 'while old forms of state intervention may be discredited and cleared away, new interventions often emerge to take their place. The state also rises.' Deregulation, of course, involves not simply removing restrictions but active *re*regulation: the new regulatory frameworks differ between countries, regions and sectors in ways that are designed to promote particular outcomes. Deregulation has not and could not ever simply be a case of eliminating controls; the huge raft of legislation and directives required to institute the Single European Market exemplifies this (Vogel 1995). This need for re-regulation gave politicians the means to continue influence over the economy in pursuit of territorially beneficial outcomes.

Since international agreements target mainly outright protectionism with clear discriminatory effects, our hypothesis is that economic patriotism will shift from measures that fall in quadrant 4 of Table 2 towards quadrants 3 and 2, and in some select cases quadrant 1. Furthermore, we expect protectionist measures to favour insiders (Q3) to move away from clearly identifiable insider support such as direct subsidies and to turn increasingly into aid that is in principle open to everybody irrespective of nationality, but in practice particularly attractive to homeland producers. The nature of the precise instruments chosen should vary considerably across policy domains.

Thus, our typology and our hypotheses identify growth areas for economic patriotic interventionism, and areas of retrenchment. Quadrant 4 – classic trade barriers – belong to the protectionist toolkit of traditional economic nationalists, and international jurisprudence and safeguards have reduced the efficacy and viability of these policy instruments. Activism within quadrant 1 remains possible under international rules, indicating likely increases in re-regulation to shape market outcomes in a manner advantageous to territorial insiders.

Policies that belong in quadrants 2 and 3 are less easily pigeonholed. For this reason, these kinds of interventions have stirred an intense debate about the 'hidden protectionism' inherent in regulatory policy-making (Jordana and Levi-Faur 2004; Vogel 1995). The majority of negotiations in international economic integration today concern not fully fledged liberalization or outright protectionism, but effects of domestic regulation for the free movement of capital, labour, goods or services (Drezner 2007). Some regulation enshrines traditional product or process standards, thus favouring insiders already acquainted with the system (Q3). Licensing procedures or professional qualifications, such as the German '*Meister*' for example, do not discriminate explicitly against foreigners but defend national quality standards that are difficult to meet for producers or service providers abroad. A virulent debate has ensued about the necessity of maintaining specific standards. However, conflicts are resolved only on a case-by-case basis where a diverse set of regulatory instances determine which standards truly serve legitimate social values (e.g., risk management or environmental protection), and which are simple protectionism clothed in convoluted political rhetoric.

Regulation that is not designed to favour insiders, but that prohibits process or product standards common abroad (Q2) constitutes another form of economic patriotic intervention. Is it protectionism to refuse textiles produced with child labour, when the countries affected by such as decision can be clearly identified? Can European Union 'precautionary principle' food standards norms prohibit hormone-treated beef, even though almost all United States beef is targeted by such a decision? Even some ardent economic liberals consider that such regulation of market rules is not always in contradiction with liberal principles, despite its discriminating effects. Ignoring these intense regulation debates characteristic of national, European and international negotiations by simply labelling all that is not *laissez-faire* liberalism as hidden protectionism is an unsatisfactory solution. Instead, the struggle over the 'right kind of regulation' needs to be understood as the result of the need to provide political answers to citizen concerns despite ambitions to facilitate economic integration. Within modern political economies, this is where what we might call the new politics of industrial policy plays out – and it is a crucial terrain of economic patriotism, both in discourse and in practice. We extend our analysis beyond simple protectionism to all cases where politicians enact economic partiality to privilege particular territorially defined groups at local, national and supra-national levels.

Let us conclude by underlining what kind of policies are beyond the limits of economic patriotism. By definition all economic policies that are apply uniformly to economic actors irrespective of their supposed origin fall outside our remit. Moreover, when the defence of territorial interests is not the primary factor in the political decision, it would be of little analytical value to speak of economic patriotism.[2] While cynics might argue that all economic policies aim to serve major political constituencies or industrial sectors, it is conceivable that some choices are truly informed by economic theories about optimal, welfare-enhancing policies. Such theory-driven rather than pragmatic economic policy would then clearly fall outside of the realm of economic patriotism (for further discussion, see Clift and Woll [2012]).

THE CONTRIBUTIONS AND STRUCTURE OF THIS COLLECTION

This collection analyses and compares political intervention in economic activity across countries and sectors, concentrating on how interventionism is refracted through different variants of liberal market capitalism. It begins by analysing who perpetuates economic patriotism as a discourse and a strategy, focusing on governments, public officials (Rosamond) and socio-economic actors (Fetzer). Analysing economic patriotism allows examining the multiple ways political actors seek to articulate economic policy objectives with territorial boundaries and how socio-economic actors, such as firms and trade unions, respond to these constraints and use them to seek legitimacy in their political struggles. Next, sectoral studies explore different forms of economic patriotism in housing finance (Seabrooke), battles over stock market ownership (Callaghan and Lagneau-Ymonet), financial market governance (Morgan) and urban policy (Crouch and Le Galès). The final two contributions analyse economic patriotism transferred to the supranational level: in agriculture (Grant) and the defence industry (Hoeffler).

The contributions exemplify different ways to engage economic patriotism – through country comparison, sectoral case studies, and focusing on shifting political boundaries – illustrating different methodological possibilities and the explanatory purchase they afford. They are also illustrative of the different forms of economic patriotism we have identified in Table 1. Rosamond, Grant and Hoeffler focus on supranational economic patriotism. Agriculture provides a defensive example, whereas European defence co-operation in reveals the strategic industrial policy objectives behind liberalization and market integration. Seabrooke, Callaghan and Lagneau-Ymonet, and Morgan study economic nationalism, the first two by means of cross-country comparison, and Morgan through a case study of the City of London. All three demonstrate the evolution of economic patriotism strategies over time from protectionist and inward-looking to support for liberalization. Finally, Fetzer and Crouch and Le Galès focus on sub-national actors. Fetzer demonstrates how firms and trade unions discursively deploy economic patriotism to protect themselves, while Crouch and Le Galès show the strategic creation of city champions that are supposed to further national interests in an integrated economy.

However, to illustrate that economic patriotism is not always as pervasive as one might expect, both Hoeffler's study of defence co-operation and Callaghan and Lagneau-Ymonet's analysis for the foreign take-over of the French stock exchange show the limits of the phenomenon, even in areas where we should have expected it to be strong.

CONCLUSION

Economic governance in open economies presents formidable challenges. The current crisis has revealed the intensity of the stakes, but gives little indication about the most appropriate political organization for interdependent economies. Analysing crisis responses only as a return to protectionism ignores the most crucial aspects of today's post-Ricardian world. It focuses on national boundaries, but assumes away that intricate web of economic interdependence that also puts pressure on policy-makers. The challenge that sovereign debt crises in countries such as Greece or Ireland pose to European economic governance are just the most recent examples illustrating that advanced industrial countries cannot just withdraw from previous integration efforts.

Politicians and other stakeholders are therefore increasingly self-assertive about the need to reconcile both objectives: facilitate the integration of markets *and* protect the interest of stakeholders within a particular territory. It is telling that even core advocates of liberalization now rediscover the potential benefits of political intervention. In 2009, the chief economist at the World Bank debated the value of industrial policy in developing countries (Lin and Chang 2009). More recently in August 2010, even *The Economist* discussed the most useful ways of pursuing industrial policy.[3]

The novel terminology of economic patriotism offers an analytical lens to study how policy-makers seek to resolve the tension between interdependent economies and political territoriality in a variety of political economic settings. It brings into focus the reconfiguration of political economic space which the interdependence of markets and multi-levelled economic governance regimes entail. These are necessary to an adequate understanding of the dialectic between the politics of liberalization and the regulatory, legal and political processes of market-shaping intervention in open economies. Understanding this dialectic, we argue, is crucial for interpreting the political economy of responses to the current economic and finance crisis within affluent democracies.

Biographical notes: Ben Clift is Senior Lecturer in Political Economy at the University of Warwick. Cornelia Woll is Associate Research Professor at Sciences Po Paris and Research Fellow at the Max Planck Institute for the Study of Societies in Cologne.

ACKNOWLEDGEMENTS

This project has benefitted tremendously from intensive discussions at workshops at Warwick University in February 2008 and Sciences Po Paris in September 2008 and June 2009, as well as presentations at the ECPR EU Section conference in Riga in September 2008, the Society for the Advancement of Socio-Economics (SASE) meeting in Paris in July 2009 and the European Consortium of Political Research (ECPR) General Conference in September 2009. We would like to thank all participants for their insightful remarks, especially Mark Blyth and Vivien Schmidt; several anonymous reviewers for the close reading and comments; and Gong Cheng for excellent research assistance. We also gratefully acknowledge the financial support from Alliance Programme of the British Council and the French Foreign Ministry and from the Max Planck Society.

NOTES

1 Dominique de Villepin argued against a possible hostile takeover of the French company Danone by PepsiCo on 27 July 2005, relying on a concept presented in Carayon (2006). Previously confined to France, de Villepin's speech brought the notion into international debates. See Christophe Jakubyszyn, 'Dominique de Villepin en appelle au »patriotisme économique »', *Le Monde*, 29 July 2005.

2 Again, territorial interest and environmental or social interests might overlap, and politicians will always favour those solutions that allow pursuing them at the same time. In these cases, the litmus test will be conflicts where eventually one of the objectives has to be chosen over the others.

3 *The Economist* (2010) 'The global revival of industrial policy: picking winners, saving losers', 5 August.

REFERENCES

Abdelal, R. (2001) *National Purpose in the World Economy*, Ithaca, NY: Cornell University Press.

Amable, B. (2003) *The Diversity of Modern Capitalism*, Oxford: Oxford University Press.

Berger, S. (2005) *How We Compete: What Companies Around the World Are Doing to Make it in Today's Global Economy*, New York: Doubleday.

Block, F. (2003) 'Karl Polanyi and the writing of the great transformation', *Theory and Society* 32(3): 275–306.

Block, F. and Evans, P. (2005) 'The state and the economy', in N. Smelser and R. Swedberg (eds), *Handbook of Economic Sociology*, Princeton, NJ: Princeton University Press, pp. 505–26.

Carayon, B. (2006) *Patriotisme économique: de la guerre à la paix économique*, Monaco: Editions du Rochia.

Chang, H.-J. (1999) 'The economic theory of the development state', in M. Woo-Cummings (ed.), *The Development State*, Ithaca, NY: Cornell University Press, pp. 182–99.

Clift, B. and Woll, C. (2012) 'The revival of economic patriotism', in G. Morgan and R. Whitley (eds), *Capitalisms and Capitalism in the 21st Century*, Oxford: Oxford University Press, forthcoming.

Costa, O., de Maillard, J. and Smith, A. (2007) *Vin et politique: Bordeaux, la France, la mondialisation*, Paris: Presses de Sciences Po.

Crane, G.T. (1998) 'Economic nationalism: bringing the nation back in', *Millennium – Journal of International Studies* 27(1): 55–75.

Crouch, C. (2005) 'Models of capitalism', *New Political Economy* 10(4): 439–56.

Crouch, C. (2008) 'Economic patriotism and the paradox of neo-liberal democracy', Paper presented at the first Economic Patriotism workshop, Warwick University, 13–14 February.

Crouch, C. and Streeck, W. (eds) (1997) *The Political Economy of Modern Capitalism: Mapping Convergence and Diversity*, London: Sage.

Crouch, C. and Le Galès, P. (2012) 'Cities as national champions?', *Journal of European Public Policy* 19(3), http://dx.doi.org/10.1080/13501763.2011.640795

D'Costa, A.P. (2009) 'Economic nationalism in motion: steel, auto, and software industries in India', *Review of International Political Economy* 16(4): 620–48.

Drezner, D.W. (2007) *All Politics is Global: Explaining International Regulatory Regimes*, Princeton, NJ: Princeton University Press.
Dubuisson-Quellier, S. (2008) *Les protestations autour du marché. La construction du consommateur par les mouvements militants'*, Paris: Sciences Po Paris.
Evans, P.B., Rueschemeyer, D. and Skocpol, T. (1985) *Bringing the State Back In*, Cambridge: Cambridge University Press.
Farrell, H. and Newman, A. (2010) 'Making global markets: historical institutions in international political economy', *Review of International Political Economy* 17(4): 609–38.
Fioretos, O. (2011) *Creative Reconstructions: Multilateralism and European Varieties of Capitalism after 1950*, Ithaca, NY: Cornell University Press.
Friedman, T.L. (2005) *The World is Flat: A Brief History of the Twenty-First Century*, New York: Farrar, Straus and Giroux.
Gamble, A. (1999) 'Marxism after communism', *Review of International Studies* 25(2): 127–44.
Gellner, E. (1984) *Nations and Nationalism*, Oxford: Oxford University Press.
George, S. (1996) 'The European Union, 1992 and the fear of "Fortress Europe"', in A. Gamble and T. Payne (eds), *Regionalism and World Order*, Basingstoke: Macmillan, pp. 21–54.
Goff, P.M. (2007) *Limits to Liberalization: Local Culture in a Global Marketplace*, Cornell studies in political economy, Ithaca, NY: Cornell University Press.
Gourevitch, P. (1978) 'The second image reversed: the international sources of domestic politics', *International Organization* 32: 881–911.
Gourevitch, P. (1986) *Politics in Hard Times: Comparative Responses to International Economic Crises*, Ithaca, NY: Cornell University Press.
Hall, P.A. and Soskice, D. (2001) *Varieties of Capitalism: Institutional Foundations of Comparative Advantage*, Cambridge: Cambridge University Press.
Hall, P.A. and Thelen, K. (2005) 'The politics of change in varieties of capitalism', Paper presented at the *American Political Science Association Annual Meeting*, Philadelphia, PA, 31 August–3 September.
Hancké, B., Rhodes, M. and Thatcher, M. (eds) (2007) *Beyond Varieties of Capitalism: Conflict, Contradictions, and Complementarities in the European Economy*, Oxford: Oxford University Press.
Hay, C. (2004) 'Common trajectories, variable paces, divergent outcomes? Models of European capitalism under conditions of complex economic interdependence', *Review of International Political Economy* 11(2): 231–62.
Helleiner, E. (2002) 'Economic nationalism as a challenge to economic liberalism? Lesson from the 19th century', *International Studies Quarterly* 46(3): 307–29.
Helleiner, E. and Pickel, A. (eds) (2005) *Economic Nationalism in a Globalizing World*, Ithaca, NY: Cornell University Press.
Hiscox, M. (2002) *International Trade and Political Conflict: Commerce, Coalitions, and Mobility*, Princeton, NJ: Princeton University Press.
Höpner, M. (2005) 'What Have we learnt? Complementarity, coherence and institutional change', *Socio-Economic Review* 3(2): 383–7.
Jordana, J. and Levi-Faur, D. (eds) (2004) *The Politics of Regulation: Institutions and Regulatory Reforms for the Age of Governance*, Cheltenham: Edward Elgar.
Keohane, R.O. and Milner, H.V. (1996) *Internationalization and Domestic Politics*, Cambridge: Cambridge University Press.
Kitschelt, H., Lange, P., Marks, G. and Stephens, J. (eds) (1999) *Continuity and Change in Contemporary Capitalism*, Cambridge: Cambridge University Press.
Lake, D. (2009) 'TRIPs across the Atlantic: theory and epistemology in IPE', *Review of International Political Economy* 16(1): 47–57.

Levi-Faur, D. (1997a) 'Economic nationalism: from Friedrich List to Robert Reich', *Review of International Studies* 23(3): 359–70.
Levi-Faur, D. (1997b) 'Friedrich List and the political economy of the nation-state', *Review of International Political Economy* 4(1): 154–78.
Levy, J.D. (ed.) (2006) *The State After Statism: New State Activities in the Age of Liberalization*, Cambridge, MA: Harvard University Press.
Lin, J. and Chang, H.-J. (2009) 'Should industrial policy in developing countries conform to comparative advantage or defy it? A debate between Justin Lin and Ha-Joon Chang', *Development Policy Review* 27(5): 483–502.
List, F. ([1841] 1974) *National System of Political Economy*, New York: Garland.
Mayall, J. (1990) *Nationalism and International Society*, Cambridge: Cambridge University Press.
OECD (2006) *Competitive Cities in the Global Economy*, Paris: OECD Territorial Reviews.
Perraton, J. and Clift, B. (2004) *Where are National Capitalisms Now?* Basingstoke: Palgrave Macmillan.
Piore, M.J. and Sabel, C.F. (1984) *The Second Industrial Divide: Possibilities for Prosperity*, New York: Basic Books.
Polanyi, K. (2001) *The Great Transformation: The Political and Economic Origins of our Time*, 2nd Beacon Paperback, Boston, MA: Beacon Press.
Porter, M.E. (1990) *The Competitive Advantage of Nations*, New York: Free Press.
Rogowski, R. (1989) *Commerce and Coalitions: How Trade Affects Domestic Political Alignments*, Princeton, NJ: Princeton University Press.
Schmidt, V.A. (2009) 'Putting the political back into political economy by bringing the state back in yet again', *World Politics* 61(3): 516–46.
Shonfield, A. (1965) *Modern Capitalism: The Changing Balance of Public and Private Power*, Oxford: Oxford University Press.
Shulman, S. (2000) 'Nationalist sources of international economic integration', *International Studies Quarterly* 44(3): 365–90.
Strange, S. (1997) 'The future of global capitalism; or, will divergence persist forever?', in C. Crouch and W. Streeck (eds), *Political Economy of Modern Capitalism: Mapping Convergence and Diversity*, Thousand Oaks, CA: Sage, pp. 182–91.
Streeck, W. and Thelen, K. (eds) (2005) *Beyond Continuity: Institutional Change in Advanced Industrial Economies*, Oxford: Oxford University Press.
Vogel, D. (1995) *Trading Up: Consumer and Environmental Regulation in a Global Economy*, Cambridge, MA: Harvard University Press.
Wallach, L. and Sforza, M. (1999) *The WTO: Five Years of Reasons to Resist Corporate Globalization*, New York: Seven Stories Press.
Yergin, D. and Stanislaw, J. (1999) *The Commanding Heights: The Battle between Government and the Marketplace that is Remaking the Modern World*, New York: Touchstone.

Supranational governance as economic patriotism? The European Union, legitimacy and the reconstruction of state space

Ben Rosamond

ABSTRACT 'Economic patriotism' (EP) and 'European integration' might normally be regarded as antonyms. The argument is made for reading some actions and discourses of the EU in terms of EP. Two assumptions are relaxed: that EP is an exclusive property of nation-state space and that is necessarily associated with the suspension of economic liberalism. By relaxing the first, the article shows how many aspects of EU discourse and practice can be thought of as EP-like. The institutionalized economic liberal biases of the EU tend to constrain the possibilities for supranational EP in its two principal guises, labelled here as 'Schmittian' and 'Listian'. The relaxation of the second assumption allows for a third variant of EP to be introduced: 'market-making' EP. This is shown to be a particular feature of Commission discourse since the mid-1980s. The move to market-making EP discourse demonstrates the particular quality of legitimacy dilemmas faced by the EU.

INTRODUCTION

'Economic patriotism' (EP) and 'European integration' would seem to be precise antonyms. The former brings to mind inward-looking policies and discourses that reinforce national territorial authority and affinity. The latter invokes a post-national project of market liberalization. The concept of EP, by virtue of its deep association with a particular geography of political economy and a particular set of economic ideas, would appear to be unfit for the task of helping us say something interesting about the processes of European integration.

The argument here seeks to question this assumption. The article relaxes two commonplace definitional axioms that tend to be associated with EP. The first of these axioms is the idea that EP involves discourses and practices that are *necessarily* protectionist and contrary to the premises of economic liberalism. The second is the intuitive understanding of EP as an exclusive property of nation-states and of national economic space. As others (Helleiner 2002; Pickel 2005) have shown, broadening the understanding of the first axiom enables EP to be understood less as a recourse to inward looking, 'beggar-thy-neighbour' politics and more as an appeal – in discourse and in practice – to the interests of a particular political-economic community. If EP is recast in this way, then there is nothing – *prima facie* – that rules out market liberal variants. Untying the analysis of EP from the second axiom is helped somewhat by the prior relaxation of the first. But doing so renders possible, at the very least, the investigation of EP-like tendencies beyond the nation-state. While nation-states are without question the most important historical forms of political-economic community, there is nothing in principle to rule out alternative renderings of 'state space' (Brenner 2004) premised upon EP-like discourses and actions. Indeed, it might be that the very vocabulary of 'patriotism' and 'nationalism' is unhelpful, drawing attention as it does to a historically particular (although dominant) form of a more generalized phenomenon of political economy.

It should be clear that the combined effect of these two analytical moves is to render the European Union (EU) admissible for study in relation to EP. By ceasing to confine the study of EP to the activities of national forms of authority in relation to imagined national communities, it becomes possible to adjudicate the EU's policy outputs and communicative discourses as potentially EP-like. This is possible even if the first assumption is held intact because elements of EU activity might be judged to be anti-liberal in character. The suspension of both axioms means that the EU's relationship to EP is yet more interesting. To study the EU is, in part, to analyse an ongoing dynamic project of market-making (Fligstein 2008; Jabko 2006). Perhaps the key argument of this contribution is that this market-making project has been increasingly shaped and underwritten by discourses and practices that anticipate and construct a European/EU political-economic community in the manner of EP as defined here. However, the final section revisits one crucial component of the conventional understanding of EP that is perhaps under-emphasized. Just as national governments' promotion of protectionism can be read as a means to secure domestic support, so an ideal-typical (liberalizing) supranational agent's appeal to an alternative spatial imaginary can be understood as a legitimation strategy. The article argues that an element of the EU's present legitimacy dilemmas can be related to its increasing tendency since the mid-1980s, through the European Commission, to appeal to the notion of the 'European economy' as a shared community of fate. By posing European integration as a set of technical and normative rationales following from the claimed existence of this political-economic space, so the EU has opened up a set of acute legitimacy questions.

EUROPEAN INTEGRATION AND ECONOMIC PATRIOTISM: BEYOND CONVENTIONAL UNDERSTANDINGS

EP is typically defined as a 'negative' policy temptation where national governments, through pressure of circumstance or because the need to secure domestic political support, engage in policies that are motivated by 'the urge to keep jobs and capital at home' (*The Economist* 2009). The popular representation thus places the EU into a particular type of relationship with EP. The resort to EP in European countries is indicative of the EU's inability to maintain internal cohesion or to act as an authoritative counterweight to protectionist tendencies amongst its member states (Cable 2009; Härtel 2006). The EU's present weakness is thus re-read as a failure to fulfil its historic project of providing open economy conditions across an increasingly integrated transnational market space (Hodson and Quaglia 2009; Quaglia *et al.* 2009). While one retort might be that the EU's lack of authoritative action in the financial crisis actually reflects an extensive institutionalized commitment to *laissez faire* (Posner and Véron 2010), it remains the case that by failing to develop proper regulatory authority over markets the EU has facilitated the return of state-led political responses at the national level.

Similarly, episodes where the EU's practices and policies derogate from open economy assumptions are seen as EP-like deviations from the core purposes of European integration. In short, the European integration project (with some notable exceptions) is broadly the antithesis of EP in philosophical and policy terms and its success is measured against the extent to which it prevents outbreaks of economic nationalism amongst its member states. This narrative locates EP within the domain of national and inter-national economic space. EP is mostly something done by national governments in the context of economic competition with other states. Successful supranational governance is defined by its capacity to eradicate EP. Both critical accounts of the EU as a spatial reordering of governance functions through a form of 'new constitutionalism' (Gill 1998, 2001, 2003) and more conventional readings of the EU as a regulatory state whose legitimate purpose is the pareto-efficient correction of market failure (Majone 1994, 1996, 2005) understand any policies that derogate from these tasks as deviations from the EU's core liberalizing mission.

The most obvious deviation, and the one which most seems to comply with the conventional notion of EP as protectionist is the Common Agricultural Policy (CAP), which originally operated through instruments that were obviously designed to distort global agricultural markets by keeping 'inefficient' producers in business (Tangermann 1983). One of the CAP's original aims was to deliver food security (Grant 1997; Swinbank 1992), and there is a strand of scholarship which interprets the CAP at its foundation as a welfare policy for farmers (Knudsen 2009). The central achievement of the CAP was the transfer of policy competence for agricultural support from the national to the supranational level (Greer 2005). Broadly protectionist policy instruments survived the spatial shift, which indicates the capacity of an entity like an EU to operate with EP-like instruments. Other examples include the accusation that the EU has subsidized the Airbus consortium in contravention of World Trade Organization (WTO) rules (Clark *et al.* 2010). The gist of the long running dispute between the EU and the United States (McGuire 1997) is that indirect instruments, such as preferential loans to Airbus from the European Investment Bank and the prioritization of EU-funded infrastructure projects that especially benefit Airbus, represent market-distorting interventions that advantage European producers. Finally, in energy policy, the EU now regularly communicates its priorities in terms of imperatives that gather under the rubric of 'energy security'. The Commission Green Paper, *A European Strategy for Sustainable, Competitive and Secure Energy* (Commission of the European Communities 2006), identifies the need for European self-sufficiency in energy given two overarching external dilemmas: global climate change and future projections of increased dependence on a small group of (often unstable) countries for gas and oil supplies. As Youngs (2009) notes, EU energy policy has become increasingly fused to, and is perhaps best thought of as a subset of, EU foreign policy.

The degree to which these exemplar policies can be classified as EP is a matter for debate. But the fact that the question can be asked in the first place seems to suggest that the spatial confinement of EP is not hard and fast. There is at least potential for governance forms beyond the nation-state to engage in such behaviour. Broadly speaking, and still holding in place the idea that EP practices are necessarily anti-liberal, there are two rationales that a governing authority might give for the use of EP-like practices. The first relates to a set of technical (and sometimes normative) arguments that reduce to the claim that comparative advantages should be nurtured before they can be properly exploited. This would be a classic Listian defence of the suspension of open economy assumptions (List 1966 [1841]). This approach would not suspend economic liberal assumptions for perpetuity; only until domestic competitiveness has been delivered. The second goes beyond arguments rooted in mostly technical economic logic. A 'Schmittian' defence of EP emerges when security imperatives trump economic imperatives – where exceptional practices are justified by 'exceptional' circumstances (Schmitt 2004 [1922]).[1] In the context of the EU, we would be looking for examples of policy where pressing external security imperatives justify the indefinite suspension of open economy and market liberal assumptions.

Having dispensed with the idea that EP is necessarily an impulse confined to the national level of action, Table 1 presents a stylized matrix of ideal typical forms of EP operable at national and supranational levels. To reiterate, in this way of thinking EP manifests itself in identifiable practices, discernible at different levels of action. For the time being, the practices understood here as EP are generally mercantilist-protectionist in character. Importantly, the distinction between sub-types of EP is also rooted in the *discursive justification* of these practices (the Listian–'Schmittian' distinction outlined above). But these communicative discourses of EP do not float freely. What is possible (at least in terms of the translation of discourse into practice) is framed within sets of rules, treaty commitments and institutional norms. Hence the placement of parentheses around mode 2 EP (Listian supranational EP), where Treaty commitments and the consolidated *acquis* render this form of EU-level action difficult, if not unlawful.

Table 1 Varieties and levels of economic patriotism (1)

	National		*Supranational*
Listian EP	1		(2)
			⇩
Schmittian EP	3	⇨	4

We return to some aspects of Listian EP in due course, but for now it is instructive to reconsider some of the examples given above. The category of 'EU industrial policy' exists, but its competitiveness enhancement rationale rules out *ad hoc* interventions to support ailing industries or to promote 'European champions' (Commission of the European Communities 2005; Pelkmans 2006). The generation of energy self-sufficiency is to be delivered through a market-based approach to 'energy security' rather than through any scheme designed to privilege European producers through direct intervention (Youngs 2009). As the CAP has been reformed since the 1990s, so it has been exposed increasingly to economic liberal logics (Potter and Titzey 2005) and to a range of ideas that transform the core policy goal of agricultural support towards the likes of environmental sustainability, rural development, animal welfare and the provision of European public goods (Garzon 2006). Indeed there is a powerful case to suggest that these conventional expressions of EP are offset by a systematic bias towards economic openness within the EU. Hanson (1998) identifies the single market *acquis* together with institutionalization in the form of voting rules in the Council as the key variables that explain this bias, while others draw attention to the active jurisprudence of the European Court in turning loose treaty commitments into a genuine economic constitution (Weiler 1991).

These observations suggest that there is limited scope for either the 'Listian' or 'Schmittian' variants to be anything other than unusual departures from normal EU practices. Yet the interplay between the national and the supranational levels is interesting. In agricultural policy, one of the most significant achievements of the past 60 years has been the movement from mode 3 to mode 4 EP. What this has involved is the establishment of the supranational level as the legitimate domain of authoritative action, which amounts to rather more than simply saying that agricultural policy has become 'Europeanized'. The legitimacy of supranational dominion in agriculture was ultimately achieved through a process of bounded internal liberalization of agricultural markets, but where – WTO objections notwithstanding – 'Schmittian' EP arguments retained some purchase. Many areas of economic policy have become 'Europeanized' and internally liberalized, but as the example of the difficulty of shifting from mode 1 to mode 3 suggests, it does not always follow that European-level policy-makers possess the capacity or the authority to operate in ways that might be commensurate with EP in mode 2. The establishment of mode 4 EP in the CAP is, of course, helped by its inscription in the founding treaties, which in turn have enabled a path-dependent institutionalization. We might also hypothesize that the difficulty of transferring mode 1 EP to the supranational level in most areas of economic governance would force EP-minded actors in those domains to seek out more 'Schmittian' discursive resources. In other words, they would need to develop a security narrative in preference to an economic narrative to justify departures from liberalism.

THE EU AND MARKET-MAKING ECONOMIC PATRIOTISM

So far, we have argued that EP need not be rooted in national state space. There is some purchase in thinking of the EU as a site for the expression of EP-like discourses and the generation of EP-like behaviour. At the same time, there are institutional, legal and discursive biases that provide limited conditions of possibility for EU economic patriotism. Perhaps the greatest potential for EP within the EU occurs in situations where policy actors articulate and communicate a set of security imperatives as justification for non-liberal economic policy initiatives.

At this point, the second assumption – that EP amounts to non-economic liberal discourse and behaviour – will be relaxed. It is here, it will be argued, that there is real potential for thinking about the EU in terms of EP.

The possibility of a relationship between market liberalism and EP has been developed by the likes of Helleiner (2002) and Pickel (2005), both of whom associate EP with its generic appeal to the concerns of particular political-economic communities. Pickel (2005) argues that economic nationalist arguments take many and varied forms, but what unites them is a broadly similar rhetorical architecture, where claims for policy innovation, or the granting of further authority or competence to the governing agent, are premised upon an appeal to the interests of the community being governed. Within national state space, this involves a discursive relationship between state managers and a subject population. While EP might be most obvious as a tactic used by office-holders or office-seekers in a democratic polity, this is not the only scenario in which EP might be useful. The affective relationship between government and electorate in democratic systems usually plays out within a settled state space: one whose boundaries are evident and one where the legitimate authority of the governing agent is settled. In those circumstances EP is an appeal to a known entity – a national economy whose interests can then be constructed in a variety of ways and be subject to political contest. But appeals to the interests of a political-economic community can be also be made in *anticipation* of the settlement of that political economic community. A focus on discourse has not been central to the rich literature on European state building (Flora *et al.* 1999; Lipset and Rokkan 1969), but this top–down view of political development focuses on the ways in which state actors come to be regarded as the legitimate governing agents of defined territorial spaces. The argument here is that EP is a technique (particularly a discursive technique) that seeks to accomplish that outcome. It not only appeals to a community; it also actively imagines and constructs it discursively. Let us return briefly to the example of Friedrich List's political economy. As is well known, in *The National System of Political Economy* (List 1966 [1841]), List pivots his argument upon a critique of Adam Smith's market cosmopolitanism, arguing instead for the primacy of national economic space as the key reference point for economic policy-making (Goff 2007: 12). This enabled him to make his famous infant industry argument because his concern was the fate of national economies as communities of fate and not universal economic welfare. List's writings are directed at the welfare of a particular national economic community of fate: Germany. Yet he formulated the most powerful expression of this position a full three decades before the formal unification of Germany. The point is not to draw precise parallels between 19th-century Germany and the EU, but to reinforce the idea that appeals to a political-economic community can be made in advance of the formal existence of that community.

The EU is read as a dynamic project of market building orchestrated through the actions of many actors, but where supranational institutions – once created – play a particularly important role as both entrepreneurs of integration and as candidate governing agents (Fligstein 2008; Parsons 2002; Pollack 2003; Stone Sweet and Sandholtz 1998). To secure supranational policy competence requires not only acceptance that a particular supranational authority is technically and normatively qualified for the job, but also widespread understanding of the space over which 'government' is to be exercised (Thrift 2005: 134). The project of market-making thus requires the spatial co-ordinates of that market to be established as a social fact, and the struggle to establish the social fact of the European economy is a fundamental feature of European economic integration since the mid-1980s. This is not to suggest that such a project has been fully and finally accomplished, but rather that recognition of EP's dynamic/historical character should alert us to the possibility that EP is not necessarily something only propagated by established governing agents with settled jurisdiction over established political-economic communities. Indeed, EP does not require the objective existence of its '*patrie*' to be recognizable as EP. In communicative discourse at least, EP can anticipate its '*patrie*' just as globalization discourse need not be underwritten by objective evidence to verify the globalization hypothesis in order to be operable (Cameron and Palan 2004; Hay and Rosamond 2002).

This refinement broadens the definition of EP to the extent that it comes to be seen as a *pathology* associated with the dynamic project of market-making. In turn this yields a third subtype of EP to add to the variants identified in Table 1. Thus Table 2 adds 'market-making' EP to characterize the ways in which appeals to particular political-economic communities become important to the consolidation of economic jurisdictions – and possibly even to their liberalization. Mode 6 EP is described in more detail below as a clear feature of the

Table 2 Varieties and levels of economic patriotism (2)

	National		*Supranational*
Listian EP	1		(2)
			⇩
Schmittian EP	3	⇨	4
Market-making EP	5		6

European Commission's discursive strategy and practices since the inauguration of the single market project in the mid-1980s. It is also worth identifying mode 5 EP as a feature of the territorial consolidation of the modern nation-state that might be comparable in interesting ways with the EU project of the late 20th and early 21st century. In the classic account of nation-building in Western Europe, the process is orchestrated and accomplished by a pre-existing, rational and goal-driven central state élite (Flora *et al.* 1999). The difference is that in the EU case market-making is being undertaken by an agent that is also emergent and not predefined and whose evolution is co-constitutive with the market space it seeks to govern (see also Bartolini 2007: 411). Common to modes 5 and 6 are two things. The first is dynamism. EP in this sense is not only the end product of historical processes; it is also fundamental to development of those processes. The second, is that this case involves the construction of 'spatially limited political mandates' (Clift and Woll 2012) where the emphasis is very much on the process by which that mandate is constructed and struggled over.

The efforts of the European Commission to premise its claims upon appeals to a particular spatial community are relatively recent. There was a marked shift in the Commission's communicative discourse on European economic integration in the mid-1980s. From the late 1950s until this time, justifications for deeper economic integration and more elaborate European-level governance relied upon the invocation of technical knowledge about the staged process which the economic theory of the time imagined for international economic integration (Balassa 1962). The idea, reproduced in Commission policy documents, is that economic unification would unfold in a predictable way. The creation of a free trade area among a group of countries would generate pressures for those countries to consolidate that free trade area into a customs union. The achievement of a common external tariff would generate technical spillovers towards the accomplishment of a common market. The benefits of the common market could not be realized without a common currency. Meanwhile the newly integrated economic space would need a centralized regulatory authority charged with the provision of rules for that space. In other words, economic integration was a technical matter that would yield eventually a centralized authority. Commission discourse in the 1960s and 1970s did not invoke this anticipated community. Instead it routinely invoked the staged, teleological process described in contemporaneous integration theory. Discussions about monetary union focused attention on a stage beyond the achievement of a common market precisely as a means to secure progress towards that very goal of a common market (Commission of the European Communities 1966: 15, 1975: 1; Commission of the European Economic Community 1967: 13; Council/Commission of the European Communities 1970: 8; Maes 2006). The 'spillover' logic of economic integration, culminating in monetary unification, is rehearsed in these documents (especially Commission of the European Communities [1973: 10–12]), thereby suggesting not only that European Monetary Union is an inevitable rather than a contingent outcome, but also drawing upon, authorizing and reproducing the logics inscribed in extant economic knowledge (Commission of the European Communities 1978: 9–18).

Since the mid-1980s, there has been a clear shift away from this mode of discourse towards the foundational claim of 'the European economy' as an actually existing entity from which certain logics follow (Jessop 1999: 2). The social fact of the 'European economy' is a precondition for establishing its deeper 'knowability'; that is, once known it can be measured. Once measured, it can be acted upon and thus governed (Miller and Rose 1990).

The term is particularly favoured in the communicative outputs of the Commission. A Eur-Lex search finds a total of 587 Commission documents (in English) that utilize the term.[2] The first use of 'European economy' in such a document was in 1979 and there was a total of four uses prior to 1985. Of the 86 documents authored by the Council that use the term, a very large number are Council endorsements of Commission proposals. Only 22 European Parliament documents contain the term. In addition, the idea of the 'European economy' is summoned up in several other prominent Commission publications.

The concerted campaign undertaken by the Commission in support of the single market initiative alighted on the concept of 'Europe 1992' as a 'cultural frame' through which the project and its institutional innovations were marketed (Fligstein and Mara-Drita 1996). The best-known output of this discursive onslaught was the 'Cecchini Report' (Cecchini 1988), a digest based upon a research programme funded by the Commission between 1986 and 1988 on the 'Costs of Non-Europe', whose findings ran to some 16 volumes of technical papers (Commission of the European Communities 1988). The counterfactual of 'non-Europe' loomed large in the report and the publicity surrounding it, thereby representing the first obvious public proclamation of a European economy, albeit one that was conjured up through the description of its actual non-existence and thus the technical and normative propriety of its future existence. The 'othering' of 'non-Europe' was at the same time allied to implications that the European economy, although not properly integrated, was something that could already be known and measured.

The summoning up of numeric indices implying an extant European economy was also evident in the landmark 1993 *White Paper on Competitiveness, Growth and Employment* (Commission of the European Communities 1993). The White Paper was remarkable for its recurrent attribution of a personality to 'the European economy'. Indeed, the text crystallized its aspirations in terms of 'an economy that is healthy, open, decentralized, competitive and based on solidarity' (1993: 11).

The White Paper mobilized data for 'Europe' (on unemployment, job creation, intensity of employment growth). This was presented, usually in terms of simple graphs plotting the variable in question on the x axis and time on the y axis as a series of macro-European trends, with no sense of member state variations or of sub-economies within the European whole. Moreover, the data is presented alongside functionally equivalent information for the United States and Japan (*ibid.*: 72–4). This presentational device has at least three notable qualities.

First, by implication 'Europe'/the EU is an economy that is as *knowable* as any other. The EU is knowable, not least because of the existence of statistical information that habitually represents it as an entity and thereby *normalizes* that representation.[3] Second, the availability (and manufacture) of data on the European economy as a discrete space provokes the corollary that this space is inhabited by discernible 'European' subjects. The concept of the 'European firm' is as elusive to analytical capture as the 'European economy', but it became a persistent theme at this time in EU discourse along with other subjects such as the 'European consumer' (Shore 2000: 100). Third, the White Paper developed the idea of 'Europe' as one symbolic growth pole (along with Japan and the United States) in a triadic global economy. This was accomplished by again deploying comparative data that implied functional equivalence with two *national* economies. This feeds through into the White Paper's central theme: 'competitiveness' (see Rosamond 2002). Because the European economy is knowable and thus of functional equivalence to the United States and Japanese economies, then it follows that its competitiveness *vis-à-vis* these rivals can be discussed and measured.

What might this be able to tell us about EP in the context of the contemporary EU? What is being suggested here is that this process fosters a discourse that enables the 'European economy' to be spoken about in terms of an entity that is *inter alia* 'competitive' (Strange 1998), or 'threatened', or characterized by particular measurable attributes, or is the carrier of certain types of values (Manners 2002), or something which requires particular forms of government. As such, in the anatomy of contemporary European economic discourse, the idea of the 'European economy' becomes foundational to the legitimation of numerous potential claims that generally take the form 'if the European Economy is x, then y follows'.

It is worth extracting a few observations from this discussion. First, the fact that the Commission is the principal user of the concept of the concept of the 'European economy' in its communicative discourse is an interesting finding. After all, the Commission is an aspiring governing agent. Its appeal to the 'European economy' aligns with expectations about market-making EP, except that its self-appointment as a governing agent does not follow from the settlement of the space over which it seeks regulatory jurisdiction. On the face of it, this is a case of a governing agent bringing itself into meaningful existence through its discursive elaboration of the very space that it aspires to govern. Second, this also suggests that the idea of the 'European economy' appeals to a community of fate rather than invoking a set of abstract technical reasons for why integration should deepen or why policy competence should be transferred to the EU level. The choice of the word 'economy' is important, invoking as it does a state–market relation. It would be equally possible to utilize the vocabulary of the 'European market' to describe the jurisdictional domain of the EU, but that would be more evocative of a social relation without a guiding legitimate authority. The recurrent use of the word 'economy', the imagination of its subject(s) and its subsequent statistical construction is what gives the Commission's discourse its market-making EP quality. Third, the associated competitiveness narrative and its statistical reinforcement reveal another generic feature of market-making EP discourse: the appeal to the inside (the 'European economy') in relation to the outside ('globalization'). Indeed globalization as an external imperative can be taken as a rationale to either liberalize or to act counter to open economy assumptions (Hay and Rosamond 2002). However, it is *what* needs to be liberalized or should act contrary to standard neoclassical assumptions that is important. Finally, this case illustrates how ideas about economic space acquire meaning when that space is rendered 'legible' (Scott 1998) through the development of statistical descriptors.

MARKET-MAKING ECONOMIC PATRIOTISM AND DILEMMAS OF LEGITIMACY

There is a quite powerful objection to almost all of the foregoing. Within the EU studies literature there is a strand of analysis that disputes the viability of supranational agency. If supranational institutions are merely secondary agents to whom member state governments have delegated selected governance tasks (Moravcsik 1998, 2002), then the idea of a the Commission as a semi-autonomous actor engaging in market-making forms of EP is bogus. At best, it might be possible to identify more conventional forms of protectionism at the EU level in terms of the successful upload of certain national preferences. What this position also dispenses with are many of the potentially acute questions about the legitimacy of EU-level EP. If, as in the liberal intergovernmentalist account (Moravcsik 1998), integration is the consequence of institutionalized bargains among the preferences of member state governments, and if those preferences are formed in the context of pluralist democratic polities, then there is no legitimacy deficit. This would be because input legitimacy conditions have been met at the domestic level and output legitimacy conditions are subject to the EU doing what it delegated to do via the outcomes of the international bargains that bring forth the EU treaties. The logical conclusion would be to assert that EP can only be properly found where one would most expect to find it: within nation-state space.

There are good reasons to move beyond this objection. As is shown by a good deal of work informed by principal–agent theory (upon which this sceptical position is based), agents will frequently detach themselves from the preferences of the principals or indeed remain wedded to the principals' original preferences rather than moving in accordance with how those preferences change over time (Pollack 2003). But if nothing else (and the evidence from EU Studies of autonomous agency being exercised by supranational institutions is extensive), the fact that the Commission in particular makes such a play of appealing to a political economic community called 'the European economy' should be taken as evidence of 'would-be' supranational governing agency. If we remember that legitimacy is something that is striven for as well as already accomplished, then it becomes possible to move beyond the position that only established communities of fate can be sites of EP.

In short, this is a point about legitimacy and the conditions under which genuine appeals to a genuine EP are possible. This relates to what Seabrooke neatly calls the 'devotional element of economic patriotism' that varies spatially across economic systems and in turn yields differential patterns of 'belief-driven economic actions' (Seabrooke 2012). Returning to the point above about EP being a feature of 'normal politics' in advanced industrial democracies, it would seem to follow that EP requires, as a precondition, an affective bond between governments and subject populations. EP, in other words, is discourse and practice rooted in fairly old fashioned understandings of the demand and support mechanisms that feature within mature political systems. An affective public implies, at a deeper level, a state engaged in a social contract with that public. That affective contract is expressed in legitimacy terms, not only (or indeed necessarily) through institutions of representative democracy, but also through the (near) accomplishment of the state's fiscal authority (Cameron 2006) and (maybe) the achievement of 'solidaristic' institutions of welfare (Flora *et al.* 1999; Wincott 2006).

On the face of it the 'devotional'/affective dimension of EP is more or less absent from the case of the EU. The debate about legitimacy in the EU is now well developed, nuanced and contested (Føllesdal 2007), but most analyses converge on the observation that the legitimacy underpinnings of the EU's economic order are thin. An interesting debate concerns the degree to which this thinness (a) is significant or (b) matters. On whether it matters, one view is that the EU is built upon 27 national legitimacy bargains that provide adequate democratic support for the integration project. This position bleeds into a minimalist defence of the pre-existing legitimacy underpinnings of European economic governance, a view associated with the writings of Moravcsik (2002) (see above). The position is most fully developed in the work of Majone (1994, 1996, 2005) who categorizes the EU as a form of 'regulatory state'. The regulatory state is a form of state that concentrates on building the conditions necessary for the operation of a market order. In the EU's case, this means that the emergent supranational 'state' has no redistributive role to play (i.e., no fiscal/welfare competence) and is barely visible in terms of stabilization functions (the provision of internal and external security). This leaves a weak form of output legitimacy associated with the successful delivery of the conditions required for functioning of a liberal market order. This means, in Majone's terms, that the EU is legitimate if it delivers what it exists to supply: a continental market order.

By extension, derogation from this mission – by lapsing into protectionism itself or failing to prevent economic nationalism amongst its member governments – would constitute a legitimacy failure. This provides an interesting supplement to some of the points made earlier about why the EU tends not to specialize in the delivery of protectionist policies. Also Majone's formulation explains why the EU as authoritative agent is less able to invoke or appeal to economic patriotic sentiment as classically understood. If its extant legitimacy is rooted in essentially liberal tenets, then classic EP discourse would seem to be counter-intuitive in the EU context. Low levels of competence in welfare, redistribution and fiscal policy limit the EU's capacity to behave like a 'government' that speaks to the interests of 'its' political-economic community. The absence of wholesale stabilization functions gives no immediate hook for Schmittian justifications for EP, although it is interesting to note how some economic programmes (such as energy policy – see above) have become fused to EU foreign and security policy and how technical questions from the 1960s of labour mobility have grown into a policy of perfect citizen mobility and ideas about the EU as an area of 'freedom, security and justice' within the EU-27 of the early 21st century.

The foregoing suggests not only that the scope for the EU acting in an EP-like way might be constrained, but also that the use of the term EP for EU practices may be misleading because the lack of a sufficient level of affective legitimacy. This is – perhaps – another way of making the familiar point that the EU is not really a state. In this sense only a state would be able to properly engage in EP because only such formations have both the jurisdiction and legitimacy to do so. Does this, therefore, rule out the thought experiment that this article seeks to perform? Is supranational economic patriotism simply a contradiction in terms? And should the study of EP in Europe be confined to national outbreaks of mercantilist activity that confront complex interdependence and take place within the context of variegated overlapping jurisdictions?

However, the contribution has argued that there is evidence within the EU of would-be governing agents seeking to speak to an aspirant political economic community. With this broader conception of EP and the more dynamic sense of legitimacy, it is possible to understand appeals to the 'European economy' not only as a legitimating strategy, but also as an act that opens a 'Pandora's box' of legitimacy dilemmas. The case of the European Commission is that of a would-be governing actor appealing to a community of fate without either democratic or fiscal legitimacy. The modern Commission is a path-dependent descendent of institutional design decisions taken at the height of 'high modernist' (Scott 1998; Walters and Haahr 2005) notions of delivering utility through enlightened technocratic means. The one card up its sleeve is a thin notion of output legitimacy that ties its fate to the performance of market management tasks. As Wincott (2006) argues, the idea (associated with Majone [2005]) that this is an adequate legitimacy basis for the EU is not merely a technical consequence of what a resource-poor EU is actually able to do. It is also normatively loaded in favour of neo-liberal conceptions of market efficiency and governance. It also means that when the Commission appeals to the 'European economy' as a political economic community, it runs the risk of disallowing debate on what sort of economy this should be.

CONCLUSION

The claims of this contribution may be summarized as follows. The application of the term EP to the EU is, on the face of it, not without merit. The relaxation of the idea that EP must be a property of national state space is clearly fundamental to any such discussion and there is no reason why the tendencies labelled 'nationalism' or 'patriotism' cannot be applied to post-national entities, particularly when those entities exhibit some of the characteristics of the EU. A much more fundamental and potentially fatal objection to this thought experiment is that EP-like appeals to particular communities require, as a prerequisite, affective legitimacy bonds between government and governed. The EU lacks these because of the nature of its economic governance regime, which technically and normatively clings to a very thin and arguably impoverished conception of output legitimacy. Present classifications of EP tend to rely upon rather static observations of politics, whereas the argument here seeks to introduce EP as an integral component to any project of market-marking because any attempt to create economic jurisdiction (even when predicated on liberal principles) requires the anticipation of, elaboration of and appeals to political-economic communities.

Biographical note: Ben Rosamond is Professor of Political Science at the University of Copenhagen.

NOTES

1 The adjectives 'Listian' and 'Schmittian' are deployed here as heuristic devices to classify two subtypes of EP. They are not intended to import in full their original authors' concerns to the analysis of the EU. This is especially true of the latter.

2 EUR-Lex is the online archive of the *Official Journal* of the EU. It holds full text copies of all treaties, case law, legislation and legislative proposals, and is available at http://eur-lex.europa.eu/en/index.htm (accessed 24 March 2010).
3 The extent to which the statistical construction of the European economy has been accomplished can be seen by referring to the data collected and presented by Eurostat at http://epp.eurostat.ec.europa.eu/portal/page/portal/eurostat/home (accessed 24 March 2010).

REFERENCES

Balassa, B. (1962) *The Theory of Economic Integration*, London: Allen and Unwin.

Bartolini, S. (2007) *Restructuring Europe; Centre Formation, System Building and Political Restructuring between the Nation-State and the European Union*, Oxford: Oxford University Press.

Brenner, N. (2004) *New State Spaces*, Oxford: Oxford University Press.

Cable, V. (2009) *The Storm: The World Economic Crisis and What it Means*, London: Atlantic Books.

Cameron, A. (2006) 'Turning point? The volatile geographies of taxation', *Antipode* 38(2): 236–58.

Cameron, A. and Palan, R. (2004) *The Imagined Economies of Globalization*, London: Sage.

Cecchini, P. (with Catinat M. Jacquemin A.) (1988) *The European Challenge: 1992*, Aldershot: Wildwood House.

Clark, P., Chaffin, J. and Weitzman, H. (2010) 'Aircraft makers both claim WTO win', *Financial Times*, 23 March, available at http://www.ft.com/cms/s/092a7554-368c-11df-8151-00144feabdc0,Authorised=false.html?_i_location=http%3A%2F%2Fwww.ft.com%2Fcms%2Fs%2F0%2F092a7554-368c-11df-8151-00144feabdc0.html&_i_referer=#axzz1edMihJ1T (accessed 22 November 2011).

Clift, B. and Woll, C. (2012) 'Economic patriotism: reinventing control over open markets', *Journal of European Public Policy* 19(3), http://dx.doi.org/10.1080/13501763.2011.638119

Commission of the European Communities (1966) *The Development of a European Capital Market: Report of a Group of Experts Appointed by the EEC Commission*, Brussels: Commission of the European Communities.

Commission of the European Communities (1973) *European Economic Integration and Monetary Unification*, Brussels: Commission of the European Communities.

Commission of the European Communities (1975) *Report of the Study Group 'Economic and Monetary Union 1980'*, Brussels: Commission of the European Communities.

Commission of the European Communities (1978) *The Customs Union: Today and Tomorrow. Record of the Conference Held in Brussels on 6, 7 and 8 December 1977*, Luxembourg: Office for Official Publications of the European Communities.

Commission of the European Communities (1988) *Research on the 'Cost of Non-Europe'. Basic Findings Volume 1. Basic Studies: Executive Summaries*, Luxembourg: Office for Official Publications of the European Communities.

Commission of the European Communities (1993) 'White paper on competitiveness, growth and employment: the challenges and ways forward into the 21st century', COM(93) 700 Final, available at http://aei.pitt.edu/1139/01/growth_wp_COM_93_700_Parts_A_B.pdf (accessed 20 March 2010).

Commission of the European Communities (2005) 'Implementing the Community Lisbon programme: a policy framework to strengthen EU manufacturing – towards a more integrated approach for industrial policy', COM(2005) 474 Final.

Commission of the European Communities (2006) 'A European strategy for sustainable, competitive and secure energy', COM (2006) 105 Final.

Commission of the European Economic Communities (1967) *Tenth General Report on the Activities of the Community (1 April 1966–31 March 1967)*, Brussels: Commission of the European Economic Community.
Council/Commission of the European Communities (1970) *Report of the Council and Commission on the Realisation by Stages of Economic and Monetary Union in the Community: 'Werner Report'*, Luxembourg: Office for Official Publications of the European Communities.
Economist, The (2009) 'The return of economic nationalism', 5 February, available at http://www.economist.com/node/13061443 (accessed 22 November 2011).
Fligstein, N. (2008) *Euro-clash: The EU, European Identity, and the Future of Europe*, Oxford: Oxford University Press.
Fligstein, N. and Mara-Drita, I. (1996) 'How to make a market: reflections on the attempt to create a single market in the European Union', *American Journal of Sociology* 102(1): 1–33.
Flora, P., Kuhnle, S. and Urwin, D. (eds) (1999) *State Formation, Nation-Building and Mass Politics: The Theory of Stein Rokkan*, Oxford: Oxford University Press.
Føllesdal, A. (2007) 'Normative political theory and the European Union', in K.E. Jørgensen, M.A. Pollack and B. Rosamond (eds), *Handbook of European Union Politics*, London: Sage, pp. 317–35.
Garzon, I. (2006) *Reforming the Common Agricultural Policy: History of a Paradigm Shift*, Basingstoke: Palgrave Macmillan.
Gill, S. (1998) 'European governance and new constitutionalism: economic and monetary union and alternatives to disciplinary neoliberalism in Europe', *New Political Economy* 3(1): 5–26.
Gill, S. (2001) 'Constitutionalising capital: EMU and disciplinary neo-liberalism', in A. Bieler and A.D. Morton (eds), *Social Forces and the Making of the New Europe: The Restructuring of European Social Relations in the Global Political Economy*, Basingstoke: Palgrave, pp. 47–69.
Gill, S. (2003) 'A neo-gramscian approach to European integration', in A. Cafruny and M. Ryner (eds), *A Ruined Fortress? Neoliberal Hegemony and Transformation in Europe*, Lanham, MD: Rowman and Littlefield, pp. 47–70.
Goff, P. (2007) *Limits to Liberalization: Local Culture in a Global Marketplace*, Ithaca, NY: Cornell University Press.
Grant, W. (1997) *The Common Agricultural Policy*, Basingstoke: Macmillan.
Greer, A. (2005) *Agricultural Policy in Europe*, Manchester: Manchester University Press.
Hanson, B.T. (1998) 'What happened to Fortress Europe? External trade policy liberalization in the European Union', *International Organization* 52(1): 55–85.
Härtel, H. (2006) 'The threat of economic patriotism', *Intereconomics* 41(2): 58–9.
Hay, C. and Rosamond, B. (2002) 'Globalization. European integration and the discursive construction of economic imperatives', *Journal of European Public Policy* 9(2): 147–67).
Helleiner, E. (2002) 'Economic nationalism as a challenge to neoliberalism? Lessons from the 19th century', *International Studies Quarterly* 46(3): 307–29).
Hodson, D. and Quaglia, L. (2009) 'European perspectives on the global financial crisis', *Journal of Common Market Studies* 47(5): 939–53.
Jabko, N. (2006) *Playing the Market: A Political Strategy for Uniting Europe, 1985–2005*, Ithaca, NY: Cornell University Press.
Jessop, B. (1999) 'Narrating the future of the national economy and the national state? Remarks on remapping regulation and reinventing governance', Department of Sociology, University of Lancaster, available at http://www.lancs.ac.uk/fass/sociology/papers/jessop-narrating-the-future.pdf (accessed 19 March 2010).

Knudsen, A-C.L (2009) *Farmers on Welfare: The Making of Europe's Common Agricultural Policy*, Ithaca, NY: Cornell University Press.
Lipset, S.M. and Rokkan, S. (1969) 'Cleavage structures, party systems and voter, alignments: an introduction', in S.M. Lipset and S. Rokkan (eds), *Party Systems and Voter Alignments: Cross-National Perspectives*, New York: Free Press, pp. 1–64.
List, F. (1966 1841) *The National System of Political Economy*, New York: Augustus M. Kelly.
Maes, I. (2006) 'The ascent of the European Commission as an actor in the monetary integration process in the 1960s', *Scottish Journal of Political Economy* 53(2): 222–41.
Majone, G. (1994) 'The rise of the regulatory state in Europe', *West European Politics* 17(3): 77–101.
Majone, G. (ed.) (1996) *Regulating Europe*, London: Routledge.
Majone, G. (2005) *Dilemmas of European Integration: The Ambiguities and Pitfalls of Integration by Stealth*, Oxford: Oxford University Press.
Manners, I (2002) 'Normative power Europe: a contradiction in terms?', *Journal of Common Market Studies* 40(2): 235–58.
McGuire, S. (1997) *Airbus Industrie: Conflict and Cooperation in US–EC Trade Relations*, Basingstoke: Macmillan.
Miller, P. and Rose, N. (1990) 'Governing economic life', *Economy and Society* 19(1): 1–31.
Moravcsik, A. (1998) *The Choice for Europe: Social Purpose and State Power from Messina to Maastricht*, Ithaca, NY: Cornell University Press.
Moravcsik, A. (2002) 'In defence of the "democratic deficit": Reassessing legitimacy in the European Union', *Journal of Common Market Studies* 40(4): 603–24.
Parsons, C. (2002) 'Showing ideas as causes: the origins of the European Union', *International Organization* 56(1): 47–84.
Pelkmans, J. (2006) 'European level industrial policy', *Bruges Economic Policy Briefings No. 13*, July, available at http://www.coleurop.be/content/studyprogrammes/eco/publications/BEEPs/BEEP15.pdf (accessed 24 March 2010).
Pickel, A. (2005) 'Introduction: reconceptualizing economic nationalism in a globalizing world', in E. Helleiner and A. Pickel (eds), *Economic Nationalism in a Globalizing World*, Ithaca, NY: Cornell University Press, pp. 1–20.
Pollack, M.A. (2003) *The Engines of Integration: Delegation, Agency and Agenda Setting in the European Union*, Oxford: Oxford University Press.
Posner, E. and Véron, N. (2010) 'The EU and financial regulation: power without purpose?', *Journal of European Public Policy* 17(3): 400–15.
Potter, C. and Titzey, M. (2005) 'Agricultural policy discourses in the European post-Fordist transition: neo-liberalism, neo-mercantilism and multi-functionality', *Progress in Human Geography* 29(5): 581–600.
Quaglia, L., Eastwood, R. and Holmes, P. (2009) 'The financial turmoil and EU policy cooperation in 2008', *Journal of Common Market Studies* 47(1): 63–87.
Rosamond, B. (2002) 'Imagining the European economy: "competitiveness" and the social construction of "Europe" as an economic space', *New Political Economy* 7(2): 157–77.
Schmitt, C. (2004 [1922]) *Political Theology: Four Chapters on the Concept of Sovereignty*, Chicago, IL: University of Chicago Press.
Scott, J.C. (1998) *Seeing Like a State: How Certain Schemes to Improve the Human Condition Have Failed*, New Haven, CT: Yale University Press.
Seabrooke, L. (2012) 'Homespun capital: economic patriotism and housing finance under stress', *Journal of European Public Policy* 19(3), http://dx.doi.org/10.1080/13501763.2011.638131
Shore, C. (2000) *Building Europe: The Cultural Politics of European Integration*, London: Routledge.

Stone Sweet, A. and Sandholtz, W. (1998) 'Integration, supranational governance and the institutionalization of the European polity', in W. Sandholtz and A. Stone Sweet (eds), *European Integration and Supranational Governance*, Oxford: Oxford University Press, pp. 1–26.
Swinbank, A. (1992) 'The EEC's policies and its food', *Food Policy* 17(1): 53–64.
Strange, S. (1998) 'Who are EU? Ambiguities in the concept of competitiveness', *Journal of Common Market Studies* 36(1): 101–14.
Tangermann, S. (1983) 'What is different about European agricultural protectionism?' *The World Economy* 6(1): 39–58.
Thrift, N. (2005) *Knowing Capitalism*, London: Sage.
Walters, W. and Haahr, J.H. (2005) *Governing Europe: Discourse, Governmentality and European Integration*, London: Routledge.
Weiler, J.H.H. (1991) 'The transformation of Europe', *Yale Law Journal* 100(8): 2403–83.
Wincott, D. (2006) 'European political development, regulatory governance, and the European social model: the challenge of substantive legitimacy', *European Law Journal* 12(6): 743–63.
Youngs, R. (2009) *Energy Security: Europe's New Foreign Policy Challenge*, London: Routledge.

From nationalism to European patriotism? Trade unions and the European works council at General Motors

Thomas Fetzer

ABSTRACT Research on economic patriotism has so far focused on public policy and only marginally addressed the role of non-state actors. This contribution seeks to fill this gap. It examines the emergence of a European economic patriotism discourse among trade union representatives at General Motors since the late 1990s, which underpinned the operation of the company's 'European works council', a statutory body of employee representation mandated by a 1994 European Union directive. It argues that the new trade union emphasis on 'European interests' *vis-à-vis* subsidiaries in other world regions, and *vis-à-vis* GM's global headquarter in Detroit, reflected a (partial) 'upward shift' of patriotism from the national to the European level in response to corporate globalization. It also highlights the limited and fragile nature of European patriotism, which was severely challenged during the recent global economic crisis

'Economic patriotism' (EP), a term first popularized by then French prime minister de Villepin in 2005, has attracted growing academic interest not least in response to the massive state interventions associated with the recent global economic crisis. As defined by Clift and Woll in the introduction to this collection, EP arises from the incongruity between a highly integrated international economy and the narrower territorial boundaries of communities, a 'mismatch' that provides a constant incentive for economic actors to discriminate in favour of territorial 'insiders'. Importantly, going beyond the economic nationalism framework (see Crane 1998; Helleiner and Pickel 2005), EP points to the multi-level character of this phenomenon, which is equally discernible at the level of sub-national (local) or supranational communities. In fact, the EP literature connects here to a long-standing discussion among political and economic geographers, which has highlighted that the spatial setup of politics can shift between various territorial 'scales' (see Cox 1998)

Most of the emerging EP literature focuses on public policy, while the role of non-state actors has so far received only limited attention. The contribution helps fill this gap, focusing on the case of trade union policy in the multinational automobile company General Motors (GM). Given the importance of job creation and/or retention for territorial politics, a study of trade unions is particularly well suited to take a closer look at what Callaghan and Lagneau-Ymonet (2012) call the 'demand side' of EP. More specifically, the contribution examines the emergence and subsequent development of a European economic patriotism discourse among GM trade union representatives since the late 1990s, which underpinned the operation of the company's 'European works council' (EWC), a statutory body of employee representation in multinational firms mandated by a 1994 European Union directive (see Gold 2007).

This focus on the supranational European level may seem surprising at first sight. If trade unions are thought of as potential carriers of economic patriotism, conventional wisdom would suggest looking at the national level. Since their post-war integration into nation-states through welfare regimes and industrial relations institutions (Sassoon 1996; Streeck 1998), trade unions are often described as having succumbed to the 'appeal of national identity' (Pasture and Verberckmoes 1998). However, labour sociologists and geographers remind us that the politics of job retention plays out at various spatial levels (see Harrod and O'Brien 2002; Herod 2001). In Western Europe, for example, the stronger post-war national rooting never displaced localist traditions, which continued to find expression in everyday union politics – witness the debates about 'factory consciousness' and 'Betriebsegoismus' (plant egoism) among British and German industrial relations scholars during the 1970s and 1980s (Batstone 1984; Kotthoff 1981). Since the early 1990s, on the other hand, trade union discourses reveal a growing European attachment, expressed in the widespread if vague union advocacy of the 'European social model' (Hyman 2005).

But why do trade unions embrace a specific spatial scale of patriotism? What are the conditions under which they have recently espoused, to some extent, a supranational European patriotism? These are the crucial questions I seek to explore through the case study of GM's European works council. While not denying the importance of the external environment – in particular the statutory support provided by EU legislation as a crucial precondition (see Gold 2007) – the analytical focus will be on developments inside the firm. As a matter of fact, EWC practices vary a great deal across countries and sectors, and the key question is why some councils (such as GM) have moved far beyond the EU-prescribed minimum of regular consultation exercises.

Unlike other scholars who have emphasized actor-specific factors such as the role of local union leaders as 'political entrepreneurs' (Greer and Hauptmeier 2008), my interpretation connects trade union strategies primarily to shifts in GM's corporate structures. Translated into the conceptual language of economic patriotism, I argue that there was an upward shift of the clash between economic and community boundaries, which entailed a 'rescaling' of union patriotism: prior to the mid-1990s, competition between subsidiaries *within* Europe fuelled national economic patriotism in the different GM locations, which, was subsequently superimposed by a new European patriotism in response to corporate globalization. As a result, GM trade unionists increasingly embraced 'European interests' *vis-à-vis* subsidiaries in other world regions, and *vis-à-vis* GM's global headquarter in Detroit. Importantly, the emergence of European patriotism was also dependent on a favourable 'internal' context, namely the absence of a clear national centre of GM's European operations.

The contribution draws on contemporary press coverage, published and unpublished trade union documents, as well as on internet sources and interviews with trade union representatives. In the first section, I briefly introduce the pattern of national economic patriotism that dominated among GM trade unionists prior to the mid-1990s, focusing on Germany and the United Kingdom (UK) as the two largest European GM locations. The second and main section analyses the transformation towards a European economic patriotism since the late 1990s and explicates how the absence of a clear national centre of GM's European operations helped to bring about this transformation. The third and last section argues that it was precisely the (temporary) dissolution of this favourable context owing to GM's impending bankruptcy and German government intervention which severely challenged European patriotism during the recent crisis in 2009/10. The article concludes with reflections about the implications of the case study for economic patriotism scholarship.

TRADE UNIONS AND NATIONAL ECONOMIC PATRIOTISM PRIOR TO THE MID-1990S

General Motors' presence in Europe dates back to the 1920s when the firm acquired Vauxhall Motors in Luton (close to London) and Adam Opel AG in Rüsselsheim (close to Frankfurt/Main), next to opening assembly facilities in Belgium (Antwerp) and Denmark. After 1945 GM's German operations grew dynamically, leading in the 1960s to the establishment of new plants in Bochum and Kaiserslautern. Today Germany still is by far the largest GM location on the old continent, accounting for nearly half of the 48,000 European GM employees. Vauxhall fell behind since the late 1960s despite the launch of an additional facility at Ellesmere Port (Liverpool) – a trend, which was accelerated with the partial closure of the traditional Luton plant in 2000 (Holden 2003). GM diversified its European production geography since the late 1970s, first by opening a large manufacturing complex in Zaragoza (Spain) and component facilities in France and Austria, later, after the fall of the Iron Curtain, by moving East: since the early 1990s new plants have been established in Eisenach (East Germany), Poland (Gliwice), Hungary (Esztergom) and Russia (St Petersburg). GM's merger with Saab temporarily added a strong Swedish component, too[1] (Bordenave and Lung 2003).

GM also increasingly integrated its European subsidiaries, starting in the mid-1970s with a gradual standardization of Opel and Vauxhall models, and accelerating after 1986 when the company established a European headquarters in Zurich in response to the Single Market (Dassbach 1989: 442f.). Ever since, car and truck models were developed and produced on pan-European platforms, with two or more locations sharing manufacturing and/or assembly. GM managers frequently threatened to shift production between locations to obtain trade union concessions (Mueller and Purcell 1992).

Against this backdrop, national economic patriotism discourses unfolded among trade union representatives, particularly in the British and German GM subsidiaries Vauxhall and Opel. Competition between locations usually involved plants situated in different countries, rather than those within the same state (Rüsselsheim vs. Antwerp, Ellesmere Port vs. Zaragoza, etc.), which encouraged a national framing of local union interests. In other words, national economic patriotism reflected a 'boundary clash' between the traditional local and national trade union communities and the emergence of GM's corporate Europeanization. Trade union campaigns highlighting alleged dangers to 'German production' or 'British jobs' frequently occurred since the early 1980s, for example with regard to the distribution of production for GM's small Corsa vehicle (1982–6), the reallocation of engine and transmission production (1988–90), or, from the early 1990s, the distribution of headcount reductions in the course of European restructuring (see Fetzer 2005: 266–73).

Such union campaigns had their 'ebbs and flows', and their core concerns changed over time, from competition for investment and production volumes to rivalries over productivity levels and the cross-border distribution of profits. The climax was reached in the late 1990s: national trade unions at various GM locations engaged in concession bargaining deliberately designed to obtain future investment guarantees at the expense of other plants (*ibid.*: 330–8).

National economic patriotism among trade union representatives was not only expressed in competitive rivalries but also in attachment to country-specific notions of national autonomy. In Germany, labour representatives launched protests against the new GM Europe headquarters' interference in Opel affairs since the late 1980s, demanding more subsidiary and brand autonomy in product development, manpower and budgetary matters (*Rüsselsheimer Echo* 1990). On the one hand, European management centralization threatened to erode the effectiveness of co-determination – lobbying for a greater range of powers for Opel managers was thus a 'surrogate' campaign to preserve traditional German trade union rights (*Rüsselsheimer Echo* 1989). On the other hand, national corporate autonomy was seen as necessary against Zurich's 'excessive' focus on cost reduction at the expense of investment into new products and technologies. A high point of this dynamic was reached in 1997 when the works council, supported by Opel management, entered into open conflict with Zurich over the introduction of a new template for intra-company performance benchmarking (Rehder 2003: 179–81).

In the UK, by contrast, national autonomy was not so much addressed in corporate terms, as British trade unions lacked their German counterparts' role as company stakeholders through co-determination. Instead, national autonomy became associated with broader initiatives for state control and national market protection. Until the late 1970s most of this concentrated on lobbies for government intervention, for example in the form of so-called 'planning agreements' (Wilks 1981), and on trade union support for the campaign against British membership in the European Community (EC). However, the defeat of the EC opposition movement and the neo-liberal shift of government policy since 1979 led to the reorientation of national autonomy strategies towards more market-based initiatives. GM was now directly pressured to accept that British plants should supply the British market – backed up with the mobilization of employees, consumers and public opinion. Exploiting the still influential 'buy British' approach among UK car buyers, the unions accused GM of deliberately depriving UK plants of the supply of the 'home market' (Fetzer 2005: 266–72).

FROM NATIONALISM TO EUROPEAN PATRIOTISM?

By the late 1990s, little seemed to indicate a shift towards European patriotism among trade unionists at General Motors. The creation of the company's European works council[2] in 1996 had little impact initially; occasional EWC meetings did not appear to mitigate the investment competition between different locations, and the associated strength of national economic patriotism (Hancké 2000). Already by the early 2000s, however, the situation had changed dramatically, as the EWC acquired the status of European managements' negotiation partner. A first agreement was concluded in 2000, which gave long-term employment and wage guarantees for employees in GM's European power train operations that were to be transferred to a joint venture with Fiat. In 2001 two further agreements followed in relation to European restructuring measures (Herber and Schäfer-Klug 2002; Klebe and Roth 2000). In October 2004, the EWC again negotiated a European framework agreement for the reduction of headcount levels without forced redundancies or plant closures. In parallel, the body also became involved in the process of investment allocation for the new Vectra/Saab 9-3, 9-5 ranges (Bartmann 2005). In 2006/7 the EWC played a crucial co-ordinating role in the 'site selection process' for the next generation of GM's new Astra vehicles involving the plants in Bochum, Antwerp, Ellesmere Port, Trollhättan and Gliwice (Banyuls *et al.* 2008).

It is not the purpose of this contribution to provide an exhaustive description of this complex transformation. Rather, its main objective is to highlight that the shift towards European trade union co-operation at GM since the late 1990s was nurtured by the emergence of a supranational European economic patriotism, which responded to corporate globalization processes that were perceived as endangering employment security across the European continent.

The new discourse of European economic patriotism

General Motors started to shift towards the globalization of corporate structures and strategies since the early 1990s. This process was not linear; it suffered setbacks owing to corporate and market constraints, and its degree was contested within the company. Still, there was a significant shift towards the integration of European operations into global company structures. New car models were developed on global platforms, which were designed to rationalize the various model ranges sold by GM brands throughout the world (Bordenave and Lung 2003). Between 2004 and the 2009 crisis, this process accelerated as Detroit increased its corporate control over the regional company groupings in Europe, Asia and Latin America (Banyuls *et al.* 2008). In parallel to global reorganization GM's production geography also changed owing to the company's massive investments in Eastern Europe and Asia. Joint ventures were launched in Russia and China, and GM took over the Korean manufacturer Daewoo. As a consequence, the relative position of GM's traditional European operations declined (Bordenave and Lung 2003).

It was against this backdrop that trade unionists started to invoke 'European interests' *vis-à-vis* GM subsidiaries in other world regions and *vis-à-vis* GM's global headquarter in Detroit. This discourse was already discernible during the first cross-border union encounters prior to the EWC creation in the mid-1990s. German Opel works councillors spoke about the necessity for a new 'European thinking' when GM was investing large sums in other parts of the world. British union representatives warned that GM's new plants in Asia would constitute a threat for long-term employment prospects in Europe (Betriebsrat Adam Opel AG 1994). After the EWC establishment in 1996, its first chairman praised the 'production location Europe', warning that accelerated investments in Asia, partly financed from European profits, would come at the expense of necessary improvements of products and facilities on the old continent (Betriebsrat Adam Opel AG 1997).

After the millennium this rhetoric intensified. There was a great deal of trade union anxiety about the expansion of GM operations in other parts of the world, expressed, for example, in frequent complaints about newspaper interviews of leading GM managers alluding to Detroit plans for a longer-term shift of GM activities to Eastern Europe, China, Korea and India. The changing GM production geography and the global platform approach were portrayed as a dangerous combination because they appeared to force West European locations into ever new rounds of cost competition with the new GM plants in Eastern Europe and Asia. Global car architectures, a EWC leaflet warned in March 2007, meant that 'a single plant can manufacture very different GM brands and models and that production can be transferred between plants even beyond Europe within six weeks' (GM Workers Blog 2007a).

'Economic patriotism' is a useful concept to interpret this new trade union discourse. Essentially, this was an upward shift of the dilemma that underpins the rationale for economic patriotism, namely the clash between a highly integrated international economy and the narrower territorial boundaries of communities. Prior to the mid-1990s *national* economic patriotism in the different GM locations had been fuelled by competition between subsidiaries *within* Europe; now, corporate globalization schemes favoured the emergence of a regional, European patriotism discourse. This did not mean the end of national trade union patriotism. Indeed, national and European patriotism often co-existed, best illustrated in comments of a Belgian EWC representative in the wake of the Astra allocation decision in 2007: while expressing satisfaction about the fact that European co-operation allowed the Antwerp plant to (temporarily) stay open despite having lost out on Astra production, he nevertheless criticized the selection decision as driven by brand considerations rather than productivity, which would have favoured the Belgian over German and British sites (GM Workers Blog 2007b).

Still, the new rhetoric of 'European interests' was a significant novelty. On the one hand, it must be seen against the backdrop of the broader notion of 'Europe' as a global economic competitor that had gained ground among European policy-makers and interest groups since the early 1990s (see Rosamond 2002, 2012). On the other hand, the earlier defensive nationalisms were transposed to the European level. Still, in 1996, for example, German labour representatives had argued that it had been thanks to 'German profits' alone that GM had been able to invest in other *European* operations in Belgium, Spain and Sweden (Betriebsrat Adam Opel AG 1996). Now the same argument was shifted to the European level: profits made in Europe should be reinvested there rather than used for helping GM's global expansion plans.

In fact, intriguingly, the new European patriotism discourse among GM trade unionists represented a curious mix of the different national approaches described earlier. Given the large size of GM facilities in the Federal Republic, there was a strong German 'imprint' here, in particular with regard to demands for management and brand autonomy. Until the mid-1990s, as we have seen, such demands had been deployed to request more independence for national management and the Opel brand. Now they were 'europeanized' – EWC spokesmen frequently argued that GM's European workers were paying the price for a misconceived strategy of global product standardization that was out of tune with 'European' market demand. They claimed that GM's 'European brands' Opel, Saab and Vauxhall, needed more autonomy and a more European product profile to achieve a turnaround in sales, and hence a stabilization of employment prospects (GM Workers Blog 2007c).

However, there was also a component that followed earlier British union approaches focusing on national market control. Time and again EWC statements argued that GMs' European sales, including those of non-European GM brands (e.g., Chevrolet) should be sourced from plants in Europe. The joint EWC bargaining position with regard to the Astra allocation in 2007, for example, rested on the assumption that the plant without Astra production would be compensated by the allocation of non-European GM models destined for sale on European markets. A EWC press release prior to the decision pointed out that 'an important principle for the employee representatives would be that cars which should be sold in the European market should be produced in the European plants' (GM Workers Blog 2007d). It should be added that such demands co-existed uneasily with parallel lobbies for a stronger role of European operations *within* the globalization process, e.g., the promotion of European leadership for global product development and greater export opportunities for European brands in other world regions.[3] Trade union aspirations, in the terms suggested by Clift and Woll (2012) in the introduction to this collection, oscillated between 'strategic (inter)-regional integration' (liberal patriotism) and 'defensive regionalism' (conservative patriotism).

As these remarks indicate, the new European patriotism discourse was not merely empty rhetoric but shaped practical trade union strategies at GM during the 2000s. On the one hand, European patriotism informed union approaches in the negotiations with GM management. Here, the EWC often pointed to the company's mediocre market performance since the mid-1990s, which it saw caused by GM's failure to develop innovative 'European' car models, e.g., with regard to engine technology, or safety standards, and the lacking cultivation of European brand images (GM Workers Blog 2007c). In light of the fact that European market demand indeed differs from America and Asia in some crucial respects (Jürgens 2004), the EWC argued that GM's business success depended on the retention of a distinctly European style, which in turn would guarantee European production and employment.

At the same time, the EWC used the European patriotism discourse to build up a united front of workforces across the continent. The EWC created its own internet forum, the 'gmworkersblog', on which 'European solidarity' became a buzzword – defined not only as an intra-European affair but, more importantly, as the necessity to stand united in the defence of European interests within the global GM network. Special efforts were made to propagate 'European interests' as a means to overcome intra-European competition. During the 2007 Astra allocation process, for example, EWC leaders discouraged plant representatives from concluding local agreements not only by pointing to the dangers of an intra-European race to the bottom but also by highlighting the risks inherent in GM's globalization even for the 'winners':

> the allocation of a future global product like the next Astra doesn't make a plant and the jobs 'safe' anymore. After getting the new product the workers, unions and works councils can easily be blackmailed by management to make further concessions, otherwise the plant can lose its production to a 'cheaper' plant worldwide. (GM Workers Blog 2007a)

Clearly, not all these attempts to 'produce' unity on the basis of presumed joint 'European interests' were successful in downplaying the importance of intra-European conflicts and the massive cost-cutting schemes to which the EWC signed up in the process (see below). It is also striking how much EWC positions reflected an essentially *West* European notion of patriotism that was to defend German, British, Belgian and Spanish plants against competition not only from Asia, but also from *Eastern Europe* However, these ambiguities notwithstanding, the new globalization-driven European trade union patriotism undoubtedly played an important role for the dynamic development of GM's European works council since the late 1990s.

The facilitating context: trade unions as 'risk communities'

As has been argued elsewhere (Fetzer 2008), the 'discovery' of 'European interests' in response to GM's corporate globalization can be interpreted as the 'external' expression of a 'risk community', whose cohesiveness stood and fell with the perception of a common threat. Crucially, however, this 'risk community' also had an internal dimension, which provided the necessary facilitating context for the emergence of European patriotism (*ibid.*: 296–300). The key aspect here was that General Motors Europe, in contrast to EU-based automobile firms like Volkswagen, Fiat or Renault, lacked a clear national centre in terms of corporate decision-making and production operations – circumstances that have routinely been emphasized as facilitating EWC operations by industrial relations scholars (Kotthoff 2006; Marginson *et al.* 2004). As mentioned earlier, GM's production facilities were widely spread across the continent; by the late 1990s substantial manufacturing and/or assembly operations existed in nine European countries. As for corporate decision-making, the creation of the European headquarter in Zurich in 1986 strongly enhanced the autonomy of GM's European management even *vis-à-vis* the largest national subsidiary, the German Adam Opel AG. This pattern contrasts with the situation in EU-based automobile producers, which continue to display a strong focus of 'production geography' on the respective home countries (Dicken 2007: 301–3) and lack an independent European management level – European strategies are decided upon in the national headquarters in Wolfsburg, Paris or Turin.

As a consequence, the interests of national trade unions and works councils at GM were *more evenly* affected by processes of corporate restructuring than in the case of EU-based car firms. At the same time, it was more difficult for even the largest national group – German Opel labour representatives – to successfully 'play the national card' in dealing with restructuring. Here, the 'domino' concession bargaining of the late 1990s, while marking the 'high point' of national economic patriotism, also provided a useful lesson about the limits of such negotiation tactics. Designed to secure long-term employment prospects in the Federal Republic, national concession bargaining caused a competitive spiral, which threatened to degenerate into a 'race to the bottom'. Among German representatives, in particular, this episode strengthened the case for at least a minimum degree of cross-border understanding to protect local/national collective labour standards in a longer-term perspective (Herber and Schäfer-Klug 2002). It is also worth noting that German representatives themselves rarely formed a cohesive group owing to tensions within and between works councils in the different locations.

Clearly, as already alluded to earlier, the new European patriotism did not mean that labour representatives abandoned their local and national allegiances. In fact, the EWC continuously faced the task of reconciling diverging interests. Next to providing a broad 'safety net' through European framework agreements ruling out plant closures, one of its most important objectives became the elaboration of accepted rules for 'fair competition' between locations, e.g., with regard to the transparency of investment tenders and the definition of 'bottom lines' for wage concessions (Bartmann 2005). Nonetheless, suspicions about a 'German bias' in GM's European strategy continued to be voiced by unionists from other locations, in the UK, for example, at the time of the Luton cutbacks in 2000/1 (Minutes of a special meeting of the Vauxhall JNC 2000), and in Belgium in relation to the Astra allocation procedure in 2007 when GM managers publicly emphasized the need to retain a good brand image in the Federal Republic.

Still, the GM context was much more favourable to the articulation of 'European interests' and European economic patriotism than that of EU-based companies. In the case of Volkswagen, for example, cross-border contacts between trade unionists also became more important since the mid-1990s, and they even reached beyond Europe (Weiler 2006). Yet, these contacts were always conducted under the leadership of German labour representatives (Carley and Hall 2006: 67). VW's supervisory board remained the crucial arena for decision-making, while the EWC never acquired the prominent role it achieved at General Motors (Weiler 2006).

CHALLENGES TO EUROPEAN PATRIOTISM: TRADE UNIONS AND THE GM CRISIS 2009/10

That the absence of a clear national centre indeed represented a crucial facilitating condition for the emergence of European economic patriotism among GM trade unionists became abundantly clear during the company's recent major crisis. That crisis, culminating in June 2009 with the insolvency of the American parent company under chapter 11 of the US bankruptcy code, led to protracted negotiations about a possible sale of GM's European operations. Among the several bidders a consortium led by the Canadian–Austrian company Magna appeared to have won the day by November 2009 when, in a surprise move, GM decided to retain its European subsidiaries and to cancel a preliminary agreement with the consortium.

On the face of it, the crisis should have further strengthened European trade union patriotism, given that the issue of European autonomy from Detroit – a staple of EWC demands since the late 1990s – soon became one of the crucial questions in the takeover negotiations between GM and Magna. It turned out, however, that the crisis instead led to serious tensions among GM's European trade unionists, most visibly expressed in the open clash over Magna's takeover bid, which was welcomed by German and Belgian representatives, while being opposed for a long time by their counterparts in Spain, the UK and, to a lesser extent, Poland (EIRO 2009). The EWC was effectively sidelined, and there was little European co-ordination in the subsequent restructuring negotiations with the prospective new owner Magna. And, while all national unions had struck deals with Magna by late October 2009, reactions to GM's U-turn in early November again revealed the deep internal divisions: in the UK, Tony Woodley, general secretary of the UNITE union, described the GM announcement as 'fantastic news', while GM's decision was met with a great deal of criticism and even a one-day strike action in the German GM plants (EIRO 2009).

While we saw that the European works council never managed to fully overcome tensions between local and national GM labour representatives, this clash was of a different quality because of the heavy involvement of the German government in the Magna–GM negotiations, which was itself in part triggered by joint lobbies from several regions in which Opel plants are situated (Hesse, Nordrhine-Westphalia, Rheinland-Pfalz, Thuringia – Tagesshau 2009). There can be no doubt that German labour representatives were actively implicated in the initiatives of this federal 'crisis cartel' from the outset – within months, the central Opel works council chairman Franz became a German media celebrity, featuring as the 'saviour' of Opel plants in the Federal Republic. At the same time, against the backdrop of the upcoming federal elections, the GM saga turned into a crisis management competition between the two coalition parties CDU (Christlich Demokratische Union) and SPD (Sozialdemokratische Partei Deutschlands), and both sought close co-operation with Franz and national union leaders. This pattern was particularly discernible in the bidding process in the first half of 2009 – the strong German government preference for the Magna consortium over the rival contenders Fiat and RHJ International was fully in line with trade union positions (*ibid.*).

Conversely, the new conspicuous role of the German government became the main bone of contention for labour representatives in other European GM locations. In Spain and the UK, in particular, it was widely believed that the German government put strong pressure on General Motors to agree to a Magna takeover, because Magna's future business plan privileged German locations over those in other European countries. In the Spanish Zaragoza plant, for example, workers went on strike to protest against Magna's plan for a partial relocation of Corsa production to Germany (Autoevolution 2009). In the UK, UNITE leader Woodley denounced what he saw as a 'disgraceful political stitch up' between Magna and the German government and called on the EU to 'block the deal immediately' (*PoliticsHome.net* 2009). In fact, these protests of non-German GM trade union representatives are likely to have contributed to the late intervention against the deal by the European Commission, which in turn provided General Motors with a legitimate argument to pull out of the takeover negotiations at the last hour.

What this analysis suggests is that the 2009 crisis upset the peculiar combination of national and European patriotism among GM trade union representatives that had emerged during the early 2000s. With the new influence of the German government, GM Europe appeared to move towards the pattern of

EU-based car makers by acquiring a much stronger national centre – providing new opportunities for some (Germany) and threats for others. As a result, notions of 'European interest' receded into the background. The 'boundary clash' at the heart of economic patriotism shifted downwards again, from the global/European to the European/national dichotomy.

GM's eventual decision to retain Opel and Vauxhall in November 2009 has had an ambiguous impact on European trade union patriotism. On the one hand, the removal of Magna's 'German bias' has enabled a 'comeback' of this patriotism, expressed in (ultimately fruitless) protests against GM plans to close the production plant in Antwerp and renewed calls for the defence of 'European interests' within GM's global structures (*Finanzen.net* 2010). On the other hand, subsequent restructuring has removed GM's independent European management centre in Zurich, as future European co-ordination is to be carried out under the leadership of the Opel headquarters in Rüsselsheim. Against this backdrop, it remains to be seen whether or not European patriotism will inspire future trade union strategies at GM as much as it has done during the last decade.

CONCLUSIONS

In this contribution, I have attempted to demonstrate that 'economic patriotism' is a useful concept for the analysis of economic actors beyond the realm of public policy. In the case study under review, the concept has helped to illuminate how and why trade unions have espoused notions of European economic patriotism in the context of a transnational company like General Motors. Put simply, the case study shows that corporate globalization produced a clash between global economic structures and strategies, and a new regional (European) expression of territorial interests that was superimposed on traditional forms of local and/or national economic patriotisms. The case study also demonstrates that this transformation was dependent on favourable contextual conditions, in particular the absence of a clear national centre of GM's European operations.

The case study has a number of broader implications for economic patriotism scholarship. First, it demonstrates that analyses of non-state actors yield valuable insights about economic patriotism. The study of trade unions provides just one among many other possible examples of how non-state actors help to reproduce territorially based economic partiality. Other relevant yet under-researched cases quickly come to mind, in particular consumer movements (Frank 1999) and business élites. Indeed, as Callaghan and Lagneau-Ymonet (2012) in this collection show, the study of a broad range of non-state actors is also useful to fully understand the 'demand side' rationale (or lack thereof) for EP in public policy-making. If there is a lesson to draw from the case study in this respect, it can only be that a strengthening of European works councils' role – beyond the modest revisions of the directive in 2009 (see Waddington 2010: ch. 7), is likely to give a boost to the politics of job retention in the European Union.

Second, the example of trade unions at GM suggests that the development of economic patriotism over time should be taken as seriously as cross-country variation, which requires us to pay close attention to longer-term continuities as well as to gradual change (see Streeck and Thelen 2005) For example, based on the General Motors evidence, it does not seem compelling to assume, as is often done in contemporary debates, that economic patriotism has had a 'comeback' in the 2000s after two decades of decline. At the same time, the case study's portrayal of the recent partial 'European turn' of economic patriotism reminds us to avoid a static conceptualization that has no place for the possibility of reproduction through renewal.

Third, the case study helps to advance the reflections about the conditions under which EP takes shape at the supranational, European level. The trade union experience at GM highlights the crucial importance of external economic challenges (here: corporate globalization). This is of course nothing new – as Rosamond (2002, 2012) demonstrates, notions of 'European' economic interests and 'European competitiveness' have been primarily defined in response to such external challenges since the early 1980s. However, like the contribution by Callaghan and Lagneau-Ymonet (2012), the contribution also shows that there is a complex relationship between perceptions of non-European challenges and intra-European fears of domination – it is only when the former are not overshadowed by the latter that supranational EP seems likely to emerge.

These remarks also point to a fourth and last aspect of broader significance, related to the multi-level framework of the economic patriotism concept. On the one hand, the case study supports the rationale for such a framework beyond the confines of traditional notions of economic nationalism. On the other hand, however, it points to differences between national and European economic patriotism – thus far the latter seems to have remained much more fragile and context-dependent. Indeed, the 'composite' character of European patriotism in the case of trade unions at General Motors suggests that it might perhaps be more appropriate to talk about 'European patriotisms' – European dimensions of distinct national allegiances, which need to be brought together and reconciled. In other words, European economic patriotism appears to be mediated through a plurality of national (and perhaps local) patriotisms, a finding, which is consistent with the thrust of a large body of scholarship dealing with the relationship between European and national identities (see Risse 2005). In turn, this suggests that we may need a stronger ideational grounding for the economic patriotism concept to fully grasp the phenomenon – including the analysis of imagined 'economic cultures' (Crane 1998). This may perhaps seem a daunting task, but it is one that promises a great deal of innovative scholarship.

Biographical note: Thomas Fetzer is Assistant Professor in the Department of International Relations and European Studies at the Central European University.

NOTES

1 In January 2010 General Motors sold the Saab brand to the Netherlands-based boutique car maker Spyker.
2 GM's European works council is officially called 'European Employee Forum'. For the sake of simplicity, the paper refers to the body as European works council (EWC).
3 The latter point, for example, was explicitly included in the 2001 restructuring framework agreement (Labournet Germany 2001).

REFERENCES

Autoevolution (2009) 'Opel Zaragoza workers go on strike', available at http://www.autoevolution.com/news/opel-zaragoza-workers-go-on-strike-12224.html (accessed 3 May 2010).

Banyuls, J., Haipeter, T. and Neumann, L. (2008) 'European Works Council at General Motors Europe: bargaining efficiency in regime competition?', *Industrial Relations Journal* 39(6): 532–47.

Bartmann, M. (2005) 'Standortkonkurrenz bei GM Europa – Wenn es ernst wird im Eurobetriebsrat', *Mitbestimmung* 51(3): 34–7.

Batstone, E. (1984) *Working Order. Workplace Industrial Relations over Two Decades*, Oxford: Blackwell.

Betriebsrat Adam Opel AG (1994) 'Protokoll der Veranstaltung in Kooperation von EMB, IG Metall und GBR Opel', Minutes from meetings, Bochum, 21–23 November, file *Europäischer Konzernbetriebsrat I*, Archive, Works Council, Adam Opel AG, Rüsselsheim.

Betriebsrat Adam Opel AG (1996) 'Rechenschaftsbericht Rudolf Müller' [Statement of accounts from Works Council meeting], 6–8 November 1996, file *GBR-Konferenzen 1993-97*, Archive, Works Council, Adam Opel AG, Russelsheim.

Betriebsrat Adam Opel AG (1997) 'Rede Rudolf Müller Europäisches GM Arbitnehmerforum 15./16. Januar 1997' ['Speech, GM European workers' forum, 15–16 January 1997'], File Europäisches GM Arbeitnehmer-Forum, Archive, Works Council, Adam Opel AG, Rüsselsheim.

Bordenave, G. and Lung, Y. (2003) 'The twin internationalisation strategies of US carmakers GM and Ford', in M. Freyssenet, K. Shimizu and G. Volpato (eds), *Globalization or Regionalization of the American and Asian Car Industry?*, Basingstoke: Palgrave, pp. 53–94.

Callaghan, H. and Lagneau-Ymonet, P. (2012), 'The phantom of Palais Brongniart: economic patriotism and the Paris Stock Exchange', *Journal of European Public Policy* 19(3), http://dx.doi.org/10.1080/13501763.2011.640788

Carley, M. and Hall, M. (2006) *European Works Councils and Transnational Restructuring*, Dublin: European Foundation for the Improvement of Living and Working Conditions.

Clift, B. and Woll, C. (2012), 'Economic patriotism: reinventing control over open markets', *Journal of European Public Policy* 19(3), http://dx.doi.org/10.1080/13501763.2011.638117

Cox, K.R. (1998) 'Spaces of dependence, spaces of engagement and the politics of scale or: looking for local politics', *Political Geography* 17(1): 1–23.

Crane, G.T. (1998) 'Economic nationalism: bringing the nation back in', *Millenium* 27(1): 55–75.

Dassbach, C.H. (1989) *Global Enterprises and the World Economy: Ford, General Motors, and IBM*, New York, London: Garland.

Dicken, P. (2007) *Global Shift: Mapping the Changing Contours of the World Economy*, 5th edn., London: Sage.

EIRO (2009) 'Trade union welcomes General Motors decision not to sell Opel', available at http://www.eurofound.europa.eu/eiro/2009/11/articles/uk0911049i.htm (accessed 3 May 2010).
Fetzer, T. (2005) 'Driven towards inter-nationalisation. British trade union politics at Ford and Vauxhall, 1960–2001', Ph.D. dissertation, European University Institute, Florence.
Fetzer, T. (2008) 'European works councils as risk communities: the case of General Motors', *European Journal of Industrial Relations* 14(3): 289–308.
Finanzen.net (2010) 'Betriebsrat und Gewerkschaft kämpfen für Opel Antwerpen', available at http://www.finanzen.net/nachricht/aktien/ROUNDUP-Betriebsrat-und-Gewerkschaft-kaempfen-fuer-Opel-Antwerpen-746813 (accessed 3 May 2010).
Frank, D. (1999) *Buy American. The Untold Story of American Economic Nationalism*, Boston, MA: Beacon Press.
GM Workers Blog (2007a) 'Union solidarity can work', available at http://www.gmworkersblog.com/languages/english/leaflet_2007_03_16 (accessed 12 March 2008).
GM Workers Blog (2007b) 'Video statement Rudi Kennes', 17 April, available at http://www.gmworkersblog.com/languages/english/video_statement_by_rudi_kennes (accessed 12 March 2008).
GM Workers Blog (2007c) 'Wir brauchen die Beteiligung aller Beschäftigten', available at http://www.gmworkersblog.com/languages/deutsch/wir_brauchen_die_beteiligung_aller_beschaeftigten (accessed 12 March 2008).
GM Workers Blog (2007d) 'EEF does not see need for plant closure', 12 April, available at http://www.gmworkersblog.com/languages/english/eef_doesn_t_see_necessity_for_plant_closure (accessed 12 March 2008).
Gold, M. (2007) 'The European Works Councils Directive: changing rationales for EU regulation of employee participation', in M. Whittall, H. Knudsen and F. Huijgen (eds), *Towards a European Labour Identity. The Case of the European Work Council*, London, New York: Routledge, pp. 19–40.
Greer, I. and Hauptmeier, M. (2008) 'Political entrepreneurs and co-managers: labour transnationalism at four multinational auto companies', *British Journal of Industrial Relations* 46(1): 76–97.
Hancké, B. (2000) 'European works councils and industrial restructuring in the European motor industry', *European Journal of Industrial Relations* 6(1): 35–59.
Harrod, J. and O'Brien, R. (eds) (2002) *Global Unions? Theory and Strategies of Organized Labour in the Global Political Economy*, London, New York: Routledge.
Helleiner, E. and Pickel, A. (eds) (2005) *Economic Nationalism in a Globalizing World*, Ithaca, NY: Cornell University Press.
Herber, A. and Schäfer-Klug, W. (2002) 'How a European works council learned to negotiate', *Mitbestimmung* 9: 50–4.
Herod, A. (2001) *Labor Geographies: Workers and Landscapes of Capitalism*, New York: Guilford Press.
Holden, L. (2003) *Vauxhall Motors and the Luton Economy, 1900–2002*, Woodbridge: Boydell Press.
Hyman, R. (2005) 'Trade unions and the politics of the European social model', *Economic and Industrial Democracy* 26(1): 9–40.
Jürgens, U. (2004) 'Gibt es einen europaspezifischen Entwicklungsweg in der Automobilindustrie?,' *Discussion Paper SP III/301*, Berlin: Wissenschaftszentrum.
Klebe, T. and Roth, S. (2000) 'Die Gewerkschaften auf dem Weg zu einer internationalen Strategie?', *Arbeitsrecht im Betrieb* 12: 749–57.
Kotthoff, H. (1981) *Betriebsräte und betriebliche Herrschaft: Ein Typologie von Partizipationsmustern im Industriebetrieb*, Frankfurt/M., New York: Campus.

Kotthoff, H. (2006) *Lehrjahre des Europäischen Betriebsrats. Zehn Jahre transnationale Arbeitnehmervertretung*, Berlin: Sigma.
Labournet Germany (2001), Europäischer Rahmenvertrag zwischen dem Management und dem Europäischen Arbeitnehmerforum von General Motors', 1 October 2001, available at http://www.labournet.de/branchen/auto/gm-opel/olympia-eu4.html (accessed 12 March 2008).
Marginson, P., Hall, M., Hoffmann, A. and Müller, T. (2004) 'The impact of European works councils on management decision-making in UK and US-based multinationals: a case study comparison', *British Journal of Industrial Relations* 42(2): 209–33.
Mueller, F. and Purcell, J. (1992) 'The Europeanization of manufacturing and the decentralization of bargaining: multinational management strategies in the European automobile industry', *International Journal of Human Resource Management* 3(1): 15–34.
Pasture, P. and Verberckmoes, J. (eds) (1998) *Working-Class Internationalism and the Appeal of National Identity: Historical Debates and Current Perspectives*, Oxford and New York: Berg.
PoliticsHome.net (2009) 'Disgraceful political stitch-up behind Vauxhall job cuts', available at http://page.politicshome.com/uk/article/2535/disgraceful_political_stitch_up_behind_vauxhall_job_cuts_says_woodley.html (accessed 3 May 2010).
Rehder, B. (2003) *Betriebliche Bündnisse für Arbeit in Deutschland. Mitbestimmung und Flächentarif im Wandel*, Frankfurt, New York: Campus.
Risse, T. (2005) 'Neo-functionalism, European identity, and the puzzles of European integration', *Journal of European Public Policy* 12(2): 291–309.
Rosamond, B. (2002) 'Imagining the European economy: competitiveness and the social construction of "Europe" as an economic space', *New Political Economy* 7(2): 157–77.
Rosamond, B. (2012), 'Supranational governance as economic patriotism? The European Union, legitimacy and the reconstruction of state space', *Journal of European Public Policy* 19(3), http://dx.doi.org/10.1080/13501763.2011.638119
Rüsselsheimer Echo (1989) 'Hoffnung auf kürzere Wege nach Zürich', 17 March.
Rüsselsheimer Echo (1990) 'Opel: Entscheidungsspielraum noch kleiner', 21 February.
Sassoon, D. (1996) *One Hundred Years of Socialism. The West European Left in the Twentieth Century*, London and New York: I.B. Tauris.
Streeck, W. (1998) 'The internationalization of industrial relations in Europe: prospects and problems', *Politics & Society* 26: 429–59.
Streeck, W. and Thelen, K. (2005) 'Introduction: institutional change in advanced political economies', in W. Streeck and K. Thelen (eds), *Beyond Continuity: Institutional Change in Advanced Political Economies*, Oxford: Oxford University Press, pp. 1–39.
Tagesschau.net (2009) 'Chronologie: Der Kampf um Opel', available at http://www.tagesschau.de/wirtschaft/opelchronologie100.html (accessed 3 May 2010).
Vauxhall Motors Ltd. (2000) 'Minutes of a special meeting of the Vauxhall Joint Negotiating Committee', 12 December, file *JNC Minutes, Vol. 7*, Archive, HRM Department, Vauxhall Motors Ltd.
Waddington, J. (2010) *European Works Councils and Industrial Relations: A Transnational Industrial Relations Institution in the Making*, London, New York: Routledge.
Weiler, A. (2006) *EWC Case Studies: Volkswagen AG*, Dublin: European Foundation for the Improvement of Living and Working Conditions.
Wilks, S. (1981) 'Planning agreements. the making of a paper tiger', *Public Administration* 59: 399–419.

Homespun capital: economic patriotism and housing finance under stress

Leonard Seabrooke

ABSTRACT Part of the state's job is to promote wealth creation that also provides public goods to enhance the broader population's life-chances. These systems for organizing economic life in a national political economy generally have to conform with widely held conceptions of how the economy should work to be legitimate and sustained. Support for the institutions that underpin citizens' welfare can be understood as a form of 'economic patriotism' – where there is a consistent preference for economic activity to be channelled through particular institutions that serve a defined population. This article traces the role and development of mortgage institutions in Denmark and the US. I examine the challenges to these institutions from the recent financial crisis, including calls for their abolition or reform. I suggest that economic patriotism and everyday politics explains both the origins of these institutions and also why they will persist through current domestic, regional and international politico-economic troubles.

1. INTRODUCTION: ECONOMIC PATRIOTISM, WELFARE TRADE-OFFS, AND EVERYDAY POLITICS

We often nod to the link between the financial sector and the real economy during periods of high financial stress. The recent financial crisis has often been interpreted as demonstrating how complex financial instruments had few ties to the real economy, as well as how the most mundane of instruments, a mortgage, can bring down the international system. The most obvious link between financial policies and social policies can be seen in how housing is financed. There is great variety in how governments regulate the relationship between financial markets and housing, which is a reflection of how different societies see the need for housing. In making choices about their 'welfare trade-off' some societies opt for high taxes and high welfare that provides social housing. Other societies favour low taxes and low welfare, but then have to build assets over their life through housing and pension fund contributions (Castles 1998; Kemeny 1980, 2005). Governments and financial markets have a clear interest in innovating to meet the political and economic need for housing. How citizens in different countries save and borrow reflects their particular welfare trade-off.

In this article I suggest that the concept of economic patriotism implies that particular actors persistently select a certain good among an open range of goods, while nationalist actors assert the superiority of a national good and exclude others from competing for attention (see Clift and Woll 2011). What matters here is the conception of how the economy should work among the broader population, since this is the touchstone for legitimating changes to policies and markets. This conception may reflect egalitarian and/or meritocratic values in a way that is consistent with the established literature on welfare regimes (Esping-Andersen 1990; Kenworthy 2004).

This contribution is concerned with the ties between housing finance systems and economic patriotism in Denmark and the United States of America. Mortgage securities institutions are interesting for studies of economic patriotism because of their mission to mediate between private capital and public value. They provide a means of tracing how economic patriotism discourses concerning how the economy should work are changing within states, as well as between them. Mortgage securities institutions also provide a means to reflect upon the institutional specificities of how states built international financial capacity based on compromises and arrangements between government, financial communities and the 'ordinary' population (Seabrooke 2006) – and how these arrangements may clash with other conceptions of community that are tied to housing (Flint 2003). As mortgage securities institutions were built upon rights discourses from the broader population, changes to how they behave call us to question how ideas, frames and discourses about how the economy should work are evolving. They call us also to identify how everyday politics and economic patriotism go hand in hand as a society and its particular form of capitalism evolves, as well as how other notions of belonging – such as the European or international community – may impinge on particular forms of economic patriotism.

The article proceeds as follows. First, I outline how economic patriotism relates to the literature on everyday politics, since economic patriotism to provide change on the ground requires the 'masses', not only élites, to include patriotism in their belief-driven economic actions. I then contrast the cases through the 'varieties of residential capitalism' framework developed by Herman Schwartz and Leonard Seabrooke (2009). The cases highlight how different conceptions concerning the role of housing in how the economy should work. The following two sections trace the development of mortgage securities institutions in the United States (US) and Denmark – these institutions are typically called government sponsored enterprises (GSEs) in the US case and mortgage credit institutions (MCIs) in Denmark. I trace their development and link the rise of institutional forms to economic patriotic discourses. In concluding I reflect on how the mortgage securities institutions have responded to the recent financial crisis. I suggest that the first implicit and then explicit guarantee given to the government sponsored enterprises in the US case was justified on patriotic grounds and an assertion of homeland redistribution over more narrow economic interests. In the Danish case the absence of an explicit guarantee given to their mortgage credit institutions followed a desire to trumpet the benefits of the Danish model to the world while reasserting the importance of egalitarian principles. This model has now come under serious pressure from the European Community and new international financial regulations that discriminate against financial systems geared towards private housing financial instruments. Finally, I reflect on how both responses reflect the contradictions between the internationalization of housing finance markets and spatially limited political mandates.

2. ECONOMIC PATRIOTISM AND EVERYDAY POLITICS

Successful housing finance systems are necessarily mass phenomena. They require a source of investment, a form of implicit or explicit governmental guarantee to stabilize investment, and, most importantly, popular will. In the US case the GSEs were created by government for the community, while in Denmark the MCIs were created by community associations and then placed under tight statutory and regulatory control. Both cases provide examples of hybrid institutional forms that remind us that, even in a more globalized world economy, there is a great deal more institutional diversity than commonly assumed. There is, at the same time, a reinforcement of distinct welfare state regimes while also increasing convergence on reform trajectories for the regulation and governance of the international financial order (Hay 2006). I suggest that the different kinds of housing finance systems invite us to look not only at coalitional politics behind the creation of varied institutional forms, but also at 'everyday politics' in how the broader population engages with property and finance in everyday life. The wellspring for support for housing finance systems comes from ideas and norms associated with particular conceptions of economic patriotism, since everyday notions of how the economy should work for the population support and enable the institutions under focus in this piece.

The work on 'everyday politics' (Hobson and Seabrooke 2007) has already been linked with changes within the international financial order. Such work, including that on the 'financialization' of everyday activities (Montgomerie 2009), typically seeks to understand how new financial practices are created through government regulation and the role of private institutions, and particularly to understand how actors alter everyday understandings on economic and social life. As such, a conception of everyday politics is important for understanding not only élites during a period of crisis, but also during periods of seeming 'normality' (Seabrooke 2007). In taking up new practices or rejecting them for the maintenance of the status quo, non-élite actors are able to provide impulses to élites for institutional change (Kerkvliet 2009). This more fluid conception of politics is also more fitting for societies in which there is a weak connection to notions of class solidarity, or where there are 'everyday makers' who do not require an ideological position on a traditional political axis in order to promote their own conception of how the economy should work (Bang 2005). In such cases, as with those discussed below, consensus among élites that is insufficiently communicated to the public can raise dissent and a change in everyday financial practices (Schmidt 2007). This is especially the case during a period of crisis, where there are interests for and against the status quo. The defence of mortgage institutions when placed under financial stress provides one way to distinguish different forms of economic patriotism and their relationship to housing finance systems. I suggest that this is especially the case with the public pronouncement of guarantees and/or bail-outs.

3. VARIETIES OF RESIDENTIAL CAPITALISM AND ECONOMIC PATRIOTISM AS RIGHTS DISCOURSES

The US and Danish cases have been chosen because they reflect two distinct types of 'residential capitalism' from the four distinguished by Herman Schwartz and Leonard Seabrooke (2008, 2009). Schwartz and Seabrooke distinguish four 'varieties of residential capitalism', separated by the degree to which residents rely on the state or the market and the source of funding for housing. The four types are 'corporatist', 'liberal', 'statist-developmental', and 'familial'. Corporatists systems have high personal debt on mortgages and low rates of ownership, with a welfare safety net waiting for those who fall out of the system. Liberal systems are high personal debt on mortgages and high rates of ownership, a combination permitted by financialization. Statist-corporatist systems are low on both debt and ownership and social housing plays an important role. Familial systems are low on personal debt but high on ownership as family members ensure that the younger generation have property access on their terms, and where financial institutions are less engaged through barriers such as extremely high deposit rates. Among these types of residential capitalism, the Danes represent the most crucial case of the corporatist system because of its size (biggest housing bond market in Europe), while the US is the most crucial case for the liberals because of size and impact on the world economy, as we have seen with the most recent international financial crisis.

Denmark and the US are also of interest because they have the mortgage bond systems that have the longest legacies and, prior to the current crisis, were considered 'best practice' models to be exported to transition economies (OECD 2005). In both cases the mortgage institutions were created by what could be understood as economic patriot discourses that sought to link the private acquisition of wealth and property with a common public good. Their creation typically followed a rights-based discourse following a period of crisis, where institutions were created (publicly or privately) to provide not only access to credit but also to compensate those who suffered from war, disaster or prolonged discrimination. Mortgage institutions were able to extend their role under the conditions permitted by the expansion of the post-war welfare state. However, with the shift to neo-liberal policies in the 1980s, these same institutions were deregulated and privatized, often with an explicit aim to integrate them into the international financial order.

In the US case housing is considered as asset that different racial groups and economic classes should be enabled to acquire. It is no surprise that aggressive mortgage securitization emerged within this society, and that access to credit was politicized in accordance with demands to economic and civil rights. As such, politicians have a clear incentive to increase credit for housing. It is also not surprising that governments create institutional innovations to meet political and economic needs. The creation of the 'sibling' institutions Fannie Mae, Freddie Mac and Ginnie Mae was to mediate the interests of private capital and public values. As we now know, the most recent US property boom made it harder for many Americans to be 'prime' borrowers through the siblings and led to the boom in sub-prime mortgage securitization. Sub-prime mortgages attracted a lot of investment, from home and abroad, because they were lucrative and because they were hidden within seemingly safer mortgage pools. Poor judgment from credit ratings agencies compounded problems. At base, the now 'toxic' sub-prime mortgage-backed securities are tied to institutional innovations that emerged from American conceptions of economic patriotism. This debate is alive and kicking today, especially with calls for the abolition of Fannie and Freddie.

In the second case, little Denmark is remarkable for having the biggest housing bond system in Europe. Unlike the US system that 'recycles' credit, the Danish system is based on a 'balance principle' covered bond market that does not recycle capital in the same manner as US-style mortgage securitization. Danes carry more personal debt than other Europeans, and to an extent that would make the most bloated of Americans blush. Danes can do so because of their high taxes and high welfare state, and because only half the population own property despite their impressive wealth.

Economic patriotism in this context meant that there would be no explicit guarantee for the housing bond system, but implicit guarantees during the period of financial stress. In Denmark the transformation of community-led MCIs from mutual borrowers associations into publicly traded companies permitted the most concentrated mortgage bond market in Europe (IMF 2007: 14). It is particularly noteworthy that these Danish institutions have transformed through harmonization with directives for European financial integration and now face new challenges explained below.

4. ECONOMIC PATRIOTISM AND MORTGAGE CREDIT IN THE US

The key connection between American economic patriotism and housing finance comes through the popular conception of the 'American dream' that directly informed the construction of consumer debt markets from the mid-1800s onwards, including the establishment of attitudes towards the acceptability of housing-related debt (Calder 1999). Following this normative foundation, the US has a long history of attempts at mortgage securitization, including a failed try in the 19th century that burnt English investors, as well a 1920s collapse of real estate bond market schemes in New York (Snowden 1995). The origins of US mortgage institutions can be found in attempts to alleviate economic instability among those heavily indebted in the private market through explicit or implicit government guarantees. In the 1930s institutional experiments included the establishment of the Federal Loan Bank system and then a Homeowners' Loan Corporation (HOLC) that had one in ten residences encumbered and was then required to engage in massive foreclosures. In 1938 the National Mortgage Association of Washington was created and soon renamed the Federal National Mortgage Association and given the nickname 'Fannie Mae' (Seabrooke 2006: 125–6).

The experience of institutional building during the Great Depression, akin to the creation of other national projects during this period of 'embeddedness' (Blyth 2002), married public purpose with private capital. The increasing stress within this system was to expand access to owner-occupier residential properties, while continued reforms within the domestic financial system sought to foster credit access for the middle classes. Of course, the 1960s civil rights movement raised numerous concerns about who exactly had access to credit, particularly given the experience of 'redlining' communities, where some banks would literally draw lines around neighbourhoods they were willing to accept deposits from but to which they would not lend money. Under the auspices of the Civil Rights Act of 1968 (Title VIII), Ginnie Mae was created from Fannie Mae to cater particularly for low income borrowers and minority groups. Furthermore, the Community Reinvestment Act (CRA) of 1977 explicitly sought to tackle redlining and empower low-income and minority borrowers, in part through bolstering the capacity of groups such as the National Community Reinvestment Coalition (NCRC) to provide a watchdog function (Seabrooke 2006: 130–2). In the 1970s the US government permitted a secondary market for mortgages, and specifically to permit the capital from mortgages to form a 'pool' that was then sold to investors (Seabrooke 2006: 125–6). The institutional innovation combined private market investment with government-sponsored enterprises chartered to uphold public values. The US government's 'conjectural guarantee' to support Fannie Mae and Freddie Mac built a strong perception that there was a line of credit from the Treasury should the institutions have any problems fulfilling financial obligations to their investors (Schmid 2003). As such, this 'conjectural guarantee' permitted the institutions to behave in non-market ways and subsidize mortgages through a large wholesale market that lowers the costs of capital. All of this was in line with the patriotic idea that homeownership was a private good and a common public aspiration.

During the 1980s the US sought to further enhance the role of the siblings within the domestic and international financial systems through regulation that promoted a more active secondary market for mortgage-backed securities.

This market was to be supported by domestic and international capital, including a drive from Alan Greenspan and others to aggressively promote foreign investment in American debt as an aspect of foreign economic policy (Seabrooke 2001). Domestically, the changes were justified by the notion that by more efficiently recycling capital through the domestic system, mortgage institutions could boost homeownership not only for the middle classes but also for lower-income groups. In the late 1980s changes to the Home Mortgage Disclosure Act (HMDA) of 1975, which required mortgage lenders to collect information on borrowers, was expanded to data about who was denied loans, including information on income, gender, race and location. Such legislation provided a further boost to watchdogs seeking to enforce CRA regulation. In general the system here was that mortgage institutions could issue mortgage-backed securities from pools of capital derived from financial institutions that could specify that they had met the financial and social criteria required for the siblings Fannie and Freddie boomed throughout the 1980s and 1990s (Stuart 2003: 110). By 2005 the market for outstanding mortgage-backed securities from these institutions was approximately \$3.8 trillion. By the late 1990s one-third of Freddie Mac and Fannie Mae outstanding debt issues were owned by foreigners, compared to around 13 per cent for the US mortgage-backed securities market in general (Roll 2003: 36). As such, Fannie and Freddie were able to attract significant foreign investment to subsidize the costs of capital to increase home ownership among the American middle and lower-middle classes. This demonstrates how economic patriotism can be linked to international investment, rather than the exclusion of foreign capital.

Patriotic goals have been critical for the siblings. Fannie Mae, for example, stated in 2003 that it is first and foremost an '*instrument of the national policy* that promotes homeownership because it is good for families, communities, and the nation' (2003: 13, emphasis added). This instrument became increasingly blunt after 2000. During the 1990s the siblings relaxed their standards to provide greater access to mortgage credit for lower-income and minority groups with no real wage growth (Sidney 2003; Stuart 2003). The American Dream ideal was entangled with a market that was increasingly predatory and discriminatory. Fannie Mae and Freddie Mac's social purpose was distorted not only by its highly questionable leadership, but by a changing regulatory environment that impeded the watchdog function of community-based groups (Seabrooke 2006: 206–13). Such restrictions allowed a greater place for non-banks to operate in mortgage markets, to bloat the sub-prime market and engender crisis.

5. ECONOMIC PATRIOTISM AND MORTGAGE CREDIT IN DENMARK

Denmark has a longer history of a sophisticated mortgage bond system than the US, and its development reflects community-led developments to fuse private capital and public value. The origins of the Danish mortgage-backed securities system can be found in the late 18th century, when a mortgage bank was formed in response to a 1795 fire in which nearly a thousand houses were burnt to the ground. The community response was to form a co-operative for the reconstruction of houses and extension of mortgage credit. In 1850 the first Danish Mortgage Act recognized mortgage credit associations, particularly given the spread of land ownership among farm workers from the aristocracy and a political desire to provide mortgages to those considered near-creditworthy (Bogason 1992). Importantly, the state came to regulate what was a community-driven activity that followed a rights discourse on the capacity to access a dwelling through mutual associations.

Within this context MCIs in Denmark have come under heavy statutory conditions to marry private capital and public value. Most importantly, they must maintain a 'balance principle' (IMF 2007: 6). In what is essentially an augmented covered bond market, all loans handled by private financial institutions dealing with homeowners must be supported by mortgage bonds, and these bonds must, in turn, be backed by already existing mortgages. Danish MCIs are considered by the key regulator, the Danish Financial Supervisory Authority (DFSA, *Finanstilysynet*), to be 'average general risk' rather than 'high general risk' (like commercial banks) owing to their special regulatory status (IMF 2007: 8). Danish MCIs boast that no bondholder has lost money in the history of the system, including through wars and depressions, and that Danish housing debt is much safer than the government debt of many of its fellow European Union (EU) member states.

Importantly, akin to the widespread perception that the US government would – and did – bail out the siblings, investors' perception of the Danish system is that it benefits from a 'broad political commitment to its integrity'. This commitment is also a consequence of the fact that Denmark has Europe's most concentrated mortgage market, with the top five lenders holding 95 per cent of the market (IMF 2007: 4).

Like their US counterparts, the Danish mortgage institutions underwent reform in the 1970s, primarily with further standardization of mortgage financing. The biggest reforms occurred in the 1980s and 1990s as Danish mortgage institutions were encouraged by the EU to comply with a more uniform European standard. A government-induced housing crisis in Denmark in 1987, created by changes to the tax code, produced a domestic environment for institutional change that coincided with European financial directives, In 1989 Denmark sought to conform with the EU's Second Banking Directive, which required legal changes to the status of Danish mortgage institutions – a challenge that has recently been recently reignited.

The key change here was the transformation of mortgage companies from mutual borrowers' associations into publicly traded companies. The regulatory changes also permitted banks to acquire mortgage companies, presenting a clear case of Europeanization introducing financial liberalization and internationalization (Abdelal 2007). As a consequence, Danish mortgage institutions that were originally established as mutual associations and foundations were joined by companies owned by commercial banks. The 1989 changes also generated more interest in the market from foreign investors, with an increase from 5 per cent in the 1990s to 15 per cent in 2006 (IMF 2007: 14). Unlike the US case, this was not an aim of foreign economic policy.

Following the Second Banking Directive Danish mortgage institutions changed their operations from a wholesale to a retail basis. In contrast to the US siblings, who do not deal with individual customers but financial institutions, the Danish mortgage institutions have directly engaged the public in competition. At the same time integration with EU Capital Adequacy Directives required the removal of collective responsibility for mortgage pools and increased stress on individual ownership (OECD 1995). As stated above, the origins of the Danish mortgage bond system come from a discourse about the right of ordinary Danes to access mortgage credit, particularly after a crisis.

In this context, an important aspect of Danish mortgage institutions is that they provide access to mortgage credit that is unusual in most of continental Europe. For example, the institutional arrangements in Denmark permit a 5 per cent down payment for a mortgage for freehold property, compared to 20–30 per cent in Germany. In this sense it does more to absorb 'non-conforming' borrowers than many other European states, despite the absence of a subprime market (IMF 2007: 14). Here Denmark differs strongly from the US in a way that reflects their different welfare trade-offs and conceptions of economic patriotism. In the US the siblings support for low-income and minority groups serves as an inadequate welfare proxy (Howard 2006). Denmark, on the other hand, has a vigorous welfare state, often considered the most generous (Hay 2006) and among the most decommodified (Esping-Andersen 1990). In this context the status of Danish mortgage institutions is important within a broad yet homogenous social consensus on the types of institutions required to allow Danes to maximize their life-chances (Campbell and Hall 2009).

A very important element of the Danish case is the relationship to another *patrie* with which it has an ambivalent relationship – the European Union. In particular, the introduction of products and regulations commonly viewed as 'American'-style recklessness has been encouraged by the EU and, for mortgage bond systems, the European Mortgage Federation (EMF). While convergence within the European mortgage bond system has been far from complete owing to persistent national legal frameworks (Stephens 2000), it is significant that the Danish government voluntarily opted to extend draft EU legislation to its mortgage market. At the same time, lobby groups, such as the EMF, continue to apply pressure for the removal of government regulations that prevent a totally flexible market, such as legally enforceable interest rate caps (EMF 2005: 12). Pressure for financial innovations within the housing finance sector from European and international markets has also led to discontent among financial institutions within Denmark, who have otherwise maintained a long-standing corporatist tradition (Børsen 2007). As explained below, there is a new challenge on the horizon that can be identified as a clash between different conceptions of how to organize housing finance for two different *patrie* – the Danes and for Europe.

6. ECONOMIC PATRIOTISM AND HOUSING FINANCE UNDER STRESS

In their introduction to this collection, Ben Clift and Cornelia Woll (2012) put the notion forward that economic patriotism suggests that the interests of the homeland carry more sway than the individual choices of élites. Through the above cases I hope to demonstrate how mortgage securities systems reflect different conceptions of economic patriotism. Successful mortgages systems are necessarily mass phenomena, certainly within advanced liberal or 'hybrid' economies like the US and Denmark (Campbell and Pedersen 2007), and therefore engage everyday politics in a substantive way.

In this final section, I look at how these systems have come under stress during the most recent international financial crisis. The most important move here has been the placement of Fannie Mae and Freddie Mac under 'conservatorship' (which is not government ownership since they are 79 per cent not 80 per cent owned by the government). Also important are recent calls for Danish MCIs to be reformed to reduce Danish housing-related indebtedness under pressure from the new Basle III international finance regime and also the EU. I suggest that in both cases economic patriotism is important in establishing the political limits of the possible for institutional reform.

In mid-2008 Fannie and Freddie's top management attempted to save the institutions with packages from Wall Street. They failed. A programme for 'conservatorship' was then established which seeks to enhance market stability and assuage investors. Essentially, the programme allowed the Treasury to support Fannie and Freddie to expand their portfolios for the next two years by around $20 billion per month, and then to reduce the size of Fannie and Freddie at a rate of 10 per cent a year thereafter (US Treasury 2008). The Housing and Economic Recovery Act of 2008 established a new Federal Housing Finance Agency (FHFA), replaced the Chief Executive Officers of Fannie and Freddie, and also put a halt to their lobbying activities. It also made plain and clear that the siblings would not be liquidated, and that dissolving the institutions requires an Act of Congress. This extraordinary demonstration of state intervention was justified by calling upon the impact that a collapse would have upon the everyday economies of American families. Henry M. Paulson, Secretary of the Treasury at the time, stated:

> Fannie Mae and Freddie Mac are so large and so interwoven in our financial system that a failure of either of them would cause great turmoil in our financial markets here at home and around the globe . . . A failure would affect the ability of Americans to get home loans, auto loans and other consumer credit and business finance. And a failure would be harmful to economic growth and job creation. (Paulson 2008)

Since 2008 the siblings have suffered ideological attacks from those who believe that government should not be involved in housing markets or financial markets. In February 2009, Phil Gramm (2009), co-author of the Gramm–Leach–Bliley Act in 1999 that removed banking market segmentation, argued that the 'politicization of the mortgage market was a primary cause of this crisis' and explicitly blamed Fannie and Freddie. Think tanks such as the American Enterprise Institute argued that Fannie and Freddie could not possibly be accommodated politically (Wallison 2008), while influential opinion-makers have suggested that the private market can and should perform the siblings' role in American economic life, with higher costs for those less creditworthy.

On the other side of this debate over how the American economy should work, groups such as NCRC have invoked the Great Depression and minority rights discourses with the aim of encouraging the government to re-engineer the siblings to meet their chartered purpose, primarily through mortgage modifications rather than privatizing the siblings (NCRC 2010). On Christmas Eve 2009, the Obama administration announced that the previous cap placed on the siblings would be lifted. In March 2010 the US House of Representatives' Financial Services Chairman Barney Frank also endorsed the siblings' renewal on the basis that there was no implicit guarantee. And by the end of 2010 the siblings securitized 98 per cent of mortgages in the US system (*Financial Times* 2011). While this is not surprising, it does point to how critical such institutions are to American economic patriotism; especially as they provide a welfare-like subsidy to support a common public good. It was a priority for the US government to restart securitization as soon as possible, because it performs a critical political and economic function within the American system, and is already identified as tied intimately to economic patriotism – chasing the American Dream. In 2011 the FHFA introduced reforms to Fannie and Freddie to make data collection more uniform, and explicitly stated that Fannie and Freddie may no longer exist but that institutional arrangements and experiments would be necessary for what is now a $11 trillion market for single-family mortgages (DeMarco 2011). In mid-2011 a bipartisan proposal, HR 1859, proposed the proliferation of private companies that had explicit government guarantees, like Fannie and Freddie, but competed with each other to enhance market competition. This would essentially spread the risk among 'mini-Freddies' but would not alter the role of government in supporting the mortgage market. In the case of housing, economic patriotism provides continued government support despite the discrediting of an organizational form by those calling for a free market.

The Danish case faces different constraints. In December 2008, the Association of Danish Mortgage Banks (*Realkreditrådet*) ran TV commercials and conferences that mimicked Carlsberg beer to reassure homeowners that Danish Mortgage system was 'probably the best in the world' and explicitly rejected any link to American-style securitization (Berlingske 2008). International market leaders, such as George Soros, advocated the Danish model of securitization (with the 'balance principle') as a way to reform the American financial system (Soros 2008) through a modification of mortgages to conform to the Danish system.

While they may credibly claim to have one of the safest system in the world, Danish compliance with European financial directives led to a change in the status of mortgage institutions. Further harmonization, mostly voluntary, brought in new financial products and commercial practices to the Danish market. These included introducing 'step loans' for housing associations that more or less replicated sub-prime 'teaser' rates, where lenders pay a low interest rate to begin with and then increase over time on the assumption that such increases would be negated by increasing property values. More importantly, Danish mortgage institutions are threatened by both Europeanization and internationalization. The publication of a white paper for the harmonization of housing finance markets in Europe in December 2007 led to immediate calls from the Danish Housing Finance Council for the protection of the unique status of Danish mortgages institutions (Realkreditrådet 2007). In 2010 there was significant pressure felt by Denmark to reform its financial system in the face of EU pressure, especially from the idea that Danes were far too heavily indebted and a threat to the European economy. On top of this came pressure from new international banking regulations, especially the formation of new rules (Basle III) from the Basle Committee for Banking Supervision that immediately followed a financial crisis closely tied to housing market volatility. In new European and international risk-weighting formulae, financial systems with heavy amounts of debt related to housing are considered riskier (Børsen 2010). Danish indebtedness outstrips US indebtedness by quite a way, but the crucial difference the two systems is really the role of the welfare state in permitting such risk tolerance and the welfare trade-offs within each society. Most Danish banks had little problem weathering the liquidity crisis owing to high capitalization (Jonung 2008: 576), but did reduce lending. It is also important to recognize that egalitarian policy frames matter in the Danish debate and arguments for a return to a 'potato diet' (*kartoffelkuren*) similar to the late- 1980s have resurfaced. European and international banking regulations, however, have little consideration for such attitudinal changes but, rather, call for an international level playing field – (raising arguments from some that international financial should legitimately recognize an 'unlevel playing field' (Warwick Commission 2009). The potential for a Danish 'opt out' of Basel III regulation, if invoked through European law, would cause a political storm but be consistent with Danish conceptions of economic patriotism.

7. CONCLUSION

In conclusion, economic patriotism matters for conceptions of how the economy should work in different societies. This article argues that if we investigate two crucial cases of different types of residential capitalism, the Danish–corporatist and the American–liberal systems, we can see how economic patriotism is at the root of how their institutions are aligned and constructed.

I suggest that housing finance provides a fine case of how resilient yet flexible these systems are and how varying international and regional engagements are providing challenges to how they are organized and funded. In both cases mortgage institutions were created to fulfil a public good with private capital, in alignment with everyday politics and socioeconomic norms in the respective societies. And in both cases economic patriotism, often expressed through rights discourses negotiated in society, establishes the legitimate limits of the politically and economically possible.

Biographical note: Leonard Seabrooke is Professor in the International Centre for Business and Politics (DBP) at the Copenhagen Business School and also Professor in International Political Economy and former Director of the Centre for the Study of Globalization and Regionalization (CSGR) at the University of Warwick.

ACKNOWLEDGEMENTS

My thanks go to the reviewers for their excellent comments on revisions. My thanks also go to Ben Clift and Cornelia Woll for their guidance during the Economic Patriotism project. This research is supported by the *Sources of National Institutional Competitiveness* (SONIC) project at the Copenhagen Business School.

REFERENCES

Abdelal, R. (2007) *Capital Rules: The Construction of Global Finance*, Cambridge, MA: Harvard University Press.

Bang, H.P. (2005) 'Among everyday makers and expert citizens', in J. Newman (ed.), *Remaking Governance*, Bristol: Policy Press, pp. 159–79.

Berlingske (2008) 'Ikke Amerikanske Tilstande', 14 September.

Blyth, M. (2002) *Great Transformations: Economic Ideas and Institutional Change in the Twentieth Century*, Cambridge: Cambridge University Press.

Bogason, P. (1992) 'Strong or weak state? The case of Danish agricultural export policy, 1849–1906', *Comparative Politics* 24(2): 219–27.

Børsen (2007) 'Nye boliglån sprænger Realkreditrådet', 3 May.

Børsen (2010) 'Nyt håb for dansk realkredit', 10 September.

Calder, L. (1999) *Financing the American Dream: A Cultural History of Consumer Credit*, Princeton, NJ: Princeton University Press.

Campbell, J.L. and Hall, J.A. (2009) 'National identity and the political economy of small states', *Review of International Political Economy* 16(4): 547–72.

Campbell, J.L. and Pedersen, O.K. (2007) 'The varieties of capitalism and hybrid success: Denmark in the global economy', *Comparative Political Studies* 40(2): 307–32.

Castles, F.G. (1998) 'The really big trade-off: home ownership and the welfare state in the new world and the old', *Acta Politica* 33(1): 5–19.

Clift, B. and Woll, C. (2012) 'Economic patriotism: reinventing control over open markets', *Journal of European Public Policy* 19(3), http://dx.doi.org/10.1080/13501763.2011.638117

DeMarco, E.J. (2011) 'FHFA, housing gses, and housing finance in a world of uncertainty', Remarks to the *Exchequer Club*, Acting Director, Federal Housing Finance Agency, 18 May, available at http://www.fhfa.gov/webfiles/21255/Exchequer_Club_051811_final.pdf (accessed 19 May 2011).

Esping-Andersen, G. (1990) *The Three Worlds of Welfare Capitalism*, Princeton, NJ: Princeton University Press.

European Mortgage Federation (2005) 'EMF position paper on the Commission green paper on mortgage credit in the EU', Brussels, 29 November: 12.

Fannie Mae (2003) '2003 annual report and proxy statement', available at http://www.fanniemae.com/ir/annualreport/index.jhtml (accessed 11 May 2011).

Financial Times (2011) 'Take Fannie and Freddie off the road', 26 January.

Flint, J. (2003) 'Housing and ethnopolitics: constructing identities of active consumption and responsible community', *Economy and Society* 32(4): 611–29.

Frankel, A., Gyntelberg, J., Kjeldsen, K. and Persson, M. (2004) 'The Danish mortgage market', *BIS Quarterly Review* (March): 95–109.

Gramm, P. (2009) 'Deregulation and the financial panic', *Wall Street Journal*, 20 February.

Hay, C. (2006) 'What's globalization got to do with it? Economic interdependence and the future of European welfare states', *Government and Opposition* 41(1): 1–22.

Hobson, J.M. and Seabrooke, L. (eds) (2007) *Everyday Politics of the World Economy*, Cambridge: Cambridge University Press.

Howard, C. (2006) *The Welfare State Nobody Knows: Debunking Myths about US Social Policy*, Princeton, NJ: Princeton University Press.

IMF (2007) 'Denmark: financial sector assessment program. technical note: the Danish mortgage market – a comparative analysis', *IMF Country Report No. 07/123*, September 2006, Washington DC.

Jonung, L. (2008) 'Lessons from financial liberalisation in Scandinavia', *Comparative Economic Studies* 50(4): 564–98.

Kemeny, J. (1980) 'Home ownership and privatisation', *International Journal of Urban and Regional Research* 4(3): 372–88.

Kemeny, J. (2005) '"The really big trade-off" between home ownership and welfare: Castles' evaluation of the 1980 thesis, and a reformulation 25 years on', *Housing, Theory, and Society* 22(2): 59–75.

Kenworthy, L. (2004) *Egalitarian Capitalism: Jobs, Income and Growth in Affluent Countries*, New York: Russell Sage Foundation.

Kerkvliet, B.J.T. (2009) 'Everyday politics in peasant societies (and ours)', *Journal of Peasant Studies* 36(1): 227–43.

Montgomerie, J. (2009) 'The pursuit of (past) happiness? Middle-class indebtedness and American financialisation', *New Political Economy* 14(1): 1–24.

National Community Reinvestment Coalition (2010) 'Working-class families arbitrarily blocked from accessing credit', *Mortgage Lending Disparities Series Paper*, Washington DC, December.

OECD (1995) *Securitisation: An International Perspective*, Paris: OECD.

OECD (2005) *Housing Finance Markets in Transition Economies*, Paris: OECD.

Paulson, H.M. (2008) 'Statement by Secretary Henry M. Paulson, Jr on Treasury and Federal Housing Finance Agency action to protect financial markets and taxpayers', 7 September, available at http://www.treasury.gov/press/releases/hp1129.htm (accessed 11 May 2011).

Realkreditrådet (2007) 'Hvidbog om realkredit i EU - optakt til øget harmonisering af realkreditmarkederne i Europa', Press release from Realkreditrådet, 19 December, avaialble from http://www.realkreditraadet.dk/ (accessed 11 May 2011).
Roll, R. (2003) 'Benefits to homeowners from mortgage portfolios retained by Fannie Mae and Freddie Mac', *Journal of Financial Services Research* 23(1): 29–42.
Schmid, F.A. (2003) 'Conjectural guarantees loom large: evidence from the stock returns of Fannie Mae and Freddie Mac', *Working Paper 2003-031A*, Federal Reserve Bank of St Louis, October.
Schmidt, V.A. (2007) 'Trapped by their ideas: French élites' discourses of European integration and globalization', *Journal of European Public Policy* 14(7): 992–1009.
Schwartz, H. and Seabrooke, L. (2008) 'The political cost of property booms', *Comparative European Politics* 6(3), special issue.
Schwartz, H.M. and Seabrooke, L. (2009) 'Varieties of residential capitalism in the international political economy: old welfare states and the new politics of housing', in H. M. Schwartz and L. Seabrooke (eds), *The Politics of Housing Booms and Busts*, Basingstoke: Palgrave, pp. 1–27.
Seabrooke, L. (2001) *US Power in International Finance*, Basingstoke: Palgrave.
Seabrooke, L. (2006) *The Social Sources of Financial Power*, Ithaca, NY: Cornell University Press.
Seabrooke, L. (2007) 'Everyday legitimacy and international financial orders: the social sources of imperialism and hegemony in global finance', *New Political Economy* 12(1): 1–18.
Sidney, M.S. (2003) *Unfair Housing: How National Policy Shapes Community Action*, Lawrence, KS: University Press of Kansas.
Snowden, K.A. (1995) 'Mortgage securitization in the United States: twentieth century developments in historical perspective', in M.D. Bordo and R. Sylla (eds), *Anglo-American Financial Systems: Institutions and Markets in the Twentieth Century*, New York: New York University Salomon Center, pp. 276–88.
Soros, G. (2008) 'Denmark offers a model mortgage market', *Wall Street Journal*, 10 October.
Stephens, M. (2000) 'Convergence in European mortgage systems before and after the EMU', *Journal of Housing and the Built Environment* 15(1): 29–52.
Stuart, G. (2003) *Discriminating Risk: The US Mortgage Lending Industry in the Twentieth Century*, Ithaca, NY: Cornell University Press.
US Treasury (2008) 'Fact sheet: treasury senior preferred stock purchase agreement', 7 September.
Wallison, P.J. (2008) 'Fannie and Freddie by twilight', *AEI Outlook Series*, American Enterprise Institute, August.
Warwick Commission (2009) *Warwick Commission on International Financial Reform: In Praise of Unlevel Playing Fields*, Coventry: University of Warwick.

Supporting the City: economic patriotism in financial markets

Glenn Morgan

ABSTRACT This contribution argues that economic patriotism constitutes a specific form of managing the relationship between open borders and the political pressures of specific territorial units in an era of neo-liberal globalization. It focuses on the case of the City of London and shows how, in the period from 1997 to 2007, the state pursued specific strategies that would support the international position of the City in ways which were firstly within global and EU rules and secondly gave credibility to the claim that this support was beneficial to the whole of British society. The financial crisis undermined this credibility. Although the City has re-established its centrality to the UK economy and there is no obvious alternative, support for it can no longer be justified as an act of economic patriotism given the strength of criticism it has endured.

INTRODUCTION

The rise of global financial markets is often seen as the highest expression of neo-liberal ideals of free, open and unfettered markets. According to this narrative, the influence of the state on these markets had to be purged by a prolonged phase of deregulation. Efforts by national governments to protect their own financial systems through restrictions on the entry of foreign competitors and on currency and capital outflows ceased in order to enable the financial markets to work freely. Surely, therefore, ideas of economic nationalism and economic patriotism are irrelevant in the financial sector, particularly in countries such as the United Kingdom (UK) which so actively espoused these processes of deregulation, globalization and liberalization. This contribution argues to the contrary. It makes the case that in the UK, during the period from the mid 1990s to the financial crash, government policies did take on a form which can be defined as involving economic patriotism. The UK government did support the City, not just in the generalized ways that had characterized British history for many centuries but in a way which was specific to this particular period of neo-liberal global markets.

The contibution consists of the following sections. In the first section, the concepts of economic nationalism and economic patriotism are discussed.

In the second section, the case of the City of London is considered. The argument is made that the City underwent fundamental organizational change in the period from 1986 through to the mid-1990s. This created a different 'City' from that previous to 1986 and from the mid-1990s, the relationship between the City and the government took on a new form in response to these changes and to the changing global environment. This new form was characterized by more direct and active state involvement in defending the interests of the City as a territorially based entity against the potential negative effects of the actions of other territorial entities, most particularly the European Union (EU) and the United States (US). Because of the nature of neo-liberal system of global regulation enforcing open markets, this defence had to be conducted using new instruments and engaging at the micro-level with City interests to provide new forms of support. In the third section, I briefly consider what the financial crisis has revealed about this particular form of economic patriotism. Finally I conclude by arguing that the concept of economic patriotism enables us to address some of the specific tensions in managing the relationship between open financial markets and democratic politics in the current era.

STATES AND MARKETS: THE NATURE OF ECONOMIC PATRIOTISM

The debate on economic nationalism described by Clift and Woll (2011) emphasizes that protectionism is not the only way to pursue national interests in the international economic arena. If national interests are the goal, the instruments to achieve this can vary from protectionism through to the advocacy of open markets. They state that economic nationalism is 'as old as the nation-states themselves' (Clift and Woll 2011). Clift and Woll (2011) argue that economic patriotism be considered as a subset of economic nationalism. In particular, it is relevant where the broader social and economic environment is characterized by an inherent tension between integrated international markets and the pursuit of territorial political interests.

Integrated international markets and particularly global financial markets emerged gradually in the 1980s and early 1990s characterized by the creation of a neo-liberal regulatory environment which enforced, through a variety of bilateral and multilateral agreements and through international organizations such as the General Agreement on Tariffs and Trade (GATT) (later the World Trade Organization [WTO]), the EU, the Organization for Economic Co-operation and Devlelopment (OECD), the International Monetary Fund (IMF), open markets in most areas of trade in goods and services as well as in capital mobility (Abdelal 2007). These factors may be seen as stripping the state of its ability to engage in autonomous policy-making and thus reducing the possibility of any form of economic nationalism. However, the pressure on the state to be active in these circumstances, to exert some sort of influence that will be positive for the voting population, does not disappear (e.g., Levy 2006). Indeed, in many ways it becomes more intense as traditional party loyalties decline and voters demand action. Economic patriotism reflects the efforts of politicians to provide a moral account of their activities in a context where policies of overt economic nationalism lack legitimacy but forces of global competition subject societies to uncertain forms of economic and social disruption. Thus, politics becomes a balancing act between, on the one hand, playing by the international rules (with all the consequences which that has in terms of losing control over economic policy), and on the other, intervening in ways which do not overtly transgress the rules but offer the possibility of protecting the distinctiveness of the local community.

Economic patriotism, therefore, is a possible policy response in environments where (a) the international economic order is rule-bound and policed by proponents of free markets in organizations granted power and legitimacy by nation-states, (b) national borders are, in the main, open to flows of goods, services and capital, (c) states have ruled out a whole series of mechanisms which would in the past have helped them combat the uncertainties and turmoil which can ensue from open borders, and (d) states are predominantly democratic in form and therefore have to respond to the demands of the electorate, no matter how mediated or muted these demands.

THE UK AND THE CITY OF LONDON

There is a long established argument that the City of London has exercised a powerful influence over the policies of the British government going back to at least the foundation of the Bank of England in 1694 (Ingham 1984; for a restatement see Talani [2011]). In particular, the City's interest has been in allowing the free flow of funds into and out of the UK, since its wealth has been primarily dependent on acting as an intermediary in financial markets. To secure this, therefore, the City sought for as long as possible to maintain sterling as a world currency, preferably with a high value in relation to other currencies, a position which generally led it to favour high interest rates. High interest rates and a high value for sterling both worked against manufacturing investment in the UK. Historical accounts emphasize that, at moments of economic crisis, the British state supported the City by keeping the value of sterling high even when this reduced potential export markets and led to unemployment and economic recession in the UK. It might well be asked, therefore, what is new about this current period and why do we require a new concept such as economic patriotism to understand what has been such a long-standing feature of the British context? There are two responses to this argument: firstly a general correction to the broad picture; and secondly a specific analysis of the current period.

In relation to the general picture, it is necessary to dispel the myth of the all-powerful City and to note how the size of the City and its impact on the British economy has fluctuated and taken different forms. Even a proponent of the 'City dominance' view such as Ingham is careful to note that this power has fluctuated, for example describing the 1930s as 'the City's low ebb' (Ingham 1984: 200). In those years, sterling moved off the gold standard, protectionism reigned, support for cartelization of British industry was increased and the City's international role was limited to managing the sterling balances of the Empire. It was by no means clear that the City would re-establish itself as a central node of world finance in the post-war Bretton Woods system. The period from 1945 through to the 1970s was a time of uncertain recovery for the City (Kynaston 2002). In the late 1940s to the mid-1950s the City, with the support of the Treasury and the Bank of England, sought ways to shift sterling back to being an international currency by making it once again freely convertible, most importantly into US dollars (Milward 1992). However, the weakness of the British economy forced the putative value of the pound down and the US dollar achieved an unassailable presence as the world's dominant currency, since sterling convertibility was not achieved until 1958 (Burnham 2007).

It took until the late 1950s and early 1960s for the City to begin to revive, and it did so initially not on the basis of sterling but through developing the Euro-dollar markets arising from the development of a pool of US dollars in Europe which City merchant banks began to package into loans. However, the broader weakness of the UK economy, the continued threats of the Labour Party to nationalize banking, the occasional conflicts between industrialists and the City over the value of sterling (Ingham 1984), the rise of takeover activity, the sterling crises of the 1960s and 1970s and rising inflation all meant that although the City was influential and important in the UK economy, its position remained somewhat fragile and contested. Although it was identified as one of the three global financial cities in the 1970s, it increasingly suffered by comparison to New York and Tokyo, both of which were characterized by high levels of internal savings that fed into the financial system and created large and powerful financial institutions (Sassen 1991).

Therefore, whilst there was no doubt a long-standing path dependent structure that favoured the interests of the City in the UK political system, this had to be activated, renewed and operationalized in response to changing circumstances. In the 1980s onwards, the most important changed circumstance came from the decline of the Bretton Woods system, the floating of currencies, the freeing of capital controls and the consequent increase in financial flows across national boundaries; in other words from financial globalization. The way that the British state related to the City consequently took new directions. This process can be characterized as consisting of two phases: the first is the Thatcherite reconstruction of the City; the second, less recognized phase on which this contribution concentrates is the relationship of New Labour to the City, as it is this phase that sees the clearest emergence of a new set of instruments, actors and policies that can be identified in terms of economic patriotism.

The Thatcherite reconstruction of the city

As the opening up of global financial markets speeded up in the early 1980s, it was still possible that the City of London would miss out on this growth and be essentially a relatively minor, regional hub in the emergent system. The US had undergone a form of deregulation in the 1970s that got rid of fixed commissions in most financial markets, for the first time since the 1920s really encouraging the development of large institutions that could use economies of scale and scope to, firstly, compete on costs and, secondly, to operate across diverse financial markets. Coupled with large, deep and liquid financial markets which already existed in the US, this was a highly attractive environment for foreign investors. The problem for London in the early 1980s was that compared to New York it was still dominated by small institutions with limited capital, often charging fixed commissions enforced by private cartels and club forms of governance ruled by long-standing traditional City élites co-ordinated through the Bank of England (Moran 1991, 2003). In order not to lose out to New York in what could be foreseen as a massive expansion of financial markets, the City had to change.

It is beyond the scope of this contribution to provide a detailed analysis of the changes over the period from the Big Bang to the end of Tory rule in 1997. Nevertheless, two points are worth making, since they bear most directly on the next period. Firstly, the organizational terrain of the City of London had completely changed between 1979 and 1997. The old segmented structure of the City, characterized by small-scale partnership firms specializing in narrow niches of the financial markets and protected against competition by cartel like agreements on who could bid for what business and how prices should be set had disappeared, was swallowed up into large investment banks. Few of these banks were of British origin, many coming from the US. The new banks also recruited on a meritocratic basis and paid according to performance linked directly to expertise and risk-taking. The ruling élite in the City, which had been linked through personal networks of shared education, social and leisure activities, began to be replaced by a more diverse group of individuals selected for their expertise, skills and market acumen. New York and City financial institutions became increasingly the same organizations with similar modes of working, a trend which gradually extended to some of the largest European and Asian banks that also came into these centres.

Secondly, and associated with this, was a limited modernization of the regulatory structure away from club governance to a form of self-regulation. Whilst it was inevitable that there would be new more formal regulation as the markets themselves were freed, the government responded to the City's argument that this should be primarily self-regulation with minimal bureaucracy. After initial problems in terms of enforcement, personnel and organizational structure leading to some amendments to the system in 2000, this self-regulatory, light-touch approach became distinctive to London. The US, on the other hand, retained the structure of the New Deal reforms, even if the Securities and Exchange Commission and the other New Deal entities and rules were constrained in their activities under Reagan, Bush and Clinton (see Krippner [2011] for an account of how the specific history of US finance shaped its development in the period of deregulation).

To summarize, by the end of the Tory period of government,the City of London had modernized significantly. It was filled with large international banks; it was open to innovative financial operators such as hedge funds and private equity. Its loose regulation enabled rapid innovation in products and processes. Its labour force was meritocratic and highly skilled. In the local area, there were multiple complementary organizations such as lawyers, accountants, auditors, as well as a dense and well-informed financial press. Its markets were deep and liquid by virtue of international (not domestic) investors. Its regulators were light touch and flexible. Its central bank was acting increasingly independently of government, targeting inflation through the use of interest rates, leading in general to a strong currency, a desirable features for any investor holding sterling-based assets. Government had been supportive of these changes and the tax system for individuals and corporations was increasingly moulded to support the role of the City. Foreign investors welcomed these characteristics of the City, not all of which were shared with New York and many of which differentiated the City from its European counterparts.

The wall of money and financial activity 1997–2007

From the perspective of 1997, the City of London had reformed itself sufficiently to compete against Wall Street as a site for global financial markets. It continued to have some disadvantages, such as the relative weakness of the UK economy and sterling, but it also had advantages over New York, particularly in terms of light touch regulation and overall a less adversarial legal culture (Kagan 2001) that could impact on firms in areas like tax, corporate governance, corporate fraud and anti-trust. Also the fact that it lacked a large internal market made it less insular than some US institutions and more willing to go out and solicit foreign investors to put their money through London. What nobody really foresaw, however, was how financial activity, still wobbling in 1997–8 from the Asian financial crisis, the Russian currency crash and the collapse of the world's largest hedge fund, Long Term Capital Management, would take off at a dizzying rate of growth and continue in spite of 9/11, the collapse of Enron, the dot.com crash and a variety of other corporate scandals and currency crashes and defaults up to mid-2007.

Two factors fuelled this escalator. The first was the rise of global imbalances associated particularly with China's growing trade surplus with the US but also with excess saving in places like Germany, Japan and the oil producing countries (Glyn 2007; Schwartz 2009). These savings, the so-called Wall of Money, were held in dollars and prompted what became known as the 'search for yield'. New York and the City of London competed head-to-head for access to these funds. Secondly, the main solution to the search for yield emerged in the US sub-prime housing market and the securitization chain which took individually risky mortgages, bundled them up in ways that converted them into high yield but seemingly low-risk Collateralized Debt Obligations (CDOs), creating a huge associated industry of other financial instruments such as credit default swaps. Clearly, New York was closest to the sub-prime markets; the global imbalances were denominated in dollars; the Wall Street institutions were capable of managing the scale and complexity of the deals. Why should the City, in some senses a pure third-party intermediary, be able to get in on this action?

It was clearly of central importance to the UK government that the City should participate in this development. At a time when manufacturing was in decline from around 20.3 per cent of GDP to around 12.4 per cent in the period 1995–2007, the benefits of a flourishing finance sector were seen as compensating for this. These effects overflowed the limited geographical boundaries in the City, having, what were deemed at the time by most politicians and economists, positive impacts much more widely, e.g., through providing employment, taxes, easy credit and mortgages (thus stimulating consumption, house building and all associated sectors – what Crouch [2008] described as 'privatisted Keynesianism'). Financial services' share of GDP rose from 5.3 per cent to 8.3 per cent in the same period, with professional services closely tied to finance (such as accounting, law and management consultancy) also growing from 2.9 per cent to 3.9 per cent between 1997 and 2007. At its highest point, in June 2007, 1,064,000, around 4 per cent of total employment, were employed in financial services. In 2007, 15 per cent of UK total income tax and 26.5 per cent of corporation tax was contributed by financial services. Financial services contributed a balance of trade surplus of £44.5bn in 2008 – compared, for example, to a deficit of £93bn in goods (all statistics in this section are taken from IFSL Research based on ONS National accounts [IFSL 2009], though see CRESC [2009] for an alternative perspective). Supporting the City in the context of global financial markets therefore became seen as an essential part of economic policy.

Supporting the city: economic patriotism in action

In this section, I argue three propositions. Firstly, the Labour government increasingly identified the City and supporting the City as an act of economic patriotism, something of value with moral overtones that reflected some essential quality of Britishness in a global competitive environment. Secondly, sustaining this advantage required a clear-eyed view of the advantages of the City and equally a willingness within certain constraints to point at and criticize the disadvantages of other systems and to resist any efforts to transfer them into the UK. Thirdly, supporting the City required the government to not only provide the right regulatory and macro-economic environment, but also a willingness to engage actively in promoting the City.

With regard to the first point, Gordon Brown was particularly prone to stress the role of the City as an example to the rest of the UK. In 2006, he stated that 'the message that the City's success sends out to the whole British economy is that we will succeed if we think globally' (HM Treasury Press Release 77/

06). In his 2006 Mansion House address to the grandees of the City just before he became prime minister, Brown lauded the efforts of the City, stating:

> by your efforts Britain is already second to none: for our openness, pro Europe, pro free trade; a world leader in stability. . . . I want to continue to work with you in helping you do your [job], listening to what you say, always recognizing your international success is critical to that of Britain's overall . . . The financial services sector in Britain and the City of London at the centre of it, is a great example of a highly skilled, high value added, talent driven industry that shows how we can excel in a world of global competition. Britain needs more of the vigour, ingenuity and aspiration that you already demonstrate that is the hallmark of your success. (*The Guardian* 2006)

Froud *et al.* (2010: 26) argue that there was 'a discursive shift that became particularly pronounced under New Labour after 1997. It amounted to a kind of naturalization of financial markets in a world where public policy and institutions had to accommodate to the play of market forces'. Yet this seems rather a dry description of what became for Brown, in particular, a much more passionate commitment to the role of the City as exemplifying the skills and qualities of the British in responding to the challenges of globalization. Brown gave this more than a pragmatic tone; he made it part of his 'moral compass'.

The second feature of this period was that at a time when measuring global competitiveness across different countries was becoming an embedded part of the public policy terrain (see Pedersen 2010), the City and the government began to engage in a series of benchmarking exercises. For example, in 2005 the City of London Corporation initiated the creation of a Global Financial Centres Index to see which were the most important financial centres in the world. In the first report written by the consultancy Z/Yen, one of the sections was headed 'Plus ca change? Well Maybe and Remember We Told You So'. The section begins with a Cassandra style warning:

> In 1990, a consensus on the global financial centres would have been London, New York and Tokyo. Today it's London and New York. But might things change? The big question is – one global financial centre or three or status quo? As we seem to have gone in 15 years from three to two financial centres, we could make a strong case that soon there will be only one. (Z/Yen 2005: 16)

Benchmarking had a very practical purpose for the City and for government. By identifying areas where other countries could be said to have advantages, most obviously in terms of taxation, it provided ammunition for those pressurizing for similar rules and resources in the UK. Global competition was brought in to the UK as a series of specific institutional features, rules, regulations and laws to which the country had to adapt. Once defending and supporting the City was made central, it was hard to avoid this logic whatever its effects in terms of internal distortions of taxation, such as, for example, the row which emerged when a private equity partner lambasted the government for having a tax system which meant that a cleaner would pay more tax than him (*The Times*, 28 June 2007).

Whilst measuring and extolling the attractiveness of the City, there was also a continuous sniping at other systems, particularly for the heavy-handedness of their regulatory structures. In relation to the US, in the period after the fall of Enron there was a growing perception that the UK had been delivered a gift in terms of extending its financial services markets. The context of these discussions was the increasing recognition that, after Enron and the other corporate governance scandals in the US in the early 2000s, followed by the implementation in the US of the Sarbanes-Oxley (known as SOX) Act in 2002, had created substantial differences between systems that had in some analyses been identified together as the 'Anglo-American' corporate governance model. The US after Enron went into a period of major reform symbolized by SOX but also involving increased Securities and Exchange Commission (SEC) activity and legal action against senior executives, such as Kenneth Lay and Jeffrey Skilling at Enron and Bernie Ebbers at WorldCom. In the UK (which had escaped the worst of these scandals in the early 2000s) SOX was seen as a form of over-regulation that would drive business towards London. In particular, it was believed that companies from emerging economies seeking listings would be more likely to come to London than New York at least in part because of the SOX framework. The way in which individual executives were targeted for wrong-doing and sent to jail if found guilty was in startling contrast to how things worked in most of the rest of the world. It was also expected that in response to SOX there would be some delisting from New York and a consequent gain of business in London.

This sense that the British system was superior to that of the US and needed to be protected appeared in many discussions of regulation. In April 2007, for example, the *Financial Times* (*FT*) reported on an interview with Hector Sants (at that time the Financial Service Authority [FSA]'s managing director for wholesale business and later chief executive of the FSA). It stated that 'as Hector Sants publishes discussion papers about market abuse, his aggressive counterparts in the US are busy handcuffing and jailing insider dealers'. Sants is quoted as saying that his style is the way forward for better regulation: 'We don't ultimately think that successful regulation comes about through a confrontational style' (*Financial Times*, 23 April 2007). John Coffee, a law professor at Columbia in New York, put the US point of view in the same *FT* pages; he noted that the SEC devotes nearly 40 per cent of its budget to enforcement compared with 12 per cent for the FSA and stated that 'The FSA is much more concerned about attracting business to the London markets than it is about being an enforcement czar' (*Financial Times*, 23 April 2007).

One report issued by the influential Institute of Chartered Accountants of England and Wales stated that 'the Sarbanes–Oxley Act is now widely dismissed by media commentators as burdensome and unnecessary regulation' (ICAEW 2007: 25) and later argued that:

> US markets might become less popular as companies opted for an environment where they could report using principle-based standards [i.e., the UK way]. The appeal of rules in the US markets might also be challenged if the promise of legal certainty were seen to be an illusion. (ICAEW 2007: 26)

The EU was also seen as a potential danger to the position of the City of London. The UK government continuously pressed an agenda against increased regulation of the financial services industry in the EU.

The third development in this period was the promotion of new instruments of support for the City. By the mid-2000s, the need for actively promoting the City of London against potential threats was increasingly taken on by the government following a series of meetings bringing together the Treasury, the FSA, the City of London Corporation, the Greater London Assembly's economic policy arm and even the left-wing Mayor of London, Ken Livingstone, in order to co-ordinate developments in the regulatory and broader environment of the City. In 2006, the then Chancellor Gordon Brown announced in his budget speech the creation of High-Level City Group to discuss proposals to 'maintain and enhance the City of London's competitiveness throughout the world' (HM Treasury 2006). The group met four times over the following two years. In the press release after the first meeting, Gordon Brown was reported as saying:

The message that the City's success sends out to the whole British economy is that we will succeed if we think globally. But we must not be complacent about that success. So today's meeting has discussed concrete steps that will allow us to take forward an agenda, bringing business and government together, to equip us to meet the challenges of global competition and promote the City and its financial services expertise throughout the world. (HM Treasury 2006)

Ed Balls, then Economic Secretary to the Treasury, reinforced the argument, stating in the same press release that:

> If we get key decisions right, as we are doing with regulation of exchanges, and continue to attract the best talent from around the world, I believe that we can entrench London as the key financial centre of the 21st century.

These meetings spawned a range of initiatives. A private–public partnership, the Financial Services Sector Advisory Board linked to UK Trade and Investment with a dedicated diplomatic staff, was set up to promote the City in key overseas markets such as China and India. It was agreed to take 'further action against unnecessary gold-plating of European Directives' and pushing 'for a more de-regulatory stance in the EU'.[1] A Financial Services Skill Council was set up and proposals were agreed to establish in London an International Centre for Financial Regulation which would offer a training site for financial regulators across the world to learn and diffuse the approach of the City. In June 2008, the Centre was announced with mainly City funding. The Financial Services Global Competitiveness Group was set up in July 2008, the aim of which was to 'meet monthly to analyse global trends affecting the competitiveness of the international financial services industry ... to help London and the UK maintain and enhance its leading place in the world's financial markets' (HM Treasury 2008). Other specific initiatives included the creation of a Rights Issues working party in August 2008, following the failure of major rights issues in the City, the creation of a Professional Services Industry group (linking financial services to the range of complementary skills necessary in law, accounting and management consultancy) and reviews of the wholesale insurance industry. Two new global markets where the City and the government were keen to establish a major UK presence were also mentioned with regularity – carbon trading and Islamic finance and working groups set up to investigate how to attract these businesses to the City of London.

In conclusion, the British government became increasingly active in ensuring that the City of London maintained its position in financial markets. In doing this, there was a concerted effort to define the virtues of the UK and the City in contrast to other competitors such as the US and the EU. The government also developed a series of initiatives which would improve the City's position by providing increased training, by identifying and developing new markets, and by creating new and more intensive liaison mechanisms between government and the City. At the same time, none of these moves undermined the ability of the government to claim that it continued to support open markets and rejected old style forms of protectionism. It was a strategy that was adapted to the integrated global financial markets and yet at the same time appeared to provide a framework for managing the politics of the UK at a time when other economic sectors were declining and disappearing.

THE FINANCIAL CRISIS AND ECONOMIC PATRIOTISM

The decline of the financial sector from 2007 and, in particular, the collapse in late 2008 following the bankruptcy of Lehman Brothers had a profound impact on the processes which have been described. Politicians and regulators in the UK hurried to distance themselves from their previous lauding of the City and all its deeds and practices. Regulators such as the previously mentioned Hector Sants gave up their 'light touch' style and quickly espoused the need for more intense monitoring of risk within financial institutions. However, debates on bankers' bonuses, on forcing the 'nationalized' banks to direct credit to cash-starved small and medium-sized businesses, on separating simple retail banking from wholesale banking, on tightening up regulation have proceeded slowly in the UK with very little effective legislation, a situation that has barely changed with the advent of the coalition government in May 2010. Further, in international negotiations, in the EU and elsewhere, the UK government has continued to make sure that nothing was agreed which would undermine the City's competitive advantage (Morgan 2010). Froud *et al.* (2010) and Talani (2011) emphasize the continuity in this later period of key aspects of the pre-crisis system. Froud *et al.*, for example, state that the 'crisis drove elected politicians to take radical measures but, in the aftermath, the undemocratic habits of market government were reasserted by unelected civil servants and financiers' (Froud *et al.* 2010: 26).

Without gainsaying this judgement, however, a perspective from the view of economic patriotism suggests a more complex and uncertain outcome. Firstly, the crisis made clearer than ever that, as in any form of economic nationalism or economic patriotism, certain groups were advantaged more than others. The adherence to the agenda of the City had made it difficult for Blair and Brown to make any moves to attack the more gross examples of inequality that had emerged during the boom years of the City, even though public disquiet was growing over the huge bonuses received by private equity partners, hedge fund managers, market dealers and others, exacerbated by their low tax liability. In the period from 2005 onwards there was increasing scepticism about the claims that support for the City was to the benefit of all rather than the enrichment of the few (Froud and Williams 2007; Peston 2008; Toynbee and Walker 2008). Emphasizing the tax take from these individuals and companies increasingly wore thin, particularly after the crisis when the rescue of the banks turned the flow of funds dramatically in the other direction (CRESC 2009). Even before the crisis, tentative discussions about codes of conduct for private equity firms and hedge funds ended up with some increased transparency but little concrete in terms of inequality issues (Morgan 2009). The form of loose regulation, as well as leading to criticisms from the US, Europe, Germany and France, was also beginning to be criticized internally by bodies such as the House of Commons Treasury Committee. Even the FSA, in its Discussion Papers on Private Equity and Hedge Funds, was beginning to puzzle over whether regulation was too weak. By 2007–8, therefore, the efforts which had been made to depoliticize the rise of finance and the City and to associate it with the 'national good' were already beginning to unravel (*cf.* Burnham 2001).

Economic patriotism in the form of supporting the City was effectively destroyed by the crisis. The lauding of the City in the way it was done by Brown and Blair has become impossible. The coalition government continues to berate banks about excessive bonuses and profits as well as poor service to small businesses; it engages in some punitive taxation of the banks, and the threat of some sort of legal restructuring of banks continues to be discussed via the government-appointed Independent Commission on Banking, due to report in late 2011. For a short period, it seemed that the meaning of economic patriotism might be completely remoulded as the state came in to save the banking system from its own excesses. Perhaps a new form of economic patriotism could have involved creating a 'socially useful system of finance', a term used by a City insider, Adair Turner, chair of the FSA when he addressed a gathering at the Mansion House in the City of London on 22nd September 2009.[2] However as Froud *et al.* (2010) show, this idea failed to take hold in the face of forces more keen to return to 'business as usual'. Nevertheless, 'business as usual' now takes place under a cloud in a way it did not prior to 200. The politics of supporting the City has become much more circumspect and less prone to wholesale endorsement of whatever the City wants.

CONCLUSIONS

In an era when national economies are increasingly interdependent and international rules set limits on what governments can do, there is a danger that electorates will feel that governments do not represent them but rather represent or bow down to the pressures of global capitalism. Therefore, in response to this governments must establish a legitimate and credible connection with their electorate, by claiming that they are pursuing the national interest in economic policy-making. This claim has to be carefully constructed and implemented, since certain discourses and practices are ruled out by the global context. Economic patriotism provides a way of making such a claim. It identifies the moral value of serving the interests of those within the territorial boundary that has been demarcated without denying the validity of economic interdependence and global rules. It provides a language for mobilizing and innovating a range of specific instruments and mechanisms which facilitate supporting territorially defined economic activities.

Turning to the City of London, this contribution has shown how the UK state has supported the activities of the City in a series of ways specific to the conditions of the current period. Thus, the specificity of the City's light-touch regulatory framework was continuously contrasted in official discourse to that of the US and the EU and given a strong moral value for the way in which it facilitated innovation and market-making, which in turn drove the British economy. This discursive positioning was accompanied in the period from 2005 by a series of micro moves to establish more firmly co-operation between the City and the government.

However, what we also learn very clearly from the example of the City, and in particular the financial crash, is that economic patriotism is in itself no solution to broader problems of managing the inter-relationship between global markets and internal political orders. Supporting the City is no longer a viable form of economic patriotism. The crash and the consequent loss of legitimacy have emptied it of any claim it might have made to the hearts and minds of the population. A pragmatic process of adjustment is currently being played out between the City and the coalition government which has continued to pursue the interests of the City in international discussions, though much more *sotto voce* than previously, particularly in relation to its internal audience in the UK.

In conclusion, the concept of economic patriotism enables us to look at how the state embeds and supports firms where open markets policed by international institutions and global rules exist. Economic patriotism reflects the effort to construct state policies which can make claims to the electorate for legitimacy. It reveals that those claims are contingent, interests shift over time as circumstances change and this impacts on how economic patriotism becomes articulated. By taking a perspective on economic patriotism which is historical, comparative, social and dynamic, therefore, we are able to see more clearly how the conflict between open markets and democratic politics is being managed in the current period.

Biographical note: Glenn Morgan is Professor of International Management at Cardiff Business School.

NOTES

1 As reported on *Money Marketing* website, 26 October 2006, http://www.moneymarketing.co.uk/news/city-group-targets-regulation/131054.article (accessed 10 September 2009).
2 For a full text of the speech, see http://www.fsa.gov.uk/pages/Library/Communication/Speeches/2009/0922_at.shtml (accessed 9 September 2010).

REFERENCES

Abdelal, R. (2007) *Capital Rules: The Construction of Global Finance*, Cambridge, MA: Harvard University Press.
Burnham, P. (2001) 'New Labour and the politics of depoliticisation', *British Journal of Politics and International Relations* 3(2): 127–49.
Burnham, P. (2007) 'The politicisation of monetary policy-making in postwar Britain', *British Politics* 2(3): 395–419.
Clift, B. and Woll, C. (2012) 'Economic patriotism: reinventing control over open markets', *Journal of European Public Policy* 19(3), http://dx.doi.org/10.1080/13501763.2011.638117.
CRESC (2009) 'An alternative report on UK banking reform', available at http://www.cresc.ac.uk/publications/an-alternative-report-on-uk-banking-reform (accessed 9 May 2010).
Crouch, C. (2008) 'What will follow the demise of Privatised Keynesianism?', *The Political Quarterly* 79(4): 476–87.
Froud, J. and Williams, K. (2007) 'Private equity and the culture of value extraction', *New Political Economy* 12(3): 405–20.
Froud, J., Moran, M., Nillson, A. and Williams, K. (2010) 'Wasting a crisis? Democracy and markets in Britain after 2007', *The Political Quarterly* 81(1): 25–38.
Glyn, A. (2007) *Capitalism Unleashed: Finance, Globalization, and Welfare*, Oxford: Oxford University Press.
Guardian, The (2006) 'Gordon Brown's Mansion House speech', 22 June, available at http://www.guardian.co.uk/business/2006/jun/22/politics.economicpolicy (accessed 20 October 2010).
HM Treasury (2006) 'First meeting of the high level group', *Press Release 77/06*, 18 October.
HM Treasury (2008) 'Group to focus on keeping London globally competitive', *Press Release 74/08*, 14 July.
IFSL Research (2009) 'Economic contribution of UK financial services 2009', available at http://www.thecityuk.com/assets/Uploads/Economic-Contribution-of-UK-Financial-Services-2009.pdf (accessed 10 October 2010).
Ingham, G.K. (1984) *Capitalism Divided? The City and Industry in British Social Development*, Basingstoke: Macmillan.

Institute of Chartered Accountants of England and Wales (ICAEW) (2007) *Emerging Issues: How Differences between US And UK Securities Markets Create Pressures and Point to Opportunities for International Policy, Investment, Business and Accounting* (London: ICAEW).

Kagan, R. (2001) *Adversarial Legalism: The American Way of Law*, Cambridge, MA: Harvard University Press.

Krippner, G. (2011) *Capitalizing on Crisis: The Political Origins of the Rise of Finance*, Cambridge, MA: Harvard University Press.

Kynaston, D. (2002) *The City of London Volume IV: A Club No More*, London: Pimlico.

Levy, J. (ed.) (2006) *The State after Statism*, Cambridge, MA: Harvard University Press.

Milward, A. (1992) *The European Rescue of the Nation-State*, London: Routledge.

Moran, M. (1991) *The Politics of the Financial Services Revolution: The USA, UK and Japan*, Basingstoke: Macmillan.

Moran, M. (2003) *The British Regulatory State: High Modernism and Hyper-Innovation*, Oxford: Oxford University Press.

Morgan, G. (2009) 'Private Equity in the UK context', *Transfer: European Review of Labour and Research* 15(2): 209–28.

Morgan, G. (2010) 'Legitimacy in financial markets: credit default swaps in the current crisis', *Socio-Economic Review* 8(1): 17–46.

Pedersen, O.K. (2010) 'Institutional competitiveness: how nations came to compete', in G. Morgan *et al.* (eds), *The Oxford Handbook of Comparative Institutional Analysis*, Oxford: Oxford University Press, pp. 625–57.

Peston, R. (2008) *Who runs Britain?* London: Hodder & Stoughton.

Sassen, S. (1991) *The Global City: New York, London and Tokyo*, Princeton, NJ: Princeton University Press.

Schwartz, H.M. (2009) *Subprime Nation: American Power, Global Capital and the Housing Bubble*, Ithaca, NY: Cornell University Press.

Talani, L.S. (2011) 'The impact of the global financial crisis on the City of London: towards the end of hegemony?', *Competition and Change* 15(1): 11–30.

Toynbee, P. and Walker, D. (2008) *Unjust Rewards: Exposing Greed and Inequality in Britain Today*, London: Granta.

Z/Yen (2005) 'Report for the Corporation of London on Global Financial Competitiveness', reports available at http://www.zyen.com/long-finance/global-financial-centres-index-gfci.html (accessed 10 September 2010).

The phantom of Palais Brongniart: economic patriotism and the Paris Stock Exchange

Helen Callaghan and Paul Lagneau-Ymonet

ABSTRACT France is famous for promoting national champions, notably by preventing foreign takeovers, but in 2005–2006, the French government allowed the New York Stock Exchange to take control of Euronext, a French-led pan-European company that includes the Paris Bourse. By mapping the public discourse surrounding this striking case of non-intervention, we explain why opponents of the transatlantic merger failed in their appeals to 'economic patriotism'. Discursive strategies designed to justify discrimination against territorially defined outsiders ran into several hurdles, including weak patriotic sentiments for the company concerned; a lack of patriotic alternatives to the proposed merger; and the questionable patriotic credentials of those demanding intervention. Our findings advance research on demand side of 'economic patriotism', including its discursive dimension. Beyond that, they inform research on business–government relations, and on the political implications of corporate ownership structures.

1. INTRODUCTION

The Paris Stock Exchange – located, until the 1990s, at Palais Brongniart in the Opera district of the French capital – has over the past three decades changed in ways that seem difficult to reconcile with the *dirigiste* image of French governments. In 2006, after successive cross-border mergers, this former symbol of national economic sovereignty became a subsidiary of the New York Stock Exchange (NYSE). Four years later, Euronext Paris and other continental European members of the now American-run group experienced significant downsizing and the relocation to London of crucial IT infrastructures and activities.[1] At the time of writing, in March 2011, NYSE-Euronext is confronted with competing takeover offers from Deutsche Börse and Nasdaq/ICE. If either of these deals goes through, Paris will suffer a further loss of influence.

The relative weakness of political efforts to prevent the Paris stock exchange from falling into foreign hands is surprising, for several reasons. The cross-border merger took place in a country with a long-standing record of transatlantic defiance and of political intervention in the market for corporate control; it coincided with heavy-handed attempts to prevent cross-border mergers in other sectors of the French economy; it concerned a sector that is arguably of high economic and political significance and with regard to which the French government has formal legal instruments of intervention at its disposal. Why did the same government that took legislative action to prevent a rumoured takeover of Danone by PepsiCo allow NYSE to gain control of Euronext?

By mapping the public discourse surrounding this striking case of non-intervention, we explain why opponents of the transatlantic merger failed in their appeals to 'economic patriotism'. Discursive strategies designed to justify political discrimination against territorially defined outsiders ran into several hurdles. Patriotic sentiments were difficult to mobilize for a company as perceivedly 'Anglo-Saxon' as Euronext; the patriotic credentials of key opponents to the merger were weak, because many of them had prepared the ground by profitably selling their shares abroad; and instead of a patriotic alternative, 'imperialist' advances by Deutsche Börse were seen as a likely outcome of failure to merge with NYSE.

Our contribution advances research on economic patriotism by helping to explain *when* governments choose to discriminate in favour of territorially defined insiders. While the heuristic provided by Clift and Woll (2012) usefully distinguishes different levels (supranational, national, local), ideological affinities (liberal or conservative) and policy objectives (favouring insiders or resistance to outsiders) of economic patriotism, it does not offer clear predictions as to *when* politicians choose to privilege territorially defined groups. The other case studies assembled in this collection do not provide sufficient leverage on this question, because they focus on instances of economic patriotism in a variety of different contexts, while neglecting cases in which political action was conspicuously absent.

We maintain that understanding variation in the supply of territorially based discrimination requires looking beyond state action to the *demand side* of economic patriotism, including its discursive dimension. As Pepper Culpepper (2011) has recently shown, economic policy-making is significantly shaped by the amount of media attention devoted to the issue in question. Put bluntly, 'business power goes down as political salience goes up' (Culpepper 2011: 177), because business groups have tools and resources that allow them to dominate fights in low-salience domains. However, 'quiet politics' is difficult to engineer. Given the distributional consequences of economic policy-making, there are always some people, both within and outside the business community, who have an interest in raising the salience level in order to rally the broader public behind their cause. Broad mobilization requires framing demands in terms of some widely shared 'public interest'. Appeals to patriotic sentiments are frequently employed, presumably because such sentiments are widespread and easily tapped without need for complex technical argumentation. Economic patriotism, in other words, is a discursive strategy as much as an objective concept.

By identifying limitations to this discursive strategy, our case study contributes to explaining why governments sometimes refrain from pursuing the kind of state action classified by Clift and Woll (2012). Whereas their approach is implicitly based on a narrow policy-maker focused rationality ('Will this policy win me electoral support'), we argue that policy-making, especially economic policy, is a broader path-generation process (Djelic and Quack 2007) which is shaped over time by a plurality of demands coming from stakeholders and constituents. We share the assumption that vote-seeking politicians need to act on high profile issues. However, we go one step further by noting that the salience level of any given policy measure is discursively engineered. Our contribution lies in identifying factors that determine whether those interested in political intervention succeed in raising the salience of the issue by framing it as a matter of economic patriotism. As a single case study of a 'dog that did not bark', our contribution cannot pretend to engage in rigorous hypothesis-testing. Nevertheless, it offers a first cut at filling a research gap recently identified by Vivien Schmidt, namely to move beyond asserting that discourse matters, by exploring empirically when, where and why it matters– and when it does not (cf. Schmidt 2010: 21).

Our empirical evidence derives from newspapers, interviews and participant observation. Eighty volumes of newspaper articles compiled by Euronext Paris between 2000 and 2007 served as our main source of press coverage. Twelve interviews held between 2006 and 2010 with prominent figures of the Paris financial centre (see Appendix) provided background information. Beyond that, one of the authors had the opportunity to witness the in-house dynamics of Euronext at first hand, through his position as an assistant to the Euronext director of international affairs in Paris from October 2001 until August 2002, and as an assistant to the Euronext director of European affairs in Brussels from August to November 2003.

We will proceed as follows. Section 2 justifies the case selection. Section 3 maps the preferences and discursive strategies of key French stakeholders concerning political intervention in the NYSE/Euronext merger. We conclude with suggestions for further research.

2. THE SURPRISING ABSENCE OF TERRITORIALLY BASED DISCRIMINATION

Our study supplements the other contributions to this collection by examining a case in which political action was conspicuously absent. The merger of Euronext with NYSE lends itself well because, *a priori*, there were strong reasons to expect political intervention. First, research on the geography of financial markets suggests that the location of stock markets has economic, regulatory and political implications. Economically, spatial proximity of issuers, investment banks, financial analysts, the stock exchange(s), asset managers and investors enhances the exchange of both formal and informal information and offers valuable network externalities. These benefits are said to explain why, contrary to predictions that information technology would spell the 'end of geography' (O'Brien 1992), financial activities remain highly concentrated in a few financial centres

(Sassen 2005; Tadjeddine and Capelle-Blancard 2009). The same benefits are also cited as a reason for the persistently strong so-called 'home bias' in investment decisions: investors tend to hold, trade and obtain superior returns from securities issued by companies that are 'familiar' to them (Wójcik 2009). From a supervisory point of view, stock market location matters because governments and regulatory authorities have only limited influence outside their own jurisdiction. Stock market regulation affects the market for corporate control, corporate governance, the protection of investors and financial regulation at large. The transfer of regulatory power over these matters to foreign institutions therefore implies a weakening of economic governance at the national level. Politically, nations throughout the history of capitalism have used the size and might of their financial centres as resources in the contest for geopolitical leadership (Cassis 2006; Ferguson 2001; Weber 2000 [1894]). Even the rapid expansion, since the launch of the Euromarkets in the 1960s, of cross-border financial transactions outside incumbent exchanges was originally promoted by the United States (US) and the British governments to secure their financial supremacy at that time (Helleiner 1994).

Second, the weakness of political efforts to prevent foreign control of the stock market coincided with a string of high-profile interventions against attempted foreign takeovers of other French companies. Building on a long tradition of *dirigisme* (Shonfield 1965; Zysman 1983), the French government lived up to its reputation as the champion of national champions by intervening in bids for the oil company Elf by its Italian rival ENI in 1999, for the pharmaceutical company Aventis by Switzerland's Novartis in 2003 and by forestalling suspected bids for Danone and for the Suez conglomerate in 2005–2006. In the same year, the government also drafted a new decree granting itself a right to veto or impose conditions on foreign takeovers of French firms in 11 sectors[2] which it declared strategic and ordered the state-owned Caisse des Dépots et Consignations to increase its investment in French equities.

Third, in contrast to the case of Danone, which triggered new legislation, a legal basis for intervention was already available to policy-makers. The French subsidiary of Euronext, which operates the Paris Stock Exchange, has a hybrid legal status: it is not an ordinary private company but a specialized financial institution *(institution financière spécialisée)*. As such, Euronext Paris is governed by French banking legislation, including the French Banking Act as amended and codified in the French Monetary and Financial Code. It is therefore subject to supervision by the Financial Markets Authority (*Autorité des Marchés Financiers*) and the Banking Commission – *Commission Bancaire* – which became the Prudential Control Authority in March 2010. The French administration can nominate a commissioner to the board of Euronext Paris to ensure implementation of the 'permanent public-interest mission' entrusted to the company by law.

Fourth, judging by their public objections to a transatlantic merger with NYSE, influential French policy-makers at the supranational, national and regional level were not indifferent to the fate of Euronext. At the European level, Jean-Claude Trichet, president of the European Central Bank and a former French civil servant, warned that a transatlantic merger might weaken EU monetary policy.[3] Pervenche Bères, French Socialist Member of the European Parliament (MEP), demanded that the European Commission intervene to 'protect the public interest'.[4] At the national level, President Jacques Chirac said that he preferred a merger with Deutsche Börse 'for reasons of principle.'[5] Jean Arthuis, president of the Finance Commission in the French Senate, and French head of the *Deutsch-Französische Freundschaftsgruppen der Parlamente*, demanded that 'the [French] government, the German government and other European governments pull themselves together and press for the creation of a pan-European stock exchange'.[6] The Parti Socialiste let it be known that it was 'completely opposed to the merger.'[7] Pierre Moscovici, international affairs spokesman for the Socialist Party (Parti Socialiste, PS) and Jean-Pierre Jouyet, Secretary of State for European Affairs at the time of the merger and chairman of the Financial Markets Authority since December 2008, declared *ex post* that they would have preferred a European solution.[8] At the local level, Jean-Paul Huchon, head of the Paris area regional assembly (Région Ile de France), regarded the transatlantic merger as a 'bad signal'.[9]

Despite these widespread reservations, and in contrast to simultaneous intervention in other cross-border mergers, French policy-makers chose not to use the full repertoire of legal and political tools to prevent NYSE from acquiring Euronext. Instead, both the French Financial Markets Authority and the French government remained neutral on the ownership question: provided that the operator of the exchange complied with the legal requirements and governance amendments to assure formal equilibrium between European and American members of its board, the capital structure of the exchange would not matter. The French chief regulator, Michel Prada, and his peers from the United Kingdom (UK), Belgium, the Netherlands and Portugal co-operated with their counterparts from the US Securities Exchange Commission to solve legal technicalities of the proposed merger. Thierry Breton, the French finance minister, successfully pushed for a formally equal governance structure, but he repeatedly insisted that, while customers and employees would be consulted, the ultimate decision on the merger lay with shareholders.[10]

3. DEMAND FOR AND OPPOSITION TO GOVERNMENT INTERVENTION

A look at the demand for government intervention in the NYSE/Euronext merger shows French business élites highly mobilized and deeply divided on the issue – possibly because the ownership composition of the stock exchange and its strategy could affect a larger part of the corporate community than that of companies in the industrial sector. While the main beneficiaries of intervention against a foreign takeover of industrial companies (management and employees of the companies concerned) usually have higher stakes than their opponents (free-market ideologues and minority shareholders), the NYSE/

Euronext merger pitched Euronext management against Euronext users (that is, French issuers and financial intermediaries), all of whom had material interests at stake.

Top managers of Euronext wanted the merger to go through. Accordingly, they repeatedly insisted that theirs was a private company. As early as 2001, Euronext Chief Eexecutive Officer (CEO) Jean-François Theodore presented demutualized stock exchanges as 'an industry like any other' and warned against 'speak[ing] of alliances as if we are diplomats'.[11] The same view was promoted by influential French economists, including members of the prime minister's Council of Economic Advisors (*Conseil d'analyse économique*). Some of the most vocal economists in the debate, including Bertrand Jacquillat (professor at Sciences Po Paris, chairman and CEO of the financial consultancy Associés en Finance) and Christian Saint-Etienne (professor at the University of Tours, lobbyist at Schell et Associés), were simultaneously members of the *Cercle des économistes*, a prominent French think tank, partially subsidized by Euronext.[12]

By contrast, many issuers and financial intermediaries, including former owners of the Paris Stock Exchange, opposed the transatlantic merger. Gérard de La Martinière, head of the powerful French federation of insurance companies and spokesman for the Mouvement des Entreprises de France (MEDEF), the French peak business federation, pleaded for 'European connections that would allow us to enlarge the capital pool while remaining in our own zone of monetary activity'.[13] The European Association of Listed Companies, chaired by Alain Joly, CEO of the French blue chip Air Liquide, complained that '[t]he proposed governance structure that puts NYSE in control, gives no assurance in the long run as to the preservation of the interests of European issuers'.[14] Claude Bébéar, supervisory board president of AXA and a leading figure of French capitalism, objected to demutualized stock exchanges *per se* and wanted them to be kept under the control of their users, at least through a shareholding pact. Michel Pébereau, supervisory board president of BNP and arguably the most powerful banker in France (Jabko and Massoc 2011) worried that a transatlantic move would dilute the influence of his bank more severely than would consolidation at the continental European level. A high-profile study of NYSE's and Deutsche Börse's takeover offers, commissioned by Paris Europlace, a public–private association charged with promoting the Paris financial centre, and conducted by Henri Lachmann, CEO of Schneider Electric, concluded that 'the transatlantic acquisition is not in the best interest of the European market place'.[15]

Apart from lobbying behind the scenes, some of the business leaders opposing the merger openly demanded state intervention. Gérard de La Martinière wanted the French government to 'bang its fist on the table'.[16] Axel Miller, CEO of the Franco-Belgian bank Dexia, complained after the merger that 'the finance ministers should have taken care of this matter ... The stock exchange is a vital instrument for growth and employment, and for the market economy at large. The failure to preserve it reveals the current political void.'[17] Their policy preferences intriguingly resembled those of the Socialist Party, which called on the government to 'immediately take ... responsible action by opposing the merger in such a way that economic patriotism, be it French or European, does not remain a mere slogan'.[18] Interestingly, perhaps for the reasons identified below, the Socialists refrained from repeating this line of attack in the run-up to the presidential elections.

The following section explains why opponents of the transatlantic merger failed to build up political pressure for intervention, despite a political climate that – in the run-up to the 2007 presidential elections – was highly receptive to appeals to economic patriotism.

4. THE DISCURSIVE LIMITATIONS OF 'ECONOMIC PATRIOTISM'

Several discursive hurdles prevented successful instrumentalization of the economic patriotism discourse by opponents of the merger. First, patriotic sentiments among the electorate were difficult to mobilize for a company as foreign and removed from people's lives as Euronext. Unlike consumer products such as yoghurt and cars, financial services do not lend themselves well to the kind of emotional attachment prone to stirring patriotic sentiments, especially since they can be construed as elements of 'Anglo-American style capitalism', even when the providers are French. In addition, the number of French jobs at stake was small. In 2006, the Paris branch of Euronext – the largest within the company – employed fewer than 400 people, mostly in positions that failed to spark feelings of solidarity in the average French worker. Moreover, direct and indirect shareholdings are still relatively scarce in France, where an extended public welfare state provides retirement pensions through taxation, contributions and intergenerational redistribution, rather than through individual capitalization and private savings (Montagne 2006).

Second, a convincing 'patriotic' alternative to the transatlantic merger was not available. In other recent cases of government intervention, blockage of a cross-border merger typically resulted either in the French company remaining independent, or in a Franco-French alliance. In the case of Euronext, failure to merge with NYSE was widely expected to result in a merger with Deutsche Börse. Proponents of intervention tried to overcome this discursive hurdle by appealing to 'economic patriotism' at the European level: Arthuis argued that 'one year after the failure of the referendum on the [Lisbon] treaty ... this new project of allowing the pan-European stock exchange Euronext to fall under the control of the New York Stock Exchange is a woeful sign and a confession of European abandonment'.[19] Ernest-Antoine Seillière, then president of the European employer federation UNICE (now called BUSINESSEUROPE) warned that, '[i]f the Americans become masters of our financial market, then this is a severe defeat for our European project'.[20] Lachmann found it 'essential that we continue to build Europe, and the Europe of stock markets should take priority over the acquisition of Euronext by the

NYSE'.[21] French conservative Member of Parliament Jacques Myard (Union pour un Mouvement Populaire, UMP), known for his vocal support for industrial policy at the national and EU levels, saw the NYSE/Euronext merger as 'further proof of the vassalization of Europe by the United States'.[22]

The resonance of appeals to economic patriotism at the European level suffered not only from the weakness of a European identity in general, but from distrust of 'imperialist' Germany in particular. This allowed opponents of intervention to neutralize such appeals by presenting the choice between NYSE and Deutsche Börse as a choice between the frying pan and the fire. According to Daniel Bouton, chairman and CEO of Société Générale, one of the two investment banks advising NYSE with Citigroup on the operation, Frankfurt was trying to 'strip Paris of its status as the main financial center on the continent, after having already obtained the seat of the European Central Bank six years earlier'.[23] Theodore had made the same point more subtly, by justifying his rejection of Deutsche Börse's merger offer on the grounds that '[t]heir vision of Europe was focused on Frankfurt ... whereas we are a 21st century company. We are represented in all our capital cities.'[24] In the same vein, Oliver Lefebvre, board member of Euronext and president of the Brussels Stock Exchange, insisted that '[t]he proposal by Deutsche Börse runs counter to the interests of the Eurozone ... By favoring such a merger, one would destroy the only cross-border example that works at present.'[25] Opponents of a Franco-German alliance drew ammunition from an off-hand comment by Kurt Viermetz, head of Deutsche Börse's supervisory board, who had boasted, in March 2006, that one could 'turn off the lights in the rest of Europe' if Euronext were to move to Frankfurt.[26] Tensions associated with previous French–German attempts to create European champions – including Sanofi-Aventis, Siemens/Alstom and earlier disappointments which turned into bitter competition between the Paris Stock Exchange and the Deutsche Börse, provided further grounds for scepticism.

Third, and perhaps most interestingly, questionable 'patriotic credentials' contributed to weakening the influence of those business leaders who called for intervention. Understanding the credibility problems afflicting financial intermediaries requires the following background knowledge about the demutualization process of the Paris Stock Exchange. Historically, most stock exchanges, including the Paris Bourse, were owned and controlled by their direct users, the stockbrokers. They were governed through a mutual structure, with member-owners contributing their time to governance and self-regulation. Profits were returned to member-owners in the form of lower access fees or other benefits. In recent years, many exchanges have changed their legal form and governance structure by separating ownership rights from membership rights – a process commonly referred to as demutualization. As a first step toward demutualization, most exchanges converted membership rights into common stock holdings, thus making members the legal owners of the corporation. After that, many exchanges went on to list their own securities on the stock market, thereby extending the possibility of ownership to outside investors

(Lee 2010). The French stock exchange, by then part of Euronext, went public in July 2001. At a time where strategic management was all about disinvestment in peripheral activities and financial consolidation in the wake of the dot-com bust, French financial intermediaries gradually sold their stakes in Euronext. They made good money[27] in return for ceding control of the exchange to international institutional investors, such as Fidelity, and activist hedge funds, including Harris Associates, Atticus and TCI.

Calls for state intervention in the name of economic patriotism by those who had sold their own means of protecting French interests sparked widespread resentment. Philippe Marini, rapporteur of the Finance Commission in the French Senate and a close ally of Jean-François Theodore, advised the historical shareholders to 'stop complaining about a situation which they themselves ha[d] brought about'.[28] He observed that '[if] large French and European banks had kept their shares instead of walking away with their capital gains a little prematurely, Euronext could very well have pursued its development autonomously and continued to integrate further European exchanges into its federal structure'.[29] Even Jean Arthuis, president of the Finance Commission in the French Senate and a strong opponent of the NYSE/Euronext merger, scolded the banks for having betraying the public interest by realizing their capital gains. In his view, this was particularly unacceptable because '[i]f anyone should have an understanding of the general interest, it is the banks. After all, when they are confronted with difficulties that pose a risk for the financial system, it is the state which comes to their rescue.'[30] Henri Lachmann, author of the above-mentioned position paper by Paris Europlace, pointed out that '[t]he French banks sold their shares and recently had the chance to regain control by acquiring a large block of shares that had been placed on the market ... Anyone who does not seize such an opportunity should not go around giving lessons on citizenship to others.'[31]

By contrast, French Euronext managers backing the merger enjoyed strong credibility because of their success in founding Euronext – which had transformed the quasi-public French, Belgian and Dutch exchanges into a highly profitable privatized multinational capable of rivalling the London and Frankfurt stock exchanges. The federally structured Euronext convinced many that cross-border stock market alliances could help Paris in its competition against London and Frankfurt – not least because its French CEO, Jean-François Theodore, was celebrated as a clever strategist in the international business press. In June 2002, the influential magazine *Institutional Investors* even gave him the front page with an explicit tribute, 'Théodore [sic] Rex'. Theodore's credibility with French Treasury officials was further aided by close network connections to top-tier civil servants. After graduating from the élite *École nationale d'administration*, Theodore had worked at the French Treasury from 1974 to 1989 before becoming chairman and CEO of the *Société des bourses françaises* and, from 2000, the head of Euronext. Likewise, his Belgian counterpart Olivier Lefebvre, president of the Brussels Stock Exchange (PhD in economics from the Université Catholique de Louvain, MBA from Cornell University) had worked at the Belgian Finance Ministry until the mid-1990s, where he had contributed to the drafting and implementation of laws reforming the national financial sector.

Apart from the discursive hurdles spelled out above, opponents of the merger faced several additional difficulties. First, intervention conflicted with the neoliberal paradigm which had guided financial sector policy-making in France and Europe since the 1980s. The decision not to intervene in the NYSE/Euronext merger coherently followed from earlier measures designed to enhance the international competitiveness of the French financial centre. First steps toward stock market demutualization were taken as early as 1984 with reforms authorizing commercial banks to branch out into investment banking (Feiertag 2005; Lordon 1997). In March 1988, universal banks, insurance companies and international brokerage houses were allowed to take control of the Paris Stock Exchange. The *Compagnie nationale des agents de change*, a hybrid organization controlled by a powerful guild of state-authorized officers under the direct supervision of the French Ministry of Finance, was dismantled and replaced by the corporation of French exchanges (*Société des Bourses Françaises* – SBF). In June 1999, the SBF absorbed the three other French market operators: the *Société du Nouveau Marché* dedicated to smaller companies; the Marché à Terme International de France (MATIF) and the Marché des Options Négociables de Paris (MONEP) for futures and options. In September 2000, the exchanges of Paris, Amsterdam and Brussels merged to form Euronext (Djelic and Lagneau-Ymonet 2009). When Euronext went public in 2001, policy-makers did not insist on a hard core *(noyau dur)* of European shareholders for Euronext, even though its management, unlike the historical shareholders, had recommended measures to ensure ownership stability.

Second, the French drive for financial sector competitiveness through liberalization was also in line with policies promoted by the European Commission. The latter aimed at the marginalization of direct state intervention in the ownership structure, governance or strategy of firms; integration of the European financial sector through competition; and co-ordination of conflicting interests through marketization (Mügge 2006). Underlying these policies was the conviction that financial market integration was more likely to result from enhanced competition between stock exchanges than from enhanced co-operation among fiercely competing stock exchanges. As Jabko (2006), Posner (2009) and Denord and Schwartz (2010) demonstrate at length, this conviction stemmed partly from the prior failure of efforts to link the main European financial markets by encouraging co-operation, and partly from a long-lasting ideological stance.

Third, party-strategic calculations meant that political leaders had strong incentives to prevent the NYSE/Euronext merger from turning into a central campaign issue in the upcoming presidential elections. The presidential candidate for the conservative party, Nicolas Sarkozy, sought to differentiate himself from the incumbent President Chirac and his archrival Prime Minister de Villepin by promising a '*rupture*' with the past. His aim was to appear as a fresh figure despite coming from the ruling party and having served as Chirac's minister for five years. To achieve this, Sarkozy deliberately distanced himself – at least during the campaign – from Gaullist diplomatic and economic policies by embracing more neo-liberal positions and by displaying admiration for the United States and the Bush administration. Meanwhile, the Socialists also lacked incentives to exploit the NYSE/Euronext merger as a campaign issue. Their party had lost the 2002 election by failing to gain the expected support from working class voters (Lefebvre and Sawicki 2005). A campaign focus on the stock exchange was not deemed a promising remedy. Moreover, in the wake of the failed 2005 referendum on the European constitution, divisions within the Socialist party over the desirability of further European integration ran deep, and the promotion of Euronext as a 'European champion' was feared to further alienate left-wing voters.

Fourth, there were some grounds for believing that a merger with NYSE might be advantageous from the perspective of economic efficiency. Advocates of the merger promised synergies from adopting a common trading technology. They also presented stock market consolidation as an inevitable pre-emptive response to competitive pressures unleashed by the European Unions's (EU) Market in Financial Instruments Directive, which was implemented in November 2007 (Hautcoeur *et al.* 2010). Last but not least, Deutsche Börse was less attractive as a partner for Euronext, because its business model featured a silo structure which integrated the entire value chain (listing, trading, clearing, settlement and delivery), whereas Euronext mainly focused on trading activities. As a result of this divergence in business models, the market capitalization of Deutsche Börse exceeded the market capitalization of Euronext to an extent that made a 'merger of equals' unlikely.

However, the above aspects do not satisfactorily explain the government's reluctance to intervene. The economic efficiency arguments, in particular, were contested. Merging firms always promise synergies. Opponents of the merger questioned some of the figures and calculations presented by its advocates. Moreover, economic rationale is not the only driver of economic policy. There are ample examples of government efforts to rescue failing companies, and discursive appeals to economic patriotism aim precisely to divert attention away from strictly economic considerations. Given the strength of the 'economic patriotism' discourse at the time, and given the fact that there were also actors with material and strategic interests to prevent the merger, the question thus remains why economic patriotism failed to trump efficiency considerations in the case at hand. By identifying discursive hurdles, we contribute to explaining why opponents of the merger failed to frame their interests in ways that could persuade a broader political audience.

5. CONCLUSION

In sum, our contribution maps the public discourse surrounding the NYSE/Euronext merger to help explain why opponents of the transatlantic merger failed in their appeals to 'economic patriotism'. Discursive strategies designed to justify discrimination against territorially defined outsiders ran into several hurdles, including weak patriotic sentiments for the company concerned; a lack of patriotic alternatives to the proposed merger; and the questionable patriotic credentials of those demanding intervention.

Whether lower discursive hurdles would have allowed the build-up of sufficient political pressure to provoke stronger government intervention is impossible to ascertain. The French state is more than a mere arena for pluralist struggles among competing interests; rather, the decision not to prevent the NYSE/Euronext merger was consistent with a long-standing policy agenda of financial liberalization, and there is no counterfactual evidence. Whether French policy-makers opted to reduce their involvement in the stock exchange business because they genuinely believed in the regulatory efficiency of market forces once installed – a view widespread among EU technocrats, especially within the Internal Market Directorate – or because they failed to fully anticipate the consequences, is equally hard to establish. While most of them might have been fooled by the time-lag between the gradual sale of shares and the evident loss of French control over the exchange, some others (including the Finance Minister Thierry Breton, previously the CEO of Thomson and France Telecom, as well as the corporate lawyer Christine Lagarde, who was Secretary of Foreign Trade at the time of the merger) acted out of conviction. Alain Madelin, a neo-liberal former French Finance Minister, for example, found it 'rather obvious that a stock market enterprise be quoted on the stock market'.[32]

Nevertheless, given the political context, it is plausible that the lack of broad electoral mobilization afforded policy-makers greater freedom to pursue their preferred agenda than they would otherwise have had. Even in statist France, elected politicians are never completely autonomous, and the timing of the merger – in the aftermath of the failed 2005 referendum on the EU constitution and in the run-up to the 2007 presidential elections – provided strong incentives for bowing to electoral demands. The discursive hurdles identified above help explain why opponents of the merger failed to rally the public behind their calls for intervention.

Our contribution advances recent research on economic patriotism by identifying variables that help explain when governments choose to discriminate in favour of territorially defined insiders. To complement previous work on government action, we focus on the demand side – including the discursive dimension – of territorially based political intervention. By examining calls for political intervention and the rhetoric employed, we show that 'noisy politics' can be as difficult to engineer as the 'quiet politics' described by Culpepper (2011). To raise the salience of a specific policy issue to front-page news level, it does not suffice to simply tap into a general current of patriotic sentiments. Even in political environments as receptive to economic patriotism as France was in the year of the rumoured foreign takeover threat to Danone, the instrumentalization of populist sentiments faces limits.

By exploring these limits, our case study also draws attention to hitherto unexplored effects of territorial ambiguities on the viability of economic patriotism. Though contested, the assignment of a territoriality to internationally operating firms is a *prerequisite* for any political intervention. Demutualized stock exchanges have an ambiguous status as listed for-profit companies, on the one hand, and as trading platforms, on the other. As such, they can be portrayed either as national champions that are to be promoted wherever they choose to play, or as an essential part of the playing field that must be kept at home (or, by those opposing both kinds of political intervention, as ordinary private businesses that are best left alone). Where they are multinational enterprises, further ambiguities arise as to whether the local, the national or the European level is the appropriate territorial reference for appeals to economic patriotism. We show that, in the case of Euronext, such territorial ambiguities represented a discursive hurdle for the proponents of intervention.

The consolidation of the stock exchange industry in other parts of the world suggests that 'economic patriotism' is not a French specialty. For instance, in Australia, a country which is not commonly known for government intervention in corporate affairs, Singapore Exchange's takeover of the main Australian stock exchange in the autumn of 2010 sparked a political outcry and was eventually blocked by the Foreign Investment Review Board on 'national interest' grounds. Similarly, at the time of writing, in early 2011, the acquisition by the London Stock Exchange of TMX, which operates the Toronto and Montréal exchanges, remains subject to Canadian political approval. Regarding the battle over NYSE-Euronext between Nasdaq, *IntercontinentalExchange* (ICE) and Deutsche Börse, it remains to be seen whether the regional government of Land Hessen will permit the relocation of trading activities or whether it will exercise its considerable legal powers to ensure the preservation of local employment and of Frankfurt as a financial centre.

Further case studies of the political discourse surrounding other cross-border mergers in France and elsewhere would allow for a comparative assessment of the relationship between rhetoric, mobilization and political action across sectors and countries. Across sectors, the takeover of the partly French-owned steel giant Arcelor by its Indian-owned rival Mittal in 2006 would make for an especially interesting comparison, because it shares not just the timing but also the multinational structure of the target company with the NYSE/Euronext merger. Across countries, comparison with the failed 2006/2007 bid by Nasdaq for the London Stock Exchange would help determine whether financial sector companies, and stock exchanges in particular, inspire stronger 'patriotic sentiments' in Anglo-Saxon economies, including Australia, than they do in France. Comparison with Deutsche Börse, which still enjoys strong legal protections against the relocation of business units, would contribute to a better understanding of the interplay between the regional, national and European levels of public actions taken to amend the industrial outcomes of market competition.

Despite a likely increase in political tensions, especially after the recent financial crisis, the phantom of 'economic patriotism' that has long haunted the French financial centre – including the Palais Brongniart – seems unlikely to reappear any time soon. While the famously strong ties between political and economic élites that underpinned post-war French *dirigisme* persist, the significance of state intervention has profoundly changed since the 1980s. Our case study shows that, by the mid-2000s, élite networks notwithstanding, the French government's commitment to financial deregulation had become strong enough to withstand calls for discrimination in favour of any territorially defined insider. Whether this commitment will survive the recent financial crisis and the consolidation manoeuvres which are reshaping the stock exchange industry in Europe, North America and South-East Asia is a question that only time can answer.

Biographical notes: Helen Callaghan is a Research Fellow at the Max Planck Institute for the Study of Societies in Cologne. Paul Lagneau-Ymonet is an Assistant Professor at University Paris-Dauphine (IRISSO), Paris.

ACKNOWLEDGEMENTS

This article is part of research project subsidized by joint-grant from Egide and the Deutscher Akademischer Austauschdienst (Hubert Curien Partnership, PROCOPE-DAAD, 21857 NF).

NOTES

1 NYSE-Euronext press release, July 15, 2010
2 Décret n° 2005-1739, December 30, 2005. After strong opposition from the European Commission, the version of the decree that was finally implemented applies only to defence-related industries and to gambling.
3 *Challenges*, 20 December 2006.
4 *Financial News*, 4 July 2006.
5 *The Independent*, 8 June 2006.
6 *Agence France-Press* (AFP), 19 June 2006.
7 AFP, 20 December 2006.
8 Question posed to Jean-Pierre Jouyet during a talk at Institut Droît Dauphine (IDD) in Paris, 21 October 2009.
9 *La Chaîne Info* (LCI), 9 June 2006.
10 Entreprise et Marché, 5 July 2006.
11 *Business Week*, 11 June 2001.
12 In January 2007, Jacques Hamon, Bertrand Jacquillat and Christian Saint-Etienne released a report on *Global Stock Exchange Consolidation* to the prime minister,

which portrayed stock exchange consolidation as inevitable and supported the tie-up between Euronext and NYSE.
13 Reuters, 9 November 2006.
14 Bloomberg News, 11 October 2006.
15 *The Wall Street Journal Europe*, 6 October 2006.
16 Reuters, 9 November 2006.
17 *Les Echos*, 18 December 2006.
18 AFP, 20 December 2006.
19 Boursorama, 7 July 2006.
20 Valeurs actuelles, 9 June 2006.
21 *Figaro*, 6 October 2006.
22 AFP, 19 December 2006. This line of argument was also promoted by Image 7, the influential French lobbying consultancy hired by Deutsche Börse. See N. Raulot (2007).
23 *Le Point*, 17 January 2007.
24 Bloomberg, 6 July 2006.
25 *L'Echo*, 27 June 2006.
26 *Futures Magazine*, 1 September 2006.
27 French intermediaries obtained seven Euronext shares, valued at 24 euros each, for every share of the previous operator of the Paris Stock Exchange. The deal was highly attractive because its shares were poorly valued, at historical cost.
28 *La Tribune*, 13 November 2006.
29 Bloomberg TV: Forum, 4 July 2006.
30 Boursorama, 7 July 2006.
31 *Le Figaro*, 21 November 2006.
32 Business FM, Good Morning News, 21 November 2006.

REFERENCES

Cassis, Y. (2006) *Capitals of Capital: A History of International Financial Centres, 1780–2005*, Cambridge: Cambridge University Press.

Clift, B. and Woll, C. (2012) 'Economic patriotism: re-inventing control over open markets', *Journal of European Public Policy* 19(3), http://dx.doi.org/10.1080/13501763.2011.638117

Culpepper, P. (2011) *Quiet Politics and Business Power*, Oxford: Oxford University Press.

Denord, F. and Schwartz, A. (2010) 'L'économie (très) politique du traité de Rome', *Politix* 23: 35–56.

Djelic, M.-L. and Lagneau-Ymonet, P. (2009). 'From playground of the French bourgeoisie to global operator: reinventing the Paris stock exchange'. Paper presented at the *MPIfG workshop on Institutional Chang*, Cologne, 21–22 June.

Djelic, M.-L. and Quack, S. (2007) 'Overcoming path dependency: path generation in open systems', *Theory and Society* 36(2): 161–86.

Feiertag, O. (2005) 'Greffe économétrique et genèse de l'école de la Banque de France (1969-1985)', in O. Feiertag (ed.), *Mesurer la monnaie, Banques centrales et construction de l'autorité monétaire (XIXe-XXe siècles)*, Paris: Albin Michel, pp. 213–45.

Ferguson, N. (2001) *The Cash Nexus: Money and Power in the Modern World, 1700–2000*, New York: Basic Books.

Hautcoeur, P.-C., Lagneau-Ymonet, P. and Riva, A. (2010) 'L'information boursière comme bien public. Enjeux et perspectives de la révision de la directive européenne Marchés d'instruments financiers', *Revue d'économie financière* 98/99(3): 297–315.

Helleiner, E. (1994) *States and the Reemergence of Global Finance: From Bretton Woods to the 1990s*, Ithaca, NY: Cornell University Press.

Jabko, N. (2006) *Playing the Market: A Political Strategy for Uniting Europe, 1985–2005*, Ithaca, NY: Cornell University Press.
Jabko, N. and Massoc, E. (2011) La France face à la crise: les limites d'une rupture, unpublished manuscript.
Lee, R. (2010) The governance of financial market infrastructure, Oxford Finance Group, January.
Lefebvre, R. and Sawicki, F. (2005) 'Le peuple vu par les socialistes', in F. Matonti (ed.), *La démobilisation électorale*, Paris: La Dispute, pp. 69–96.
Lordon, F. (1997) *Les quadratures de la politique économique*, Paris: Albin Michel.
Montagne, S. (2006) *Les fonds de pension entre protection sociale et spéculation financière*, Paris: Odile Jacob.
Mügge, D. (2006) 'Reordering the marketplace: competition politics in European finance', *Journal of Common Market Studies* 44: 991–1022.
O'Brien, R. (1992) *Global Financial Integration: The End of Geography*, New York: Council on Foreign Relations Press.
Posner, E. (2009) *The Origins of Europe's New Stock Markets*, Cambridge, MA: Harvard University Press.
Raulot, N. (2007) *On a vendu la bourse! Comment Euronext est devenue américaine*, Paris: Economica.
Sassen, S. (2005) 'The embeddedness of electronic markets. The case of global capital markets', in K. Knorr-Cetina and A. Preda (eds), *The Sociology of Financial Markets*, Oxford: Oxford University Press, pp. 17–37.
Schmidt, V. (2010) 'Taking ideas and discourse seriously: explaining change through discursive institutionalism as the fourth "new institutionalism"', *European Political Science Review* 2(1): 1–25.
Schnyder, G. (2010). 'Varieties of insider corporate governance: centre-right preferences and the determinants of reform in the Netherlands, Sweden and Switzerland'. Paper presented at the *22nd Annual Meeting of the SAS*, Philadelphia, 24–26 June.
Shonfield, A. (1965) *Modern Capitalism. The Changing Balance of Public and Private Power*, Oxford: Oxford University Press.
Tadjeddine, Y. and Capelle-Blancard, G. (2009) 'The location of financial activities: the impact of new technlogies and the financial crisis', *EconomiX Working Paper 2009-26.*
Weber, M. (2000 [1894]) 'Stock and commodity exchanges', [Die Börse (1894)], *Theory and Society* 29: 305–71.
Wójcik, D. (2009) 'Geography of stock markets', *Geography Compass* 3(4): 1499–514.
Zysman, J. (1983) *Governments, Markets, and Growth*, Ithaca, NY: Cornell University Press.

APPENDIX. LIST OF INTERVIEWEES

Interview partners agreed that notes could be taken and that their names be mentioned, but declined to be recorded. These one- to two-hour interviews took place either at their home or at their offices.

Jean-Louis Beffa (CEO of Saint-Gobain), March 2009.

Pervenche Berès (President of the Economic and Monetary Affairs Committee of the European Parliament), March 2010.

Arnaud de Bresson (General Delegate, Paris Europlace), May 2010.

Bertrand Collomb (CEO of Lafarge), June 2010.

Jacques Hamon (Professor, University Paris-Dauphine), May 2010.

Pierre de Lauzun (Deputy General Director, Fédération des Banques Françaises), May 2010.

Helmut Mader (Managing Director of Mader Capital Resources GmbH), November 2009.

Philippe Marini, (Rapporteur of the French Senate Finance Commission), September 2010.

Gérard Pfauwadel (President of Unigestion), February 2009.

Michel Prada (President of the Autorité des Marchés Financiers), October 2009.

Edouard deLencquesaing (Special Advisor, Paris Europlace), February 2009.

Jean-François Theodore (CEO of Euronext), March 2010 and September 2010.

George Ugeux (CEO of Galileo Partners), April 2010.

Cities as national champions?

Colin Crouch and Patrick Le Galès

ABSTRACT As governments, committed to neo-liberalism but still committed to pursuing national economic success, seek for policy approaches that evade international competition law, they may turn to favouring national champion cities, usually but not always capital cities. This usually also favours particular industries and firms, but only indirectly. This is not the same as policies for favouring backward or declining regions, as the champions selected are already strong and well performing. The aim of policy is to make them even stronger, with resulting tension with pre-existing redistributive territorial policies. Examples are taken from a number of European cases, but with special emphasis on London and Paris.

INTRODUCTION

Once upon a time, European states provided large material support to the making of national industrial firms, the national champions, pillars of economic modernization and economic development strategies. These were firms that dominated their domestic markets (energy, automobile, steel) and often were the bulk of the export capacity. National champions might have been private or public (Shonfield 1965), but they benefited from the financial support of the state. As this collection demonstrates, those days are largely gone, although not entirely. Even if some national champions still prevail, in energy for instance, many of them have had to deal with globalization and European processes; some have even disappeared. International and, in particular, European competition rules make it increasingly difficult for governments directly to support national champion companies or even sectors.

However, economic competition between countries has not decreased; neither has the need for governments to be re-elected by national electorates. Research on the restructuring of the state suggests that market-making and supply-side policies have become expansion areas for state activities (Levy 2006). From a more critical standpoint, Jessop (2002) suggests the current state may be characterized as a Schumpeterian workfare state mostly concerned with economic competition, the development of supply-side policies and the forced realignment of social policies. In this contribution we consider one aspect of this process: the shift from national champion firms to national champion cities. Among the realignments of social policy that this involves is frequently a shift away from regional development policy aimed at assisting backward areas to one aimed at improving further the performance of the most successful.

As made clear by Clift and Woll (2012), economic patriotism is very much at play in many countries but 'unlike economic nationalism, economic patriotism is agnostic about the precise nature of the unit claimed as *patrie*'. In our case, this does not mean that we are looking at a local economic patriotism in the sense of people defending 'their' city against others – except to the extent that national politicians, whatever districts they represent in parliament, come to identify with the political capital. Governments and economic élites, however, may well decide that the national interest requires the subordination of many local interests to that of the key city or cities that will be the national leader in global competition. Where this includes campaigns to make the city the location for iconic and lucrative international events, this may well include an appeal to patriotism of a literal kind.

A recent article in the *Financial Times* clearly made the point and worried about classic *dirigisme* issuing from the French or in our terms, the effectiveness of economic patriotism. Mentioning the threat to the City of London after the financial crisis the journalist wrote:

> the city of London cannot be complacent. Most British politicians and officials are bad at engaging with European institutions, and somewhat embarrassed about fighting for the nation, let alone the City. But the French financial establishment by contrast, is highly disciplined (if not *dirigiste*) and has no qualms about protecting the national interests. It also understands the importance of fighting in the financial weeds, be that the halls of Brussels or the darker reaches of derivatives clearing houses. So stand by for plenty more subtle tussles about infrastructure. (Tett 2010)

As the production of wealth has become more urban (Scott 2002, 2008; Storper 1997), states have shifted resources to invest massively in their capital cities and in urban infrastructures, from information technology to research, financial platforms to transport. Nothing can stop them developing national champion cities or regions, as competition policy is directed solely against favouring firms and industries, though in practice favoured locations are often associated with specific industries, even specific companies, and these can benefit from advantages being given by public policy to the geographical space. Such strategies constitute particularly literal examples of economic patriotism. Patriotism is associated with the defence and promotion of nations, lands, territories; in the strategies being discussed here, economic patriotism takes the form of advancing the interests of specific parts of the national territory. Support to leading, usually capital, cities may therefore be an important feature of economic patriotism. We must make it clear at the outset that we are not talking here about policies for aiding backward or declining regions, but the direction of resources towards leading, already successful, cities and regions as national champions.

We shall here first explain the changes in economic innovation in advanced economies that have produced this new emphasis on the economic politics of location. Second, we consider how these processes produce policies for champion cities. Examples are given, with particular reference to the key examples of London and Paris.

KEY CITIES AS MAJOR CENTRES OF NATIONAL COMPETITIVENESS

Large urban economies are the main motors of contemporary economic growth. The argument is well known, not always easy to measure, is more a question of degree than nature, and the explanation for this dynamic is not completely clear. One difficulty is to explain the process through which one region has more successfully specialized in the knowledge economy, with its high wages, skills and incomes, than the other. As Storper (2010) argues, economic development is a process with long latency effects, combining economic specialization and innovation, human capital formation, policies and institutions. We argue that the competitiveness of many countries, in particular in Europe, is heavily dependent on the competitiveness of certain city regions, often the national capital.

In many parts of the world cities have become again the key engine of economic development as they were during most of the Middle Ages (Hohenberg and Lees 1985). Two main factors have been proposed: the pressure of globalization processes; and the need for agglomeration raised by new forms of economic development. Many observers have therefore taken globalization trends and increasing networks and exchanges to be the main factors behind the city revival. Processes of globalization, including transnational migration, architectural development, financial transactions, transport flux, or dissemination of technological innovations contribute to the rise of mega cities in different parts of the globe. The phenomenon is also explained by the demands of the 'new economy'. Storper and Manville (2006) suggest that its demands for proximity are stimulated by information. Therefore, people have to work in close vicinity in big cities with diverse economic sectors to sustain the production of knowledge and the circulation of talents among sectors. Cities are giant matrices for recombining resources in order to generate innovations (Veltz 1996).

According to Scott (2008) the rise of global city regions, both in the rich part of the world and within developing countries, is first and foremost economically driven by two forces: first, concentration of economic activities reduces transaction costs and helps ensure flexibility and overall efficiency; second, city regions allow the concentration of learning processes, innovation, creativity and dissemination within all sorts of networks. These city regions result from the amalgamation of existing localities, forming an inter-territorial organization for collective actions that are more or less functionally dependent. Some can be organized around a major urban centre as in the classic model of the metropolis; some may be the network of urban centres, e.g., Milan or the 'Randstad' delta metropolis in the Netherlands. Some may cross national boundaries such as the

'Örestad' region linking Denmark and south-west Sweden. The basic argument behind this version of the mega-city is from economic geography:

> These regions are the centres of dense networked of transnational firms, they 'thrive on the productivity – on innovation- enhancing effects of dense and multifaceted urban milieux that are simultaneously embedded in worldwide distribution networks' (Scott 2002: 4).

Following John Friedmann's (1986) early intuition and the acclaimed book of Saskia Sassen (2001), many researchers have tried to identify global cities as a particular urban form. Only a small number of locations around the world seem to be able to support the most advanced, high added-value activities, the kinds of activity in which governments around the world are concerned to ensure that their economies can succeed. Firms in these cities are often networked with each other across the globe (Sassen 2001). Paradoxically, the more global and less material an economic activity, the more it is concentrated in space. Sassen (2006, 2007) has pointed out that it is services activities – increasingly constituting the highest end of the value chain – that are typically concentrated into a far smaller set of spaces than the extraction, manufacturing and distribution stages. She draws particular attention to the highly concentrated nature of commodities trading in just a few centres (New York, London, Chicago, Tokyo). In fact the concentration is even more extreme, often consisting of a few streets of high-rise buildings within these cities, as captured by such precise identifications as 'Wall Street' and 'The City of London'. Meanwhile, as Sassen points out, production of the commodities themselves is scattered around the world, often in highly unfavoured locations. She also suggests that 24 cities dominate global network connectivity, airline traffic and immigration around the world. The activities that are concentrated are in particular those that require highly educated, well-remunerated staff, leading to a concentration of wealth and cultural activities. It is as though these top-end parts of whole complexes of related activities have been extracted from the generality of activities and located in this small number of highly favoured places. Governments then become engaged in a form of competition to secure the choicer parts of the very mixed bag of investments that transnational corporations spread differentially across the world. However, Sassen also shows that the advantages do not stop there: the new growth poles of the knowledge economy help stimulate exceptional growth in distributive services, restaurants and sometimes even certain forms of local manufacturing and agriculture.

Capital cities have been particularly favoured by these processes, as these also offer proximity to political and administrative decision-makers and the headquarters (or at least national bases) of major corporations, bringing together large pools of talented labour. Even in decentralized countries like Germany and Italy, capital cities have begun to attract disproportionate shares of economic growth and highly educated people (Rodríguez-Pose *et al.* 2005). Where financial capitals are separate from political ones (as in the case of Milan in relation to Rome, or New York in relation to Washington), the former may rival the latter, but few other types of city are able to do so. Of the 78 metropolitan regions identified by the Organization for Economic Co-operation and Development (OECD) in its 34 member states, 23 were capitals and a further four financial capitals (OECD 2006: 38–41).

However, there is little evidence to suggest that, in the European context, global or world cities are a particular category of cities beyond the concentration of networks, headquarters and more diverse interests. In economic terms, therefore, the rise of the so-called global cities is rather to be related to the more general renewal and acceleration of metropolization trends which are also valid for medium-size cities in the United States (US) and Europe alike. There is indeed more to economic development than just the leading services. Following Veltz (1996, 2008) we would argue that dynamics of metropolization could be used to account for both the growth of a good number of European cities, notably regional capitals, and the effects of acceleration and accentuation of these dynamics in the largest of them. Differences are of degree, not of nature, reflecting hierarchies of cities. But differences of degrees make a big difference.

These ideas about the growth of large cities have been based on various measures of urban growth. Within the limits of this contribution we do not address the question of population growth. However, the *State of European Cities Report* by the Urban Audit[1] of the European Union (Eurostat 2007) provides evidence of the more recent socioeconomic urban trends within the Europe of 27 (and of increased diversity from the enlargement). The population of European urban areas is still expanding more quickly than the growth of the overall population. In most countries, the pattern is mixed: some dynamic urban growth in a majority of cities and some cases of decline (or of shrinking cities). The largest cities in the north of Europe in particular (Netherlands, United Kingdom) and in Spain or Greece have expanded more quickly than smaller urban areas.

Turning to economic growth, which is our concern, one must keep in mind the limits of some indicators, using regional gross domestic product (GDP) indicators in particular (Davezies 2008). Also, the production of wealth has become disconnected from the level of income through massive public redistribution processes and the mobility of the population (Davezies 2008). When comparing urban and regional growth rate, one must remember the specific regional macro-economy, which comprises four particular dimensions (Davezies 2008): development based on industry and services; public employment; transfer payments to individuals from the state; and the residential economy (consumption of inhabitants, tourism, secondary homes). There is an increasing disjunction between places where people work, live and contribute to wealth creation and places where they spend time and money. In most countries, inhabitants from capital cities have better jobs, salaries and contribute more than their share to the production of wealth; hence the very high productivity of those regions. By contrast, strong economic growth from other regions may be also related to this type of process but more often is primarily based upon the three other motors of economic growth related to massive transfers (public redistribution, pensions, but also private transfers through mobility) from capital city regions to the rest of the country.

In most European Union (EU) countries the competitiveness of the country is increasingly dependent on the economic performance of the key region, and a growing part of national GDP is produced by a smaller part of the population. Most accounts of the productivity of the larger cities conclude that it is superior by about a third to that of the rest of the country (Davezies 2008). Greater London accounts for about 25 per cent the population but 33 per cent of GDP. Paris Ile de France produces over 30 per cent of the GDP with about 21 per cent of the French population. Figures are similar in smaller centralized countries: Oslo accounts for 22 per cent of the GDP but 11 per cent of the population.

The *State of European Cities Report* by the EU Urban Audit[2] (Eurostat 2007) provides a set of figures (from GDP per capita within cities, to economic growth, employment growth and contribution to the national growth) which clearly demonstrate high levels of economic concentration to the largest cities (London and Paris), and to major cities of north-west Europe, even if a whole set of more peripheral and medium-size cities are also enjoying very consistent economic growth: national and regional capitals of Eastern and Central European countries (Budapest, Prague), Madrid, Barcelona, Athens, Thessaloniki, regional cities in the main countries (Munich, Lyon) and in the periphery (in Ireland). The picture also reveals the remaining transformation, slow growth or difficulties of old industrial areas, port cities, or Eastern European cities that do not benefit from the service growth. Services are centrally important; within the five largest urban areas in Europe (i.e., London, Paris, Berlin, Madrid and Rome), 'service sector employment accounts for between 80 and 90 per cent of all jobs' (Eurostat 2007: 44). Some regional capitals still have an industrial base. Among them it is, however, crucial to make a distinction between rapidly declining industrial cities in Eastern and Central Europe, and dynamic cities with mixed economies including a dynamic industrial part in Western Europe (such as Göteborg, Grenoble, Cork, Tampere, Linz.). But the economic weight of capital cities is massive in comparison.

Similarly, Harding (2007: 54–6) has identified urban development trends within European and some other countries between 1998 and 2003 based on two sets of data from the European Union's NUTS 3 regions: rates of economic growth; and a measure of economic 'weight' (the percentage of national GDP accounted for by a region). This enabled him also to conclude that (with some exceptions) pre-existing national urban hierarchies were reinforced, or at least the largest metropolitan regions grew faster than the rest.

The burden of the evidence, certainly within Europe, seems to be that in the post-industrial economy capital cities, and a small number of other locations, are able to build on past legacies of superior facilities and accessibility to pull away from the rest of their countries. Le Galès (2002) and Veltz (1996) have reached similar conclusions. Veltz in particular has shown how the knowledge economy makes increasing use of concentrations of people, producing a kind of archipelago economy in which the results of growth are retained within existing privileged areas. Other regional capitals or second-tier cities also have strong economic growth but, in particular in more centralized countries, the mix of large scale, growth and competitiveness is central for the economic development of most countries. This has been reflected in policy terms.

THE POLICY SHIFT: FROM ADDRESSING INEQUALITIES TO REINFORCING SUCCESS

Obviously, it cannot be concluded from the above survey that these patterns are the deliberate or even the incidental consequences of public policy. At a certain level it does not matter whether government is concerned to advance its capital or some other favoured city, or it just happens as a result of market forces; the result is the same. It is, however, a matter of interest to discover how much intention lies behind these patterns, particularly because of the frequent assumption that government policy operates to offset inequalities resulting from market forces. Perhaps government sometimes *reinforces* the market, either because it believes that 'trickle-down' is superior to redistribution, or because it believes that it has no choice. If there is a competition to attract footloose resources, the competition can be won only by maximizing one's chances of success. A football manager does not field a weak team for a crucial match in order to give the other side a chance. If this is indeed a consequence of globalized investment activity, it has profound implications for the role of the state in relation to redistribution going far beyond this particular issue.

National governments have shifted policies in order to strengthen their capital cities as national champion of economic growth; evidence that this occurs indicates that this new form of economic patriotism has been adopted. In terms of Clift and Woll's scheme in their Table 2 (Clift and Woll 2012), it is an instance of 'Quadrant 1', a liberal (rather than protectionist) policy favouring insiders, but it goes beyond their characterization of this quadrant as constituting '[s]elective liberalization in strategic sectors'. Rather, public resources of a more social democratic kind are brought to bear on the favoured cities, equipping firms in principal sectors within them then to take part in liberalized economic competition.

A more radical version of the argument suggests that the contemporary capitalist state is organizing the demise of regional equality strategies and urban competition in order to strengthen national competitiveness. Brenner (2004: 16) believes this to be the case, claiming that the aim of contemporary urban policy is not the even development of a country's regions, but the intensification of inequalities 'through the deployment of locational policies designed to strengthen the place-specific socio-economic assets of strategic, globally linked regions'. As Van den Berg *et al.* (2004: 1) express the point:

> Urban competition seems to have become the leading principle to determine the future urban system in Europe. ... Cities need to anticipate and respond

> efficiently and effectively to opportunities and threats that influence their competitiveness structurally. City governments develop policies to try to meet these challenges, but at the same time higher layers of government pursue policies that influence the position of the cities. National governments – and regional governments in federal states – draw up financial and policy frameworks that establish the social, economic and political conditions for cities to design their own policies.

We document this trend while remaining aware that contradictions remain in national policies. Shifting resources to favour national champion cities always generates massive opposition from political interests representing the rest, i.e., the majority of the population and regions. We argue that this contradiction is becoming strongly politicized in many countries, leading to contradictory policies.

There is nothing new about policies favouring key cities, and especially capitals. In many parts of the world, including much of Europe, today's leading cities do not lead because they won out in a pure market competition. They are the products of centuries of political decision-making, concentrating major cultural facilities, transport networks, great architectural endeavours and major national institutions within them. It is notable that the capital cities of small states each manage to possess these attributes in a way rarely demonstrated by neighbouring cities within the same state. Would Brussels and Amsterdam both have world-class art galleries if Belgium had remained part of the Netherlands? Where we find exceptions, there is usually a legacy of earlier political separation (as in the cases of Barcelona and Edinburgh). Once established, characteristics that render a city superior to its neighbours within a national territory establish a path dependence. A city that has inherited from the 19th century an excellent network of rail connections is also likely to be chosen to be the centre of road networks and major airports, as it is more promising to enter it into the global contest as a city that has everything in the way of transport links than to offer one city with the country's best rail links and another with the biggest airport.

During the post-war years, most national governments had developed forms of carrot-and-stick regional policies. Economic policies directed at specific territories were associated primarily with the development of backward areas, like the Italian *Mezzogiorno*, or, in industrialized countries, with the regeneration of declining old industrial areas trying to find new futures in the post-industrial economy. In Britain or France firms which located outside Paris or London benefited from subsidies, and a decentralization of economic activities remained significant until the 1970s. Large numbers of public-service jobs were moved. At the same time, particularly in France, governments developed a financial instrument to penalize the development of new investment in the Paris region. Nordic welfare states guaranteed similar level of services and investments in all regions, thus limiting the development of the capital city.

A major factor inducing change in this model was the rise of small numbers of transnational corporations having wide choices of locations across the world when they wish to establish new facilities. Once they have established themselves in an area, they are likely to build strong corporate-specific infrastructures and therefore remain there for years. Persuading some of these firms to locate an up-market facility in the national territory therefore became an important goal of public economic policy. Well-equipped, dynamic, attractive cities are valuable supports to governments when they lobby firms to choose their country as a location.

This is a very different form of locational competition from that dominant in developing countries of providing low-cost, low-tax, low-standard environments for other aspects of the same firms' activities, the 'race to the bottom' competition that has acquired prominence in the debate over globalization. These differences in the geographical location of different activities are of course two sides of the same coin. For some national governments in middle-ranking countries there may even be a choice concerning in which of the two competitions they wish to play; some large countries with extreme internal inequalities may offer different cities in different competitions. In other cases historical legacy more or less determines the game that a city will play. In this manner new patterns of global inequality are being produced, or old ones reinforced through the path-dependent nature of many of the processes involved. Rarely will governments leave the outcomes of these competitions to chance, when they have the chance to influence outcomes through actions that break no competition rules. As Crouch (2008: 3) has expressed it:

> While it might have developed initially from market forces, the process of establishing some favoured cities as the preferred locations for advanced economic activities has quickly become a major field for public policy. In many respects, urban policy has become for the advanced services-oriented economies of the early 21st century what industrial policy was for much of the 20th.

Important examples can be drawn from the cases of Oslo and Helsinki. Norway has long had a strategy primarily concerned with ensuring opportunities for development in more remote parts of the country's thinly populated, long, narrow landmass, a clear example of the old concept of development policy as compensatory. There was also a decentralization of policies away from central government, through the establishment of national implementation agencies and the regional distribution of significant policy funding (OECD 2008: 96–7). A 2005 White Paper on regional policy built on these policy developments and confirmed the new way of thinking about regional policy, by explicit reference to competitiveness concerns. It stressed innovation and the promotion of regional development in *all* regions through the regional differentiation of policy (OECD 2008: 98). Meanwhile, however, something else had been happening. Economic dynamism was becoming increasingly concentrated on just one region, that around the capital, Oslo. About 22 per cent of national GDP (excluding offshore oil and gas activities) in 2002 was produced in the Oslo region, although it represented only 11 per cent of the national population (OECD 2008: 58). Governments decided that Oslo's development could no longer be left to chance, given that competitor cities in other countries were receiving favourable policy treatment. The capital region is therefore now being favoured by public policy (OECD 2008: 77–8). In recent years policy has shifted to a proactive concern with ensuring a strong business environment to aid competitiveness in all regions of the country. As a consequence there was necessarily some shift of attention away from peripheral and rural areas, though the funding emphasis continues to be strongly in favour of the latter. Tensions created between Oslo and other regions, some of which are now experiencing a drain of skilled labour and other resources towards the capital, are becoming an important issue. Meanwhile, there is anxiety that these other local economies will be damaged, while not enough is being done to secure the international competitiveness of Oslo (OECD 2008: 144).

The story is even more telling in the case of Helsinki because of the importance of Nokia for the whole economy (Haila and Le Galès 2005). The Finnish government has accepted a need to finance major infrastructure projects in Helsinki in order to compete with other Baltic cities on the one hand, and with Scandinavian cities on the other, in particular for airports. Massive policies to invest in research clusters, in higher education and infrastructure in Helsinki have been closely connected to the need and requirements of Nokia. In this case, the idea of a national champion firm and a champion city region overlap heavily. What was good for one was good for the other, despite the protest of powerful agrarian interests. Regional innovative clusters were also developed elsewhere in the country, in particular in the dynamic remote region of Oulu – another major Nokia site – but that did not prevent the shift of resources to accompany and foster the growth of the capital.

An ostensible difference between policies for champion cities as opposed to champion firms is that individual corporations do not acquire privileged positions in relation to government. However, this is not necessarily the case. An important recent trend everywhere in the politics of business is the decline of representation by associations and the rise of lobbying by individual firms. This includes a role in structuring the new global urban pattern. Sassen (2007) points out how new, private IT infrastructures link member firms and parts of firms across the world. These are not services that are shared with other individuals and organizations within the cities, but just with other global firms. This cuts these firms off from the remainder of the city in which they are located, which are left outside the global networks of the firms. It is not so much cities as their corporate élites that form the new global urban networks.

Governments necessarily deal closely with these firms when devising the new urban strategies. The firms then become government insiders, possibly erecting entry barriers against those who have not managed to gain such privileges. Competition may become distorted and displaced from the quality of products to the quality of political influence (OECD 2006). Second, only large firms can usually participate in this kind of relationship with government, leading to public policy overlooking the role of small and medium-sized enterprises, as several cases of local development policy in the United Kingdom (UK) demonstrate (Burroni *et al.* 2005). Some of the problems raised by the old national champion enterprise strategies may therefore return with the new approach. There is, however, the major exception that the firms are only coincidentally national, in the sense of belonging to the nation states forging policies with them. In former national champions approaches, governments selected favoured national firms and sought to advance them in global competition. In the new policy, governments seek to have parts of their national territories selected by transnational firms, so that these territories might advance in global competition.

However, strong resistance is also deployed against these trends, either because other regions and cities organize to limit champion city privileges, or because many of the inhabitants of champion cities themselves are less interested in economic growth than in quality of life. Ongoing debates on the extension of the airports bear witness to those tensions. Also, although both London and Paris, for example, are clearly escalator regions for the rest of the country, it is not clear that their productivity remains as high as it used to be. Some economists argue that there is far too much transfer and redistribution from the capital city to the rest of the country, creating a threat to the competitiveness of the whole economy.

LONDON AND PARIS

Securing locations within the national territory for activities of the kind discussed above, and then ensuring that these locations are the most competitive of their kind in the world, become a means of politically favouring selected sectors in ways that break no competition rules. The relevant policies include such things as steering major infrastructure projects – such as urban transport systems, scientific complexes, advanced education facilities – towards the cities concerned; paying particular attention to their physical environments; using political influence to attract major global iconic events to them. It is not possible to draw up an analytical scheme of policy approaches that might be deployed; this is territory for imaginative political entrepreneurialism, with governments watching out for new opportunities to improve the competitiveness of their champion locations without offending either international trade law or the population of unflavoured regions. Some further illustrations of the range of policies that can be deployed can be given through a brief discussion of Europe's two largest cities, London and Paris.

The UK has been at the forefront of many of these developments in city competitiveness, with London always as its aim. The neo-liberal project of the Conservatives during the 1980s led to a dramatic restructuring of urban and regional policy. The government argued that the development of London, if successful, would benefit the whole country through a trickle-down effect from the increased employment and tax revenues that its success will generate. As Morgan (2012) explains, the development of the City of London, the medieval London that is today synonymous with the financial sector, was a key priority. In relation to this, the government organized the regeneration of the London Docklands to accommodate an extension of the City's financial sector, pumping a large amount of public and private investment into the making of Canary Wharf and the surrounding area. This, alongside deregulation of the financial sector, enabled London to reinforce its status as a leading financial centre, attracting investment from all over the world. By contrast, investment in public infrastructure such as urban transport was at first not seen as a priority, though later the government realized it would have to build a new underground railway line to service the area.

These developments in London helped stimulate a French policy shift. As Harvey (1990) and Brenner (2004) argue, the rise of urban competition has been decisive in stimulating policy shifts, supported by private sector organized interests. The Paris Ile de France region had, until the 1990s, mainly been directly governed by state officials and had long benefited from state investment. But the priority now became clearer: attraction of investment to the region, a new phase of expansion of the business district of La Défense to rival London, major investment in prestigious cultural projects, major investment in IT, research clusters and financial infrastructures.

In both London and Paris, the shift became more marked over the years. Different governments have invested large sums to improve and enlarge dominant airports (Heathrow and Roissy Charles de Gaulle). Large-scale public transport renovation has been initiated on both sides of the Channel for existing underground and surface railways, including the Crossrail link in London and a plan to link Charles de Gaulle Airport, the business district of La Défense and the technological centre of Paris Orsay. The scale of these projects is from 20 to 40 billion euros. By contrast, support to public transport elsewhere in France was cut, and the ambitious Northern Way, supposed to provoke massive investment in the North of England, was more or less abandoned. Culture was also at the forefront of the strategy with new national libraries, new museums, and in London the Millennium Dome. Both national governments worked hard to host the 2012 Olympic Games, a competition finally won by London, much to the disgrace of Paris. In both cases, the Olympic bid was an opportunity to justify massive regeneration projects and to channel large amounts of public money to the capital city at the expense of the rest of the country.

Public policy to develop research and innovation was also clearly spatially biased. Although mechanisms to fund research are different in the two countries, in both cases the capital city region (if Oxford and Cambridge can be considered part of this) massively benefited from the shift of public investment. The most ambitious project in France, clearly set up as *Opération d'Intérêt National*, is the development of the Orsay/Saclay area in the southwest of Paris as a world-leading centre for innovation and research with massive public investment to develop infrastructures and technology transfers benefiting, first and foremost, French leading large firms who happen to have their headquarters and research centres in the Paris region.

This shift in priority has also translated in political terms. A directly elected mayor was only introduced in Paris in 1977, and the first regional council was elected in 1986. The London Mayor was established in 1999. In both countries, ministers have been appointed with particular responsibilities for the capital. In France the Sarkozy government created a junior minister for 'Grand Paris', on the grounds of the need of the Paris region to become a competitive economic centre of the global economy. In governance terms (John *et al.* 2005), large firms have become legitimate actors to play an important role in formulating London and Paris Ile de France strategic plans.

CONCLUSION

There is a clear tension between this 'champion city' approach and the policy aims of many governments to ensure even levels of economic development across their territory. In particular there is tension with strategies of regeneration or assistance to under-developed regions. While the latter is a compensatory approach, seeking to provide assistance for cities and regions previously ill favoured by both market forces and political decision-making, the new policy involves deliberately concentrating resources on those already showing success, even (or perhaps especially) where that success has been the result of earlier political favour.

For example, a government may have to decide where to locate a major new piece of infrastructure, when the country can have only one. Examples would be a major exhibition centre or national sports stadium, or a terminus for an international high-speed rail service. If it chooses a city that already has an exceptional collection of facilities, it may tip the balance favouring that city above all its competitors across the rest of the world. Indeed, without such a favourable decision, the city may clearly lose out to its rivals. On the other hand, locating the infrastructure in a poor region that has difficulty attracting investment may considerable boost its attraction – but not to the point where it becomes a global or world-regional leader; just enough to attract a few new jobs. Of course, choices are not always as stark as this. It may be possible to divide investments between the two areas, though this might produce pots of resources too small to help either achieve its goal, wasting resources. Many other examples of similar policy dilemmas can be found (OECD 2006).

Advancing favoured places within their national territories has become one of the few forms of substantive economic policy left to national governments within European and global competition regimes. It is, however, an important policy arena because of the new importance of geographical place in the global knowledge-based economy. Cities and regions that are able to achieve a strong position in the competition to join the favoured networks of that economy can reap strong rewards. Instead of engaging in races to the bottom in the global economy, based on low wages, low taxes, poor public infrastructure and environment, they participate in the opposite race which is also taking place. Governments, at least of democratic countries, are likely to be extremely concerned to enter that second kind of race.

However, this is a race with many losers. It is likely that only a few cities can enter it, which involves certain strategic choices to favour some locations and not others. It is in the nature of competitive processes that such a situation requires trying to build on existing success rather than advancing new or previously under-privileged places. This has in itself anti-egalitarian implications, but these are intensified by the fact that the strategy often involves zero-sum choices. Both policies for helping backward areas and those for generally ensuring evenness of development are thereby threatened.

Biographical notes: Colin Crouch is Professor Emeritus of Governance and Public Management at the University of Warwick Business School. Patrick Le Galès is a CNRS Research Professor of Politics and Sociology at Sciences Po, Centre d'Etudes Européennes, Paris.

NOTES

1 Data from the European Urban Audit, an ongoing project started in 2003, are available at http://www.urbanaudit.org/

2 *Ibid.*

REFERENCES

Brenner, N. (2004) *New State Spaces, Urban Governance and the Rescaling of Statehood*, Oxford: Oxford University Press.

Burroni, L., Crouch, C. and Keune, M. (2005) 'Governance caleidoscopica, debolezza istituzionale e sviluppo locale', *Stato e Mercato* 3/2005: 423–54.

Clift, B. and Woll, C. (2012) 'Economic patriotism: reinventing control over open markets', *Journal of European Public Policy* 19(3), http://dx.doi.org/10.1080/13501763.2011.638117

Crouch, C. (2008) 'Globalisation and city competitiveness: new trends in urban development policies', unpublished report, Paris: OECD.

Davezies, L. (2008) *La République et ses territoires, la circulation invisible des richesses*, Paris: Le Seuil.

Eurostat (2007) *State of European Cities Report*, Report prepared by ECOTEC Research and Consulting Ltd in cooperation with NordRegio and Eurofutures, based on the Eurostat European Urban Audit, available at http://ec.europa.eu/regional_policy/sources/docgener/studies/pdf/urban/stateofcities_2007.pdf (last accessed December 2011).

Friedmann, G. (1986) 'The World City hypothesis', *Development and Change* 17(1): 69–83.

Harding, A. (2007) *What Policies for Globalizing Cities? Rethinking the Urban Policy Agenda*, Paris: OECD.
Harvey, D. (1990) 'From managerialism to entrepreneurialism: the transformation of urban governance', *Geografiska Annaler* 71B(1): 3–17.
Haila, A. and Le Galès, P. (2005) 'State restructuring versus the cities in Finland: the coming of age of metropolitan governance in Helsinki?', in H. Heinelt and D. Kübler (eds), *Metropolitan Governance: Capacity, Democracy and the Dynamics of Place*, London: Sage, pp. 117–32.
Hohenberg, P. and Lees, L. (1985) *The Making of Urban Europe*, Cambridge, MA: Harvard University Press.
Jessop, B. (2002) 'Liberalism, neo-liberalism and urban governance: a state theoretical perspective', *Antipode* 34(3): 452–72.
John, P., Tickell, A. and Musson, S. (2005) 'Governing the mega-region: governance and networks across London and the south east of England', *New Political Economy* 10(1): 93–108.
Le Galès, P. (2002) *European Cities, Social Conflicts and Governance*, Oxford: Oxford University Press.
Levy, J. (ed.) (2006) *The State after Statism, New State Activities in the Age of Liberalization*, Cambridge, MA: Harvard University Press.
Morgan, G. (2012) 'Supporting the city: economic patriotism in financial markets', *Journal of European Public Policy* 19(3), http://dx.doi.org/10.1080/13501763.2011.638134
OECD (2006) *Competitive Cities in the Global Economy*, Paris: OECD.
OECD (2008) *OECD Territorial Reviews: Norway*, Paris: OECD.
Rodrigues Pose, A., Petrakos, G. and Rovolis, A. (2005) 'Growth, integration, and regional disparities in the European Union', *Environment and Planning A* 37(10): 1837–55.
Sassen, S. (2001) *The Global City*, Princeton, NJ: Princeton University Press.
Sassen, S. (2006) *Cities in the World Economy*, Thousand Oaks, CA: Pine Forge Press.
Sassen, S. (2007) *A Sociology of Globalization*, New York: W.W. Norton.
Scott, A.J. (ed.) (2002) *Global City-Regions: Trends, Theory, Policy*, Oxford: Oxford University Press.
Scott, A.J. (2008) *Social Economy of the Metropolis: Cognitive-Cultural Capitalism and the Global Resurgence of Cities*, Oxford: Oxford University Press.
Shonfield, A. (1965) *Modern Capitalism*, Oxford: Oxford University Press.
Storper, M. (1997) *The Regional World: Territorial Development in a Global Economy*, London and New York: Guilford Press.
Storper, M. (2010) 'Why does a city grow? Specialization, human capital, or institutions?', *Urban Studies* 47(10): 2027–50.
Storper, M. and Manville, M. (2006) 'Behaviour, Preferences and cities: urban theory and urban resurgence', *Urban Studies* 43(8): 1247–74.
Tett, G. (2010) 'London faces battle to stop trading shift to Eurozone', *The Financial Times*, 2 March.
Van Den Berg, L., Van Den Meer, J. and Pol, P.M.J. (2004) *Social Challenges and Organising Capacity in Cities*, Aldershot: Ashgate.
Veltz, P. (1996) *Mondialisation, villes et territoires*, Paris: PUF.
Veltz, P. (2008) *Le nouveau monde industriel*, Paris: Gallimard.

Economic patriotism in European agriculture

Wyn Grant

ABSTRACT In several sectors, national growth strategies have led governments to transfer economic patriotism to the European level to ensure continued control over these sectors. This contribution explores how European agriculture and the CAP constitute a policy regime which seeks to discriminate in favour of particular social groups, firms or sectors understood by policy-makers as 'insiders' because of their territorial status. The case of agriculture, where policy is made at the EU level, illustrates how supranational economic patriotism co-exists and complements national ambitions and explains why European integration is not necessarily synonymous with the liberalization of the sector in multilateral arenas. The contribution explores how CAP reform, the re-emergence of food security discourse and a complex interplay of productionist and consumptionist discourses present opportunities for discriminatory economic patriotic interventionism in favour of European agricultural producers.

INTRODUCTION

The examination of the Common Agricultural Policy (CAP) permits an analysis of supranational economic patriotism. In this particular case, in terms of the typology of forms of economic patriotism developed in the contribution by Clift and Woll (2012), this takes the form of conservative economic patriotism leading to defensive regionalism. It seeks to maintain a protected space for European agriculture challenged by global liberalizing forces.

There is always some 'disjuncture between the rhetoric and the reality of economic patriotism' (Clift and Woll 2012). However, in the case of the CAP it is more than 'cheap talk' but has a profound effect on the selection of policy choices. The contemporary dialogue about agriculture within the European Union (EU) is a complex interplay of productionist and consumption discourses. Consumption discourses are here interpreted widely to cover not just food in terms of its safety and quality, but also the external public goods it provides such as cherished landscapes or the maintenance of biodiversity. Recent food shortages and discussions about food security have led to the revival of productionist discourses, but this remains highly contested terrain. The shift from the production to the consumption regime means that economic patriotism in agriculture is no longer concerned just with what should be produced but to an increasing extent with what should be consumed. Economic patriotism in agriculture today thus focuses on the regulation of consumption (where territorial discrimination can come into play) rather than production and trade limitations.

What kind of climate does the agriculture and food sector provide for policies based on economic patriotism? The persistence of 'agricultural exceptionalism' is one characteristic of the sector (Grant 1995; Halpin 2005). 'Agricultural exceptionalism holds that the farming industry is different from most economic sectors in modern societies.' Although productionist understandings of exceptionalism have been eroded to some extent, they have also been reinvigorated by 'newer versions of agricultural exceptionalism that emphasised the public goods provided by the agricultural sector' (Daugbjerg and Swinbank 2008: 633). Even productionist understandings of exceptionalism may yet be reinvigorated (Daugbjerg and Swinbank 2008: 651).

Exceptionalism is a two-edged sword as far as economic patriotism is concerned. On the one hand, it stems from a perspective that the farming sector contributes to broader national interests and goals, providing a potential link to economic patriotism. A secure and safe food supply and stable and reasonable food prices are seen as highly valued and agricultural exceptionalism argues that unregulated markets will fail to deliver these valued objectives in food supply. Exceptionalism thus provides a justification and a protected policy space for initiatives that may be characterized as economic patriotism. However, it also has its limits because it is not transitive to other policy sectors, rooted as it is in what is perceived to be the particular economic, social and cultural context of agriculture. It does not offer a broader model for or legitimation of economic patriotism.

What is clear is that there are very different interpretations among member states about what sort of Common Agricultural Policy the European Union (EU) should have. At one end of the spectrum, countries like France and Ireland have favoured the perpetuation of subsidies and protection. France has organized the G-21 group of countries within the EU to advocate the need for continued support for agriculture: all member states are involved except four liberally oriented northern member states and Malta and Cyprus. At the other end of the spectrum, countries like Sweden and the United Kingdom (UK) have advocated a more market-oriented, commercial agricultural policy in which subsidies are limited to the provision of public goods, typically various environmental benefits resulting from agricultural activity. What is also evident is that each member state, including the UK, is eager to defend the policy design that maximizes the budgetary benefits it derives from the CAP.

What is evident is that agriculture constitutes 'a policy regime which seeks to discriminate in favour of particular social groups, firms or sectors understood by policy-makers as "insiders" because of their territorial status' (Clift and Woll 2012). Agriculture is nothing if it is not territorial: indeed, in certain contexts the word *terroir* is invested with a special meaning. This is consistent with understandings of local patriotism and therefore with the argument that economic patriotism is agnostic about the precise shape or nature of the unit claimed as *patrie.*

TWO COMPETING DISCOURSES

Two competing discourses have shaped the debate about the CAP for many years: neo-liberal and protectionist. There are, of course, many variants of these discourses, and there has also been a strengthening environmental discourse which wants intervention for different purposes and using new policy instruments. However, for the sake of clarity, two simplified accounts of these discourses will be presented here.

For neo-liberals, the persistence of agricultural 'exceptionalism' is an affront to what is otherwise seen to have been a triumph for the market economy. Agriculture should be treated as a sector like any other, subject to the forces of supply and demand and the information signals transmitted through the price mechanism. Existing policies cannot even be defended on equity grounds as they push up the cost of food for consumers, with food accounting for a larger proportion of the income of the less well off. They also involve a transfer of funds from taxpayers to relatively wealthy farmers (who derive most of the CAP subsidies). The logical conclusion is to 'scrap the CAP'.

In practice, very few policy-makers or analysts adopt such an extreme position. Agriculture is not really a sector like any other because it is difficult to achieve a stable equilibrium between supply and demand because of phenomena such as the cobweb cycle well-documented in agricultural economics. The underlying factors at work here are the length of the production cycle for many products, the costs of product substitution and the variability of the weather which modern agronomy can only offset to a certain extent. Most market-oriented policy-makers would also accept the 'multifunctionality' argument that agriculture is about more than producing food and that public goods it delivers, such as cherished landscapes, merit subsidy. However, those of a neo-liberal disposition would certainly want to explore whether visitors could be 'charged' for the beauty of the countryside. Rather than perpetuating direct intervention in the market, liberals would favour innovative risk-based or insurance-related instruments to stabilize the market.

Those in the protectionist camp would argue that European farmers should not be sacrificed to their competitors elsewhere in the world. Agriculture contributes something to Europe that is unique and irreplaceable and has cultural as well as economic value. Regionally distinctive landscapes have evolved over the centuries as a result of humanity's interaction with the land. They provide distinctive, high-quality products whose geographical origin constitutes part of their value and which in turn contribute to local cuisines. The 'family farm' and the countryside provide a stability and continuity that has real value in an increasingly urbanized and frenetic society.

The reforms of the CAP have attempted to provide reconciliation between the two points of view. Protection and subsidies have largely been maintained (the Organization for Economic Co-operation and Development [OECD] Producer Subsidy Equivalent for the EU has not declined by much), but the form of the subsidies have changed (Grant 2010). They are less productionist in the sense that they do not require the farmer to over produce in order to claim the subsidy. This allows the farmer to respond more readily to market signals and largely eliminates the stored surpluses that attracted such critical attention to the CAP. There has also been a greater emphasis on meeting environmental and other standards, although there has not been as a great a shift from Pillar 1 (which covers market guarantee payments) to Pillar 2 (concerned with rural development and agri-environmental schemes) payments as many reformers hoped for.

THE REVIVAL OF THE FOOD SECURITY DISCOURSE

The food security device is being revived in a way which shifts the balance from consumptionist to productionist discourses. This increases the political opportunity space for economic patriotism arguments which seek to shield producers through defensive regionalism.

Food security was one of the main drivers for the original formulation of the CAP. The drafters of the policy had direct personal memories of the shortage of food in Europe after the Second World War. The Cold War produced new fears about disruption of sea lanes supplying Europe. Hence, 'to assure the availability of supplies' became one of the objectives for the CAP enshrined in the Treaty of Rome. However, over time the problem in Europe became not a shortage of food but a structural surplus. One response was to dispose of this surplus on world markets through export subsidies, a policy that was unpopular both with local farmers in the country concerned and with third countries seeking to supply the market.

In the last two years the food security discourse has been revived as world food prices increased in response to a tightening balance of supply and demand. They then fell back, but have since increased again, reflecting an expected pattern of greater volatility. Most analysts consider the long-term trend will be upwards. On the demand side, the growing prosperity of emerging countries like China has led to a change in diet. In particular, meat consumption is increasing, which means that more animal feed is required for livestock which in turn places pressure on grain prices. On the input side, modern agriculture is fossil-fuel-intensive and these costs, particularly the oil price, are likely to rise in the medium to long term.

A longer-term perspective would attempt to identify structural challenges that affect the price of food and the adequacy of its supply. Barling (2008) identifies seven converging factors. He regards the overarching one as climate change 'which will have potentially far reaching consequences for food production and supply, not least upon the reliability of harvests'. Rising oil prices will affect energy costs along the whole food chain, while water shortages are another key input factor. The use of land with competition from growing urbanization and maintaining soil quality is a fourth factor. The adequate skill base and cost of labour is often overlooked, while demographic pressures and rising affluence and a transition to a more meat and dairy protein and fat based diet creates important pressures on food production (Barling 2008: 17).

Sometimes an inappropriate analogy is drawn between food security and energy security where European governments have been more inclined to develop policies. However, it should be remembered that energy security is characterized by the presence of near-monopoly suppliers, particularly in terms of Russia as a supplier of gas to Europe, although also to an extent the Gulf states in relation to oil. In contrast, 'Currently no single country accounts for more than 13% of UK food and drink imports. In 2006, 68% of food imports in the UK were from other Member States of the EU i.e. from low risk, stable trading partners' (Defra 2008: 15).

WHAT IS MEANT BY FOOD SECURITY?

There is clearly a link between food security and economic patriotism as the policy remedies advanced are usually neo-mercantilist in character. It provides an opportunity for politicians to claim that they are standing up for the interests of their citizens who are being buffeted by seemingly uncontrollable economic forces. However, the concept is more complex than it might appear on the surface. As the UK Cabinet Office (2008a: 32) notes, 'These debates can get confused, not least because "food security" is a term devalued by use in too many contexts. It is often read as "self-sufficiency". A more thorough exploration of what it entails is required.'

Defra (2008: 2) offers a working definition of food security: 'There are many ways to define food security but in this paper we take it to mean consumers having access at all times to sufficient, safe and nutritious food for an active and healthy life at affordable prices.' This is expanded in terms of three dimensions of food security. 'Availability is about how much food there is and how reliable is the supply' and corresponds to traditional understandings of food security. 'Access covers the transportation and food distribution system which gets food to where it is needed.' Concerns about this aspect of food security have been accentuated by the development of 'just in time' delivery systems and have been a particular issue in the UK since the 'petrol protests' of 2000. 'The very efficiency of supply chains under normal circumstances increases their vulnerability under abnormal ones' (Cabinet Office, 2008b: 78). From a UK government perspective, 'There is a legitimate public policy interest in the resilience of the logistic systems and infrastructure that support the UK's food supply chain, and in good contingency planning' (Cabinet Office 2008b: 72). One response has been to allocate a civil servant responsible for food to the Cobra civil emergencies team within the Cabinet Office.

There is a tension between the affordability dimension, which prioritizes the interests of consumer, and the traditional productionist objectives of the CAP. One of the original CAP Treaty objectives was 'to ensure that supplies reach consumers at reasonable prices', but as 'reasonable' was never defined or quantified, it had little real impact on the conduct of the policy which pushed up prices beyond world market levels as it pursued strategies of defensive regionalism.

POLICY RESPONSES TO THE FOOD SECURITY CHALLENGE

What are the policy strategies that may be deployed in response to the food security challenge and how do they relate to understandings of economic patriotism? Four categories of response are distinguished here: market; protectionist; technological; and sustainability. One of these approaches – the market one – is essentially neo-liberal in character and might be seen to represent a repudiation of economic patriotism. However, one can keep in play the possibility of a neo-liberal economic patriotism, utilizing the typology developed by Clift and Woll (2012), although, as will be discussed below, doing this raises some interesting questions about the typology. This would involve taking actions that are consistent with a market-oriented approach in that they seek to provide information that influences consumer decisions in the direction of favouring agricultural products that come from within Europe. Such actions fit most readily into Quadrant 2 of the typology.

An example is animal welfare labelling on which the Commission has issued a communication. This also is a means of providing information to consumers and is therefore consistent with a liberal approach. It clearly relates to Quadrant 2, 'resistance to outsiders' through 'risk regulation or competition rules that prohibit standards common abroad' (Clift and Woll 2012). On one level, the debate about animal welfare labelling seeks to maximize animal welfare, although in practice this presents difficulties of measurement and enforcement. On another level, it responds to a demand from European livestock producers for a 'level playing field' with their foreign competitors. In general, producers outside the EU are less likely to be able to meet such standards than European farmers. Those within the EU are better placed to meet them as part of a general quality 'offer' and this is how it is perceived by consumers. The evidence that is available from Eurobarometer surveys[1] and other sources suggest that consumers perceive such products to be healthier, to taste better and to generally represent better quality. In other words, a well-reared product is seen as a quality product rather than one that advances animal welfare. A healthy animal assures a healthy product and one that tastes better. What is good for animals is good for humans. What this also suggests is that there may be productionist drivers behind a consumptionist discourse, i.e., welfare labelling may be a more effective way of marketing products and hence protecting existing modes of organization of production.

The second category of response is that of protectionism which falls within Quadrants 3 and 4 of the Clift–Woll (2012) typology. In Quadrant 4 they cite classic barriers to trade as their example. It represents a reversion to a traditional form of economic patriotism that uses traditional measures to control market access such as tariffs and quotas.

However, some more ingenious policy responses may be found within Quadrant 3. A clear example that fits into Quadrant 3 arises from the notion of 'Geographical Indications' (GIs) as it does involve regulation to maintain traditional product and process standards. It is a clear example of territorial discrimination coming into play. It also involves 'the favouring of insiders' as the top row of the typology requires. The EU has been pushing GIs in both multilateral and bilateral trade negotiations, e.g., Parma ham should come from Parma and should be prepared in a particular way. This case has a broader importance because it captures so well the multi-levelled element which is central to the intellectual project of economic patriotism. One has national governments campaigning for local interests within an EU strategy to be negotiated at the World Trade Organization (WTO).

It is interesting that geographical indications are given a central role in the recent Commission Communication on Agricultural Product Quality Policy (European Commission 2009). The Commission intends to develop the use of GIs as advertised ingredients on the labels of processed products. It is also intended to include GIs within the scope of the 'anti-counterfeiting trade agreement' and the forthcoming 'European observatory on counterfeiting and piracy'. This form of intervention is actually perfectly consistent with a liberal approach as it involves seeking to overcome information asymmetries that arise from the provision of fraudulent information to consumers. It should be noted, however, that both GIs and animal welfare labelling could shade into hidden protectionism so that liberal and less-liberal elements coexist.

This provokes some reflections about the typology. Quadrants 1 and 4 fall clearly within two familiar ideological stances, the liberal and the protectionist ones respectively. Quadrants 2 and 3 are 'less easily pigeonholed' (Clift and Woll, 2012), but they are the more interesting ones in terms of policy and instrument innovation, which can be considered in terms of information provision, technology and sustainability dimensions. They are contested as they are open to charges of hidden protectionism. If, however, what one is seeking to do is to maximize information to consumers, can this be interpreted as protectionism? Leaving aside complex questions of international trade law, some difficult questions about intent arise. For example, in terms of Clift and Woll's typology, animal welfare labelling could be seen as market integration according to home standards by underpinning standards of animal welfare in the EU and therefore as liberal economic patriotism. However, it could also be seen as defensive economic patriotism that targets lower foreign standards to the benefit of EU producers. The position taken here is that any effort to provide more and better information to consumers and thus reduce information asymmetries is a form of liberal economic patriotism.

The technological response to perceived challenges may be developed in different ways, more or less market oriented, and this conditions its relationship to economic patriotism. In principle, however, a form of economic patriotism that emphasized investment in research and information might be seen as more modern and less open to accusations of being protectionist. This partly depends on who appropriates the benefits of such research, but publicly funded research should in principle be available to all potential users.

The sustainability response is interventionist, but points to a different form of interventionism which is framed in terms of consumption. As noted above, it might, for example, involve providing more accessible and fuller information to consumers. It also involves penalizing external negative externalities such as pollution and rewarding positive externalities such as forms of farming that promote biodiversity. As one is seeking to overcome market failures, it is consistent with a liberal analysis.

Within the EU, member states have different perspectives on the best response to the food security challenge. 'The UK believes that functioning markets are fundamental to ensuring global food security' (Defra 2008: 27) and calls for a programme of continuing liberalization. This stance stems from the view that the government's 'core role in the UK food system is to correct market failures where they arise (the food economy may be distorted by market failures caused by poor information, imperfect competition, the failure to price externalities, and the under-provision of public goods)' (Cabinet Office 2008a: 38). In practice, many tasks relating to activities such as food safety and combating obesity are delegated by government to the retailers. (Marsden *et al.* 2009). The UK Government makes it clear that 'an isolationist attitude to national food security is unlikely to be part of the solution' (Cabinet Office 2008a: viii). In particular, any autarchic goal of self-sufficiency is dismissed as a feasible or desirable approach to policy.

In contrast France has seen the food security debate as an opportunity to defend traditional remedies of subsidy and protection, representing what is termed here the 'protectionist' approach. French farm minister Michel Barnier stated, 'What we are now witnessing in the world is the consequence of too much free-market liberalism. We can't leave feeding people to the mercy of the market. We need a public policy, a means of stabilisation and intervention' (Hall 2008). The European Commission responded by dismissing French calls to curtail food imports as self-defeating and backward-looking. 'Autarky is not the future. We are not aiming at a closed market where we are self-sufficient,' a spokesman for farm commissioner Mariann Fischer Boel stated. Barnier favours domestic production and requiring imports to match EU welfare needs – moves the spokesman said would invite retaliation: 'It is not in our interests to become a fortress. If we erect new barriers, so will our trade partners,' he said. 'We are a major trader in agricultural products. We are the biggest exporter and importer of farm products in the world. What we believe in is trade. We are seeing increasing exports of our high-quality food products' (Bounds 2008).

What this contrast in approaches emphasizes is the fundamental difference between British and French perspectives. Britain has a history of liberalism, France a *dirigiste* one of state intervention and protectionism. From a British perspective, the market is an effective way of transmitting consumer preferences through the price mechanism. National institutional and political configurations are likely to shape the discourses and policy choices of economic patriotism.

Land is in principle a finite resource. Additional land may be brought into production by discontinuing policy measures such as set aside and higher prices may encourage some marginal land to be brought into production, but as a generalization the fixed amount of land available for agricultural production holds. If anything, in the longer run the quantity of available productive land is likely to decline because of factors of urbanization, the loss of land to rising sea levels, etc. One response to a perceived scarcity of food supply is to make the existing area of land more productive through the deployment of technology. This is in no sense an area which is uncontested in policy terms. The intensification of agriculture in Europe has brought with it many negative externalities such as water pollution, an increased carbon footprint and loss of biodiversity. Even relatively benign innovations such as the use of polytunnels to boost soft fruit production in the UK raised a number of issues about social and environmental sustainability, notably an adverse landscape impact and an increased risk of flooding.

Advocates of genetically modified (GM) crops saw the food security crisis as a window of opportunity to advance their use in Europe and to seek the removal of regulatory barriers. However, it could be argued that they do not represent a 'silver bullet' that would solve the problems of food supply and that in particular they are more likely to make a contribution in relation to tropical rather than temperate crops. Political opposition to their planting, even their importation, remains strong in northern Europe. Possibly if they had been developed by publicly funded research organizations rather than by multinational companies that displayed very little political sensitivity, they might have received a more favourable reaction. One conclusion that has come out of the food security debate is a view that public funding of food chain research has been run down too far, limiting the availability of technological solutions that would permit the expansion of production in an environmentally friendly way. This would imply an increase in public funding which would be consistent with a version of economic patriotism that emphasized investment in research and innovation.

Thinking about how the food security debate might be mapped on to a sustainability agenda is still at a relatively early stage, but it is likely to become a more important component of the debate as it progresses. The UK government would claim that it is already taking it into account because of its emphasis on the consequences of policy change. Barling (2008: 18) suggests that a starting point could be 'the "triple bottom line" of economic, environmental and social sustainability'. However, these are very broad brush concepts and tend to conflict with each other.

A series of food scares have been key drivers of demands for the increasing regulation of consumption. Paul (2009: 41) notes:

> [T]he context of post-WWII Western Europe is particular in the sense that it provided the following generations with a certain degree of largely unquestioned trust in food supply and food [safety].
>
> That trust first came to be challenged in the course of the 1980s, when issues such as salmonella, listeria, *E.coli* bacteria and the discovery of anti-freeze in wines provoked public alarm.

The most important of these in terms of its impact on public trust in existing food regulation systems was that of bovine spongiform encephalopathy (BSE) which led to avoidable human deaths from a food-related illness. Some of these issues could be constructed in terms of economic patriotism, notably the long-running dispute on the import of hormone-treated beef from the United States. Moreover, although genetic modification was developed in Europe as well as the United States, the public reaction was influenced by perceptions that the main developers of the technology were American multinationals.

What are the consequences of the revival of the food security discourse and the effective collapse of the Doha Round for the future direction of the CAP? Some analysts have been heard arguing that food security concerns justify the old policy of storing large quantities of surplus produce. However, such a stance has little support among policy-makers and there is little appetite for the revival of old, discredited and expensive policy instruments (Grant 2010).

The CAP Health Check proceeded largely as planned. However, it is freely admitted by the Commission that was largely a tidying up exercise and a more crucial decision-making process has been started by the publication of a Commission communication (European Commission 2010) on the future of the CAP in 2010 to initiate debate on the shape of the CAP after 2013. Despite the collapse of the Doha Round, export subsidies will probably be phased out by 2013 as the EU offered in the context of the negotiations, even though they have been used to shore up the dairy sector. If world commodity prices continue to increase, there is less need for these subsidies anyway, as profitable sales can be achieved on the commodity markets without subsidy. That logic could be extended to subsidies in general, but farmers would point out that their input prices such as fuel and fertilizers have increased.

The greatest impact of the Doha failure will be on market access where high tariff barriers will remain in place, even if some are eased by bilateral deals. Such barriers, which can be as high as three figures in percentage terms, are a clear demonstration of neo-mercantilism. But they are survivals from the past, rather than evidence of a new era on economic patriotism. No one has suggested extending them to manufactured goods, reinforcing the sense that agricultural is 'exceptional': it exists in a world of its own and does not impact on policy discourses in other worlds. This is exemplified by the fact that the policy instruments used in agricultural policy are distinctive to the sector and there is little or no transfer of policy instruments either to or from other policy areas (Grant 2010).

PRODUCTIONISM AND CONSUMERISM

Economic patriotism is in its origins primarily a productionist perspective, but, as has been argued, it is open to a consumerist reading. In its classic form it involves making choices in favour of firms and sectors to boost their competitive performance. Yet the current era is one in which the act of consumption is seen as more central to social life than that of production. This is particularly apparent in the food chain, but one can observe 'broader changes in modern societies towards what social scientists term reflexive consumption, whereby people think of themselves as active, discerning consumers whose choices contribute to their sense of identity.' With the decline in the defining power of old economic and political formations associated with workplace, class and nation there is a 'growing personal focus on consumption and leisure activities and the cultural resources and goods that surround them' (Lowe *et al.* 2008: 228).

Agriculture and food was for a long time the prototypical example of the politics of production and it should be emphasized that many of these features of the policy-making process have not disappeared, even if they have been increasingly eroded and challenged. In some contexts, an attempt has been made to reinvigorate them, but using a market logic rather than one of subsidy and protection. A politics of production is concerned with the organization of the production process and the battle about who should benefit from the surplus value that is generated. In many sectors, it was a battle between employers and employees, but agricultural workers have generally been a weakly organized group, a few exceptions aside.

The politics of production in agriculture was usually characterized by tightly knit policy communities in which farming interests were the policy-makers and consumers and other actors were the policy-takers. They were typically organized around an agriculture department in government which had a close and clientilistic relationship with a farmers' organization or organizations, usually dominated by larger-scale farmers. The complexity and distinctiveness of the policy-making process made it very difficult for outsiders to have an effective impact on the decisions that were taken.

Evidence of the erosion of the traditional politics of production is to be found in the weakening of the traditional domestic politics duopoly of an agriculture department in government closely linked to a national farm organization. Most countries still retain an agriculture department (and the EU DG-Agri), a situation that gives agriculture a privileged position in relation to other sectors of industry. It means that agriculture has its own voice within government and the agriculture department usually also has a key role in the farm related aspects of international trade negotiations. However, there is an emergent trend for traditional agriculture departments to be replaced by ministries with a much broader mandate. Thus, in Britain the Ministry of Agriculture, Fisheries and Food was replaced by a Department of Environment, Food and Rural Affairs (Defra).

The traditional farm organizations persist and, given that farm ministries survive in most countries and that the generous provision of subsidies continues, might seem to be as influential as ever. However, there is some evidence of a process of 'hollowing out' of these organizations. As the number of farmers decline, it is sometimes difficult to maintain the levels of resources necessary to sustain an effective role in the policy-making process. Staff numbers may not appear to decline that much, but often experienced staff members may be replaced by inexperienced recent graduates hired on low salaries. There may be more emphasis on the provision of selective incentives for members, but this directs attention away from the representational role. One survival strategy might be to transform farm organizations into more broadly based bodies looking after rural interests, recruiting the growing numbers of 'hobby farmers' and other countryside dwellers. However, that can set up new tensions within the organization over policy that then hamper its effectiveness.

More moderate farm organizations that based their strategy on a dialogue with government often find themselves increasingly challenged by more militant movements, led by farmers who have particularly suffered from processes of change, often smaller-scale farmers. This has long been a feature of farm politics in France, but the more militant bodies seem to have gained even more ground, bolstered by the use of popular anti-globalization discourses. In Britain, the National Farmers' Union (NFU) offered the classic example of an 'insider' group locked in a close relationship with government. However, the emergence of Defra and the hard financial times experienced by some farmers led to an increase in questioning of this strategy and the emergence of a direct action group based on the French model, Farmers for Action. The NFU decided to move its headquarters of London and signalled that it would to some extent move away from its traditional 'insider' strategy.

The traditional production-oriented policy community has increasingly been challenged by groups emerging from a politics of collective consumption. Their agendas come from outside farming: the environment; health; global social justice. Because they do not share the assumptions that have underpinned agriculture and food policy for so long, they are able to challenge the way in which issues have been framed and to penetrate and disrupt issue networks based on production-based paradigms of policy. Policy models based on economic patriotism are likely to be seen by them as at best irrelevant and at worst as threatening to dealing with the policy challenges presented by food safety, obesity and the environment.

Michelsen (2008) has carried out a careful quantitative assessment of these propositions in relation to the case of Denmark. He notes the suggestion of 'a moderate change of agriculture and food policy through the introduction of collective consumption interests parallel with production interests.' He found that 'an originally positive attitude to agriculture was replaced by positive attitudes to non-farming issues of food on the official political agenda,' and that 'The critical assessment of available Danish network analyses also supported [this] thesis' (Michelsen 2008: 23). Denmark is a country that has a strong national economic interest in the success of its agriculture and food sector, which is an important contributor to exports; indeed food security issues were initially interpreted in terms of impacts on exports. What is evident in the Danish case is a clear shift from an agenda emphasizing production-based agricultural policy to a collective consumption-based food policy, a shift that is likely to be replicated in some other EU member states.

MULTILEVEL GOVERNANCE

A key area of interest in relation to agriculture in terms of economic patriotism is that of multilevel governance. Distinctive national configurations can be detected in member states – in the UK, France and Germany: respectively, neo-liberal, *dirigiste* and ordo-liberal. However, as Clift and Woll (2012) note, 'Regulation of economic activity is today much more internationally intertwined and can no longer be neatly separated into national governance and trade relations. Instead, much regulation has become transnational.' In the case of agriculture, some of the traditional economic nationalist instruments are feasible and indeed strongly present. Tariffs, subsidies and favoured market access (in relation to countries outside the EU) are all deployed, while the UK is increasingly emphasizing public procurement as a key instrument to pursue its food policy objectives. This enables government purchasers to prioritize food purchases that meet sustainability criteria. The Commission is more than a neutral umpire brokering a compromise, but has developed its own vision of how the CAP should evolve which maintains some elements of economic patriotism while also advancing understandings derived from sustainability (Swinnen 2008).

One more general question is how well the concept can travel outside France, particularly within an EU context. Is EU supranational market-making compatible with economic patriotism?' The EU has shown that it can seek to identify and foster 'European champions', but the divergences among leading member states over how to respond to food security challenges shows how contested are interpretations of economic patriotism. One view is unlikely to prevail, but any compromise position may be riven with so many contradictions as to make it ineffective as a frame for policy.

CONCLUSION

Given that traditional industrial policy has acquired a bad reputation, a key question is how 'the new politics of industrial policy plays out – and this is one of the crucial terrains of economic patriotism, both in discourse and in practice' (Clift and Woll, 2012). As far as agriculture is concerned, there are substantial elements of continuity with the 20th century. Some of the forces for change have been weakened, while old discourses such as food security have been revived. However, there will not be a simple reversion to the policies of the past while the importance of climate change as a driver will ensure that the sustainability discourse makes an important contribution to the framing of policy.

The revival of food security narratives has certainly provide a rallying point for those who would like to see traditional productionist approaches to agriculture restored. These discourses can be seen as having a close link to understandings of economic patriotism. However, policy responses to a tighter world food supply and demand balance are highly contested. The exceptional nature of agricultural policy makes it difficult to generalize from it other policy arenas. It does provide a setting in which one can examine how multilevel governance affects the viability of economic patriotism.

The EU level is not incompatible with economic patriotism. It has been suggested here that it is a novel co-existence of liberal market-oriented elements with regulated, co-ordinated capitalist ones, for example in terms of efforts to reduce information asymmetries between producers and consumers. The balance of forces at the European level is highly complex and to some extent unpredictable, although enlargement has to some extent tilted the balance more in the direction of a liberal interpretation. Regulation survives through protection and subsidy, although the budget is more a mechanism for redistributing funds rather than pursuing particular policy goals. Policy has moved in a more market-oriented direction and it is difficult to see that being reversed, given the forces that have driven that adjustment, even if some of them have weakened more recently.

Biographical note: Wyn Grant is Professor of Politics at the University of Warwick.

NOTE

1 Eurobarometer survey data available at http://ec.europa.eu/public_opinion/index_en.htm

REFERENCES

Barling, D. (2008) 'Reframing UK food security: prices, capacity and sustainability', *Food Ethics* 3: 17–18.

Bounds, A. (2008) 'EU rejects call to limit food imports', *Financial Times*, 28 April.

Cabinet Office (2008a) *Food Matters: Towards a Strategy for the 21st Century*, London: Cabinet Office Strategy Unit.

Cabinet Office (2008b) *Food: An Analysis of the Issues*, London: Cabinet Office Strategy Unit.

Clift, B. and Woll, C. (2012) 'Economic patriotism: reinventing control over open markets', *Journal of European Public Policy* 19(3), http://dx.doi.org/10.1080/13501763.2011.638117.

Daugbjerg, C. and Swinbank, A. (2008) 'Curbing agricultural exceptionalism: the EU's response to external challenge', *The World Economy* 60: 631–52.
Defra (2008) *Ensuring the UK's Food Security in a Changing World*, available at http://archive.defra.gov.uk/foodfarm/pdf/Ensuring-UK-Food-Security-in-a-Changing-World_170708.pdf (accessed 1 December 2011).
European Commission (2009) 'The Communication on agricultural product quality policy', available at http://ec.europa.eu/agriculture/quality/policy/communication_en.htm (accessed 1 December 2011).
European Commission (2010) 'The CAP towards 2020', available at http://ec.europa.eu/agriculture/cap-post-2013/communication/com2010.672-en.pdf (accessed 1 December 2011).
Gamble, A. (2006) 'The European dimension', *The British Journal of Politics and International Relations* 8(1): 34–49.
Grant, W. (1995) 'Is agricultural policy still exceptional?', *The Political Quarterly* 66(3): 156–69.
Grant, W. (2010) 'Policy instruments in the Common Agricultural Policy', *West European Politics* 33(1): 22–38.
Hall, B. (2008) 'Europe's CAP holds "answer" to food crisis', *Financial Times*, 27 April.
Halpin, D. (2005) 'Agricultural interest groups and global challenges: decline and resilience', in D. Halpin (ed.), *Surviving Global Change: Agricultural Interest Groups in Comparative Perspective*, Aldershot: Ashgate, pp. 1–28.
Lowe, P., Phillipson, J. and Lee, R.P. (2008) 'Socio-technical innovation for sustainable food choices: roles for social science', *Trends in Food Science and Technology* 19(5): 226–33.
Marsden, T., Lee, R., Flynn, A. and Thankappan, S. (2009) *The New Regulation and Governance of Food*, Abingdon: Routledge.
Michelsen, J. (2008). 'Changes of agriculture and food policy – the Danish case', Paper prepared for the workshop on *Regulatory Reform and Policy Changes* at the XV NOPSA Conference, Tromsø, August.
Paul, K.T. (2009) 'Food safety: a matter of taste?', Academisch Proefschrift, University of Amsterdam.
Swinnen, J. (ed.) (2008) *The Perfect Storm? The Political Economy of the Fischler Reforms of the Common Agricultural Policy*, Brussels: Centre for European Policy Studies.

European armament co-operation and the renewal of industrial policy motives

Catherine Hoeffler

ABSTRACT This article explores economic patriotism within the evolution of European defence procurement policies. As European integration advances, the nature of the *patrie* underpinning interventions in defence industries evolves, and becomes partially post-national. That said, 'national' boundaries endure, and special relationship among national actors continue to exist. European co-operation in armaments production involves an ambiguous blend of partial liberalization *and* the implementation of industrial policy at a new level. Tensions among actors about both the nature of defence industrial policy (liberal vs protectionist) and its level of implementation (national/European/global) explain the evolution of the European prerogatives in this sector.

1. HAGGLING OVER DEFENCE: THE STATE'S DEMISE IN THE ARMAMENT SECTOR?

The armament industry has historically been one of the most regulated sectors. Military sovereignty, defined as the state's capacity to possess arms and maintain security of supply in defence acquisition, is one of the fundamental features of modern nation-states (Tilly 1990; Weber [1922] 2002). Even for liberal economists like Adam Smith, the need for military sovereignty legitimized both the dominant role of the state's industrial interests in the armament sector and the exclusion of market forces from this field (Smith [1776] 1998). However, European armament policies have profoundly changed since the end of the Cold War. Market-based reforms and the development of European co-operation increasingly appear to challenge the control of the state over its defence sector and the pursuit of national protectionist regulation.

Arms-producing countries such as France, Germany and the United Kingdom (UK) have promoted more co-operation and integration in order to harmonize their armament procurement policies and create a demand large enough to sustain European national firms, since fragmented national markets were too small in a context of budget decline (Schmitt 2000).

Backed by political will, co-operation in armament matters has steadily increased. Supported by the development of the European Security and Defence Policy (ESDP), governments have called for the creation of a European armament policy (Masson 2003) and have created many European rules and organizations regarding armaments. In particular, Europe has seen the creation of OCCAR (*Organisation conjointe de coopération en matière d'armement*), which represents the integration of armament programmes management, the Letter of Intent regarding intra-community equipment transfers; the creation of the European Defence Agency (EDA) in 2004; and more recently the 'defence package' in 2009, which contained a directive on transfers and one on defence public contracts. The novelty of these developments is twofold. First, it is the first time that organizations and rules regarding procurement have been institutionalized at the European level – against former *ad hoc* multinational co-operative venues – thus leading to a partial denationalization of defence procurement. Second, these organizations and rules are framed in liberal terms. The market is the driving norm-shaping European endeavours: co-operative programmes should be implemented in a market-oriented manner, focused on competition and cost-effectiveness, while national defence markets are liberalized.

Do these changes mark the end of the specificity of defence markets and a move away from nationally embedded protectionist practices? Are European market-oriented rules and organizations curtailing governments' capacity to pursue national industrial policy strategies in the defence sector? In the following, I will argue that these changes do not signal the end of defence industrial strategies, but rather their reinvention at the level of the European Union (EU). States' industrial strategies, defined as the various instruments with the objective of maintaining national sovereignty, no longer proceed only at the national level and through national protectionism. On the contrary, arms-producing countries have promoted market-oriented procurement and liberalization at the European level as industrial strategies intended to support national and European firms. This contribution suggests that the economic patriotism categories developed by Clift and Woll (2012) in this collection provides insights into the development of EU competences in defence procurement by demonstrating the evolution of the nature and types of national industrial strategies.

Focusing on the Europeanization of defence procurement, this contribution shows that governments use the European level as a new territory for economic patriotism in the armament sector. Although there is no shift of loyalty to the EU level, supranational market-making regulation is promoted as a means to sustain European firms. Using the different analytical categories of economic patriotism sheds light on why states promote this partial denationalization and marketization of defence procurement, but also on the conflicts and combination between different options. The new emphasis on market forces does not mean the demise of national strategies but instead their new framing at European level (Jabko 2006).

This contribution is structured as follows. The first section deals with theoretical approaches explaining the development of European competences in this policy domain and discusses their connection with categories of economic patriotism. I then analyse the reinvention and reinforcement of industrial policy logics in defence procurement at the European level from two angles. The second section explores the changes in European co-operative armament programmes and shows how states combine liberal and protectionist measures on different European territories. The third section charts the evolution of European regulation of defence markets, illustrating the combination between market liberalization and industrial strategies. Taken together, these two sections highlight the extent to which governments use the EU as a new level of industrial policy. Finally, the conclusion points out the limits of the supranational economic patriotism in defence.

2. THEORIES OF ARMAMENT CO-OPERATION IN EUROPE AND THE ISSUE OF DEFENCE INDUSTRIAL POLICY

The development of European organizations and rules in this industrial sector has been analysed through a range of theoretical approaches. While some authors underline the exogenous causes for renewed European integration such as changes in military environment after the Cold War and the development of a European defence policy (Britz and Eriksson 2005), the impact of American industrial mergers at the beginning of the 1990s (Guay and Callum 2002) or globalization (James 2002), others have looked more thoroughly into the endogenous causes and mechanisms of change in Europe. In doing so, this latter group contributed to integrating the understudied armament policy sector into European studies, in particular by highlighting the influence of European institutional actors or firms in the process (Fligstein 2006; Guay 1996, 1997; Mörth 2003) as well as a process of Europeanization of armament policies (Britz 2008, 2010; Britz and Eriksson 2000; Mawdsley 2000). In particular, Malena Britz (2010) offers a fruitful perspective on the Europeanization of defence industry policies by analysing the role of marketization. Marketization refers to the process by which national authorities adopt largely similar liberal norms such as privatization, cost-effective procurement and open defence markets. This trend is indeed observable to varying degrees in the UK, Germany, France and Sweden (Britz 2008, 2010; Britz and Eriksson 2000; Hartley 1998; Hoeffler 2008, 2011; Mawdsley 2000, 2002).

Building on Britz's approach to the market as a norm (see also Jabko 2006), this contribution nonetheless suggests that studying marketization and Europeanization 'hand-in-hand' only explains one part of the story: why relative convergence led to the institutionalization of Europe in this policy domain. Yet conflicts between governments over the precise shape of European competences in armament matters show that 'going European' does not imply decreasing national interests in armament matters. The problems in the management of the A400M military aircraft stand as a notable example of renewed state intervention whenever governments felt it necessary to defend nationally defined interests. International political economy offers insight into how European rules and organizations have been shaped by national industrial strategies. European solutions represent a new level of industrial policy, but European institutions also reflect diverging national norms about the role the EU.

This contribution demonstrates that the lens of economic patriotism sheds insights onto the various dimensions of this debate, in particular the differences between national vs European intervention and liberal vs protectionist measures. The concept of economic patriotism is a useful heuristic to grasp both the changes in nature (from protectionist to liberal) and in the level of implementation (with renewed emphasis on Europe) of the national industrial strategies of arms-producing states. Following the introduction to this volume, economic patriotism is defined as 'economic choices which seek to discriminate in favour of particular social groups, firms, or sectors understood by the decision-makers as "insiders" because of their territorial status' (Clift and Woll, 2012). Types of economic patriotism vary according to different dimensions, such as the economic space of reference (national and European), and policy content (conservative or liberal).

An economic patriotism approach has three advantages. First, it does not postulate the dilution of states' industrial strategies within supranational and/or liberal measures. Second, by focusing on the territory of public policy, it highlights the potential conflicts arising from the combination of different territories (national, EU, or European co-operation outside the EU), rather than seeing the uploading of defence industry policy to the EU level as functional and automatic. Third, within the European level, it allows us to think about two different meanings that are given to the EU: namely as a territory of regulation where market making is promoted as an industrial strategy (strategic regional integration); or as a political territory where protectionism is recreated at a supranational level (defensive regionalism). Rather than opposing liberal and protectionist measures and rather than seeing co-ordination at the European level either as a zero-sum game between levels or as a functional response without conflict, economic patriotism allows us to grasp the role of the EU. Most importantly, it allows us to perceive the contested frontiers and nature of the EU. The evolution and limits of its organizations and rules can be explained by the consensus or conflicts over different nature and levels of economic patriotism.

3. CO-OPERATIVE ARMAMENT PROCUREMENT: IMPLEMENTING INDUSTRIAL POLICY IN A MARKET-ORIENTED ENVIRONMENT

Co-operative armament programmes constitute a tool of economic patriotism at the European level, both in their goals and in the territories they cover. The recent emphasis put on market-oriented procurement does not mean the demise of national industrial strategies, quite the opposite. On the one hand denationalization and market-oriented co-operation were initially considered a prerequisite for better co-operation, which in turn was supposed to sustain European industrial capacity. On the other, the very process of co-operation shows the loosening of liberal norms and the intervention of states within co-operation. European co-operation on programmes thus combines liberal and protectionist practices. As for the territories they cover, Europe is fragmented in several sometimes overlapping territories: patriotism is not so much attached to the EU as to different European organizations or subgroups of states.

3.1. *Ad hoc* programme-driven co-operation: national economic nationalism

European co-operative programmes date back to the end of the 1950s and the 1960s, involving mostly France, the UK and Germany (Hébert and Hamiot 2004). The organizational pattern of co-operation shows the clear pursuit of national industrial interests within it: states controlled the process and co-operation served national industrial interests. Co-operation was organized around *ad hoc* programmes, without structures and mechanisms of co-operation being institutionalized. Nations would co-operate within a programme with the leadership given to one state. Management was the competence of an intergovernmental organization where all positions were duplicated so that the interests of all nations would be equally defended. This was the case for instance with the DFHB (*Deutsch-französisches Hubschrauber Büro*), created to produce the Tiger helicopter. The industrial organization mirrored the intergovernmental one: industrial co-operation began with simple subcontracting contracts and built towards further integration with the creation of transnational '*groupes d'intérêt économique*'. The distribution of industrial activities reflected strategies of protecting and enhancing national technological expertise and economic involvement. The principle of '*juste retour*' encapsulated such national strategies (Hayward 1997): the industrial work-share had to match the exact financial participation of states in the programmes. The way co-operative programmes were organized clearly shows the states' control of the process and the *national* territory of economic patriotism.

This organizational pattern came to be criticized in the early 1990s, the subordination of management to national industrial interests being blamed for its lack of cost effectiveness. Incentives for change paved the way for the creation of an integrated and market-oriented procurement. Governments undertook many initiatives to promote co-operation through programmes, either by improving their efficiency or by trying to identify common military needs that could be fulfilled in co-operation; both of which aim at sustaining European firms.

3.2. Managing co-operative programmes: old protectionist recipes in new liberal bottles

The rules and organizations dealing with co-operative programmes are emblematic of the central role of national norms of defence procurement in explaining

European evolutions. The UK, but also Germany and France, has undergone transformations in the norms and organization of defence procurement along liberal norms, what Britz (2010) refers to as 'marketization'. These changes have been uploaded onto the European level, so as to organize co-operative programmes accordingly. Yet the emphasis put on partial liberalization and denationalization of co-operative procurement does not mean the demise of national industrial strategies. Firstly, market-oriented norms of procurement are not opposed to but complementary to industrial strategies. Cost-effective and market-oriented procurement was considered a prerequisite for the very launch of programmes that were in turn dependent on their market-oriented procurement. Second, practice shows that those norms did not survive long when it came to defending national interests in procurement, pointing to the renewal of state interventions in this sector.

Attempts to create a European armament agency got underway at the beginning of the 1990s (Masson and Paulin 2005; Mezzadri 2000). The 1992 Maastricht Treaty mentioned the creation of a European armament agency that was to co-ordinate national procurement policies. However, given the slow pace of the process, France and Germany decided to create an intergovernmental agency. Initially designed to be a single Franco-German institution, OCCAR was created by France, Germany, the UK and Italy in December 1996, consolidated in 1998, and given the status of legal entity in 2001 (Mawdsley 2003). Its goal is to manage co-operative programmes: it replaces bilateral or trilateral organizations such as the DFHB for the management of the Tiger helicopter.

OCCAR's goals reflect attempts to reconcile liberalization and industrial strategy at the European level. OCCAR's policy is based on the so-called Baden Baden principles announced in 1995 by the German and French governments. These principles outline the preference given to armaments produced by OCCAR members' industries, the promotion of competition, the search for cost–benefit efficiency, and a shift away from the rule of strict *juste retour* to a globalized *juste retour* (Schmitt 2000). Competition is promoted both as a functional response to excess costs, seen as the consequence of biased markets, and as a normative precept playing down traditional industrial policy tools. The change from the strict to the globalized *juste retour* is emblematic of the implementation of national industrial strategies within a liberal context. On the one hand, it is meant to blur the direct and short-term causal relations between one state and its participating industries; the defence of national interests through the rule of *juste retour* had been regarded as the cause of the co-operative programmes' inefficiency because it triggered overly complicated industrial organization, thus hampering efficiency. On the other hand, the introduction of the globalized *juste retour* was also intended to give more flexibility to programme management and to provide industries with a more stable and predictable regulatory and budgetary framework, which can be read as a new industrial policy (Levy 2006).

In practice, however, co-operative programmes reveal persistent protectionism, be it through OCCAR, the EDA or the latest directive. Measures to open

European co-operative programmes to competition in OCCAR are implemented rather restrictively and are overturned by governments when important industrial issues are at stake. Firstly, opening competition to foreign competitors is conditioned by a unanimous vote; it thus seems impossible in strategic sectors. In other words, the OCCAR principles create preference for firms stemming from participating states. The question of real competition among prime-contractors is here questionable. Historically the armament industries of the biggest arms-producing countries have already merged in the sectors that lend themselves more to co-operation (aerospace, helicopters, missiles). Thus, with the emergence of European champions through mergers, there is even less competition than before.[1] Even if competition is part of a wider search for efficiency, it appears to be more of a rallying banner and a legitimization tool (Jabko 2006) than a reality for big European firms. Secondly, even when it is promoted, market-oriented management of OCCAR programmes is overcome by states intervening to shape the outcomes so as to defend national industrial interests. Despite being the very symbol of OCCAR's creation, the abandonment of the *juste retour* has so far not been fully implemented for several reasons. It would undermine incentives for other countries to join co-operative OCCAR programmes, which would go against states' interests in fostering larger European demand. For instance, the Tiger helicopter programme, OCCAR's founding programme, remains organized around the *juste retour* principle. Following a clear 'infant-industry' strategy, the participation of Spain in 2000 was granted on condition that their Spanish industries could use it to obtain technological competencies they did not possess beforehand. The newer A400M programme, which is symbolic of the commercial approach to management (Joana and Smith 2006), still reflects national industrial strategies, as the industrial organization for the engine's production shows; against the very principle of non-intervention, states intervened to counter the wish of Airbus to grant the engine contract to Pratt & Whitney, a North American firm (*Le Monde*, 3 May 2003). The solution was eventually found in the form of a European consortium, composed of the four biggest engine firms stemming from participating A400M member states.

The conflicts between governments and Airbus over the 400M delays have participated in a shift in norms at the European level. Although competition is still promoted so as to reduce costs, the importance of national industrial strategies is acknowledged as being part of co-operative ventures. For instance, co-operative projects initiated by member states to be handled by the EDA (so-called category B projects) reflect work-share arrangements between governments: the latter negotiate the industrial plan before handing projects to the EDA, whose task is then to manage work-share compromises whenever another member state wants to join in the project.[2] Moreover, under the 2009 defence procurement directive, co-operative programmes are exempt from competition rules, as we shall see in more detail in the next section. This indicates that governments agreed to keep the European co-operative programmes out of the Commission's scrutiny, so as to use them to maintain the ability to sustain insider firms.

All these elements indicate that despite partial denationalization and marketization, co-operating through European programmes represents a form of protectionist economic patriotism at the European level, since governments have created organizations and rules that enable industrial strategies.

3.3. Fostering more co-operative programmes through the European Defence Agency

Alongside improving programme management, another way to sustain defence firms is to harmonize some of the military needs of nation states in order to foster more co-operative programmes. Facing the limits of the managerial approach through OCCAR, arms-producing states have focused more on the military side of armament policy at the European level as a new industrial strategy. From the issue of 'how to procure', debates in national and European arenas have progressively been articulated around the question of 'what to procure' in the wake of the definition of the European Security and Defence Policy. Defence integration has served as a catalyst for armament integration (Mawdsley 2004): new military needs put the necessity to maintain industrial capacity able to provide military equipment back on the European political agenda. The shift from *armament* to *defence* agency reflects the new emphasis put on military needs: the European Defence Agency was created in 2004 within the framework of a Joint Action of the Common Foreign and Security Policy.[3]

The EDA's organization and goals indeed show the interdependency between two policy dynamics at the European level, namely those of the defence and armament industry. This interdependency is organic and functional. First, the EDA occupies a nodal position between armament and defence, being on the one hand presided over by the High Representative of the Union for Foreign Affairs and Security Policy and standing under the Council's oversight, and on the other hand being embedded in the industrial side, with links to industry and OCCAR. This interdependency is also functional, since military goals are complementary to industrial ones. According to the Council Joint Action, the EDA's mission is 'to support the Member States and the Council in their effort to improve European defence capabilities in the field of crisis management and to sustain the European Security and Defence Policy as it stands now and develops in the future' (Article 2). Although industrial concerns are stated in its goals, the sole mission ascribed to the Agency is expressed in military terms. Yet the EDA is given four functions that are primarily industrial: developing defence capabilities in the field of crisis management; promoting and enhancing European armament co-operation; strengthening the European defence industrial and technological base (DTIB); and creating a competitive European defence equipment market. This shift towards military determinants can thus be understood as a necessary complement to the management approach, since only the definition of a shared perception of threat and shared military needs can provide the European DITB with large enough armament contracts. The development of European organizations and rules regarding co-operative programmes can be understood as a new means for states to pursue industrial strategies.

3.4. One European *patrie*? The fragmentation of the EU and the centrality of states' strategies

While co-operating at the European level serves national industrial strategies, the frontiers of this space of co-operation have to be clarified. Although the EDA aims to promote co-operation at the EU level, co-operation seems to be fragmented in various and changing coalitions which are inside or outside the EU.

In OCCAR, preference is given to firms from member states or from *ad hoc* participating states. Opening competition to external competitors being dependent on a unanimous vote, it is therefore very unlikely to happen in strategic sectors. In other words, the OCCAR principles create preference for insider firms on a variable basis. Moreover, the geography of OCCAR does not match that of the EU, with for instance the participation of Turkey in one particular programme.

The same pattern of restricted format of co-operation is visible with the EDA: until now, the EDA has developed only very few 'common' programmes, and only in Research & Technology.[4] Significant programmes in armament are category B projects, i.e., proposed by a coalition of states which can decide under which conditions other member states can join. The variability of coalitions is seen as a condition ensuring that historical arms-producing states can avoid free-riding strategies from other states. Moreover, the EDA is a contested organization within the EU. Although arms-producing states share an interest in fostering the harmonization of military needs, they do not share a unified conception of Europe: the EDA is thus at the crossroads of different institutional logics, which oppose the EU to North Atlantic Treaty Organization (NATO), or European industrial policy to a market-centred approach (Bátora 2009). Intense debate pitted the French plan of an extensive conception of the EDA against a more restrictive approach supported by the UK, for example. Diverging perceptions explain the current poor financing and restricted power of the EDA. All these elements point to the paradoxical conclusion that integration at the European level is dependent on it remaining optional for states, so that they can choose whether or not to use the EU channel and with which partners to work.

Another dimension of the EU fragmentation lies in the institutional architecture of organizations dealing with programmes. Many actors in the field therefore consider the organizations as complementary: the EDA should foster more programmes to be launched through the identification of common needs, whereas OCCAR could be the executive agency managing these programmes in a second phase. This conception is shared by the Council which stated in 2008 that OCCAR represents a favoured partner to the EDA and that links between both organizations should be tightened (Council of the European Union 2008). According to the Common Action, an administrative arrangement is required for the EDA to build partnerships with other non-EU organizations. This arrangement was drafted in October 2009. Yet it was vetoed in the Council by the Cypriot government, which refused a partnership with OCCAR because of the participation of Turkey in this organization.[5] This shows that there is no unified EU territory of armament programmes, since OCCAR does not officially belong to the EU architecture.

If there is patriotism in the sense that European programmes do serve national industrial strategies, the *patrie* is not so much a clear territory as varying and overlapping organizations or coalitions either inside or outside the EU framework.

4. THE MOVE TO THE LATEST 'DEFENCE PACKAGE': AN AMBIGUOUS INSTRUMENT OF SUPRANATIONAL ECONOMIC PATRIOTISM

The persistence of Article 346 has always been the symbol of the power of the states in this sector. This treaty provision allows states to exempt national defence contracts from community procurement rules on the basis of an extensive list of warfare equipment, formulated in 1958, which is related to the essential interests of national defence. States have so far made extensive use of this provision to escape single market procurement rules. The latest critical development has been the 'defence package' voted on by the European Parliament in 2009, which encompasses one Communication and two Directives, one of which deals with defence procurement.[6]

The Transfer Directive is the most visible tool of supranational economic patriotism of a liberal nature: governments agreed on a set of measures designed to facilitate trade within the EU. This section is devoted to the Directive on defence and security procurement,[7] which reduces to a very small core the competencies that will remain outside European competitive single market rules. In other words, it opens the majority of domestic defence contracts to competition at the European level. At first sight, this directive therefore seems at odds with any considerations of economic nationalism, since it deprives national public authorities of the ability to give preference to national firms. Relying on the analysis of the negotiations (the importance of which has been underlined by Eising and Jabko [2001]) and of national cognitive and institutional changes regarding defence industry policy, this contribution argues that this directive is best explained by an ambiguous combination of liberal and protectionist variants of supranational economic patriotism.

4.1. The arms-producing states' interests in liberalizing European domestic armaments market: a liberal supranational economic patriotism

A symbol of the continued industrial policy practices at the national level, Article 346 has been the target of repeated initiatives by the European Commission (CEC 1996, 1997, 2003, 2004, 2006), which has tried to limit the extensive use of this exemption. Still, before 2007, when the Commission published its proposal, governments had opposed any coercive supranational rule regarding domestic armament contracts. One key example of these oppositions is the Code of Conduct on Defence markets adopted by governments through the EDA in 2005: emblematic of soft law mechanisms, this Code was meant to co-ordinate national contracts procedure so as to reduce the use of Article 296 and make contracts more transparent and open (EDA 2005). It was used by states to convince the Commission not to push forward any directives,[8] but without success.

The adoption of the directive is partly explained by a shift in the European Commission's framing strategy on this topic (Mörth 2000, 2003), from an orthodox market approach towards the inclusion of industrial concerns. This change made the Commission's proposal acceptable, since it presented the liberalization of European armament market as the only solution to enhance European firms' competitiveness in global competition. Moreover, the Commission's will to limit the use of Article 346 has been backed by a few symbolic cases of the European Court of Justice,[9] which for the first time condemned governments for their extensive use of Article 346. However, these evolutions proved crucial only in interaction with changes at national levels. National defence industry policies also reflect liberal definitions of how defence contracts should be governed. Since the UK and Germany have always stressed the importance of market-oriented procurement more than their French counterparts, it is surprising that this directive was negotiated and approved under the 2008 French Presidency of the EU. This move from French officials, the least expected to support such a measure, exemplifies the liberal conception of economic patriotism at the European level. Firstly, states do anticipate future potential constraints imposed by marketization and therefore try to shape the process rather than reject it. For example, France had adopted in 2004 a decree[10] which was already close to the Commission's directive proposal: it aimed to introduce more competition, but with contracts procedure adapted to the specificities of the defence market. This decree was deliberately shaped so as to avoid future conflict with the Commission and make France look proactive in liberalizing. French negotiators were therefore mandated to push for this directive since the government felt it had already adopted 'virtuous' practices.[11] Another example of this anticipation of market constraints is the symbolic importance of the European Court of Justice (ECJ) cases during the negotiations: they were used as arguments to convince some reluctant negotiators that a compromise would be better than no directive at all.[12] Secondly, regarding norms, liberalization was no longer considered a threat to insider firms but rather a tool to enhance their competitiveness, echoing the Commission's framing. Thirdly, arms-producing states promoted the directive as a way to expand market opportunities for their insiders. European firms able to compete for important contracts originate from arms-producing countries such as the UK, France, Germany or Italy. Those countries therefore gain from liberalizing, since the directive should enforce more transparency in other states' defence contracts. Market integration was sought in order to compensate for the structural disadvantage of European firms in comparison with those of the United States (US), the latter benefiting from a large domestic market whilst European firms are restricted to domestic or co-operative markets.

4.2. Supranational economic patriotism without a European preference

Notwithstanding this consensus, the question of promoting the European industrial base against foreign firms has been the subject of opposition between two conceptions of the role of the EU which can be traced back to the beginning of the 1990s (Walker and Gummett 1993). In the first conception, 'Fortress Europe', defended notably by France, the EU is used as a shield against globalization. Promoting a 'European preference' refers to the category of *defensive regional integration* developed by Clift and Woll (2012). However a majority of states supported another conception which can be characterized as a strategic regional integration: it consists of opening markets without any preference given to European firms. In this respect, the directive reflects the liberal type. Nevertheless, this cannot be interpreted as a lack of economic patriotism; the directive instead represents a combination of different types of economic patriotism.

More than a convergence of conceptions, the directive reflects an 'ambiguous consensus' (Palier 2002) about the very meaning of European industrial policy:

> [T]he directive was considered as an industrial policy. But there are many different interpretations of this notion. For pro-market negotiators, opening markets is helping enterprises. In a more traditional conception, helping the firms, it's about doing protectionism. The solution? It was in the middle. This directive is a good system, which both promotes big [European] programmes and triggers more competitiveness.[13]

Indeed, for the Commission, this directive is no 'industrial policy', but is more about competitiveness and promoting European co-operative programmes. As one Commission official puts it:

> [W]ith this directive, we accept things that are not really orthodox from a market point of view. Through this directive, we do not only tolerate cooperation through programmes, we encourage it.[14]

Thus, the exclusion of European programmes from the competition rules is considered a tool at the European level in order to help promote European firms.

The absence of European preference is promoted as a liberal means of supporting European industries: for negotiators, it was supposed to encourage other governments – and most importantly the US – to open their domestic markets, as the Recital 18 puts it: 'Member States should press for increasingly open markets. Their partners should also demonstrate openness, on the basis of internationally-agreed rules, in particular as concerns open and fair competition.' As a negotiator explains:

> 'the recital 18 is a political message: instead of saying 'we close ourselves', we say 'we want you to open your market as well'. There is a shift from a European preference logic to strengthening our firms by trying to find market opportunities abroad for them.'[15]

The directive also allows member states to choose whether they want to open their market to foreign competitors, thus maintaining differences between countries.[16] However, this does not mean that the EU is not a territory of economic patriotism, but rather that the role given to the EU is to promote European firms by expanding markets on a global scale.

5. CONCLUSION: THE LIMITS OF SUPRANATIONAL ECONOMIC PATRIOTISM

This contribution has focused on how governments use the EU as a new level of economic patriotism in defence procurement. It has shown that even partially denationalized and liberal measures account for new national industrial policy strategies. Through the emphasis given to market-making functions, the EU appears to be a regulatory arena aiming primarily at sustaining firms through facilitating trade, enhancing competitiveness and expanding markets. Although less developed and only partially linked to the EU level *stricto sensu*, co-operative programmes represent the 'positive' side of integration and economic patriotism, since they allow states to discriminate in favour of national firms.

However, this does not mean that the EU represents a stabilized territory for defence procurement. The EU appears as a policy space competing with the national and transatlantic levels for the definition of defence industrial policy in government decision-making. The existence of European competences implies by no means the end of a process or an automatic uploading without conflict.

In this respect, I shall conclude by emphasizing one important limit to European industrial policy related to the definition of economic patriotism: the very identification of insiders, or put differently, a *European* industrial base in defence. As an interviewee puts it: 'it's difficult to define what is European in those defence groups. They are either national or global players.'[17] Big European firms such as EADS or MBDA are still organized along national lines to a large extent, not even to mention political interference that this 'Europeanization' has fostered. For instance, whereas French interventionism is taken for granted, German chancellor Angela Merkel has mentioned several times her wish to see the German state participate in the capital of EADS (Bruneau 2011; Von Tlesenhausen 2006).[18] Liberalization and internationalization have not erased nationally defined loyalties. They may have even reinforced national stakes instead. In addition to this possible renationalization, the EU is challenged by the transatlantic strategies of firms such as BAe, for instance. Even some French officials recognize that the survival of European firms may depend on their ability to tie themselves to American counterparts in order to enter the American market, 'because Europe is too small for such industrial players'.[19] In that respect, the limits of the EU in defence industry policy also stem from the problematic definition of the insiders, whose survival paradoxically appears to depend on their ability to succeed beyond European frontiers.

Biographical note: Catherine Hoeffler recently obtained her Ph.D. in Political Science at Sciences Po, Centre d'études européennes, Paris, and is currently a post-doctoral researcher at CEPEL, Montpellier, France.

ACKNOWLEDGEMENTS

The author thanks Ben Clift, Cornelia Woll and two anonymous referees for comments on an earlier draft of this contribution.

NOTES

1 Competition is much more important for specialized equipment manufacturers that act as subcontractors than it is for large industrial groups, which nowadays play more of an overall role of integrating the various components into weapon systems.
2 Interview with an EDA official, June 2010. This analysis draws on the 71 interviews I have conducted between January 2007 and June 2010 with politicians, civil and military ministry officials and industry representatives from Germany, France and the UK, as well as with officials from the EDA, the European Commission and OCCAR, on the topic of European cooperation in armament matters.
3 Council Joint Action, 2004/551/CFSP, 12 July 2004 (OJ L 245/17).
4 Joint Investment Programmes Force Protection and ICET, see: http://www.eda.europa.eu/Otheractivities/RandTjointinvestment/Investingmoretogether (accessed 31 May 2011).
5 Interview with an EDA official, June 2010.
6 For these three documents, see: http://ec.europa.eu/enterprise/sectors/defence/documents/ (accessed 31 May 2011).
7 Directive 2009/81/EC of the European Parliament and of the Council of 13 July 2009 on the coordination of procedures for the award of certain works contracts, supply contracts and service contracts by contracting authorities or entities in the fields of defence and security, and amending Directives 2004/17/EC and 2004/18/EC, OJ L 216, 20.8.2009, pp. 76–136
8 Interviews with French officials and EDA officials, March 2009 and June 2010.
9 C-414/97 Commission vs Spain in 1999 and C-337/05 Commission vs Italy in 2008.
10 Décret n° 2004-16 du 7 janvier 2004 pris en application de l'article 4 du code des marchés publics et concernant certains marchés publics passés pour les besoins de la défense, *JORF*, 8 janvier 2004.
11 Interviews with French officials, March 2009 and June 2010.
12 Interviews with a French official, June 2010.
13 Interview with a French official, June 2010.
14 Interview with a Commission official, DG Internal Market, June 2010.

15 Interview with a French official, June 2010.
16 The Recital 18 allows governments to choose whether they open their domestic market to non-EU industries or not. This point will be implemented in various ways. For instance, former German Minister of Defence zu Guttenberg underlined that there should be no more taboo about buying non-European weapons (Brumeau 2010). On the contrary, French Defence Minister Alain Juppé states that European preference will be clearly stated in French law (Sénat 2011).
17 Interview with an EDA official, June 2010.
18 A middle ground has been found with a coalition of institutional shareholders.
19 Interview with a French official, June 2010.

REFERENCES

Bátora, J. (2009) 'European Defence Agency: a flashpoint of institutional logics', *West European Politics* 32(6): 1075–98.

Britz, M. (2008) *Europeanization of Defence Industry Policy in the 1990s*, Saarbrücken: VDM Verlag Dr. Müller.

Britz, M. (2010) 'The role of marketization in the Europeanization of defense industry policy', *Bulletin of Science, Technology & Society* 30(3): 176–84.

Britz, M. and Eriksson, A. (2000) 'British, German, and French defence industrial policy in the 1990s', *Swedish Defence Research Establishment, User report.*

Britz, M. and Eriksson, A. (2005) 'The European security and defence policy: a fourth system of European foreign policy?', *Politique européenne* 3(17): 35–62.

Bruneau, C. (2010) 'L'A400M et l'A380 en vedette à Berlin', *Air&Cosmos*, 4 June.

Bruneau, C. (2011) 'Capital d'EADS : les pistes de l'Allemagne', *Le Figaro*, 24 February.

Clift, B. and Woll, C. (2012) 'Economic patriotism: reinventing control over open markets', *Journal of European Public Policy* 19(3), http://dx.doi.org/10.1080/13501763.2011.638117

Commission of the European Communities (1996) 'The challenges facing the European defence-related industry. A contribution for action at European level', COM (96) 10 final.

Commission of the European Communities (1997) 'Implementing European Union strategy on defence', COM (97) 583 final.

Commission of the European Communities (2003) 'European defence-industrial and market issues. Towards an EU defence equipment policy', COM(2003) 113 final.

Commission of the European Communities (2004) 'Green Paper on defence procurement', COM(2004) 608 final.

Commission of the European Communities (2006) 'Interpretative communication of 7 December 2006 on the application of Article 296 of the Treaty in the field of defence procurement', COM(2006) 779 final (not published in the Official Journal).

Council of the European Union (2008) 'Council Conclusions on the ESDP. 2903rd External Relations Council meeting, Brussels, 10 and 11 November', Annex 1.

Eising, R. and Jabko, N. (2001) 'Moving targets: national interests and electricity liberalization in the European Union', *Comparative Political Studies* 34(7): 742–67.

European Defence Agency (2005) 'The code of conduct on defence procurement of the EU member states participating in the Defence Agency', Brussels, 21 November.

Fligstein, N. (2006) 'Sense making and the emergence of a new form of market governance: the case of the European defense industry', *American Behavioral Scientist* 49: 949–60.

Guay, T.R. (1996) 'Integration and Europe's defense industry: a reactive spillover approach', *Policy Studies Journal* 24: 404–19.

Guay, T.R. (1997) 'The European Union, expansion of policy-making, and defense industrial policy', *Journal of European Public Policy* 4: 404–21.

Guay, T. and Callum, R. (2002) 'The transformation and future prospects of Europe's defence industry', *International Affairs* 4: 757–76.
Hartley, K. (1998) 'Defence procurement in the UK', *Defence and Peace Economics* 9(1): 39–61.
Hayward, K. (1997) 'Towards a European weapons procurement process', *EUISS Chaillot Paper 27*, Paris: European Union Institute for Security Studies (EUISS), available at http://www.iss.europa.eu/publications/detail/article/towards-a-european-weapons-procurement-process/ (accessed 19 December 2011).
Hébert, J.-P. and Hamiot, J. (eds) (2004) *Histoire de la coopération européenne dans l'armement*, Paris: CNRS Editions.
Hoeffler, C. (2008) 'La réforme des systèmes d'acquisition d'armement en France et en Allemagne: un retour paradoxal des militaires?', *Revue Internationale de Politique Comparée* 15(1): 133–50.
Hoeffler, C. (2011) 'Armament policies in Europe: the "farewell to arms" of the nation state? A comparative study between Germany, France, the UK and the European Union from 1976 to 2010', Ph.D. dissertation, Department of Political Science, Sciences Po, Paris.
Howorth, J. (2007) *Security and Defence Policy in the European Union*, Basingstoke: Palgrave Macmillan.
Jabko, N. (2006) *Playing the Market. A Political Strategy for Uniting Europe, 1985–2005*, Ithaca, NY, and London: Cornell University Press.
James, A.D. (2002) 'Comparing European responses to defense industry globalization', *Defense & Security Analysis* 18(2): 123–43.
Joana, J. and Smith, A. (2006) 'Changing French military procurement policy: the state, industry and "Europe" in the case of the A400M', *West European Politics* 1: 70–89.
Le Monde (2003) 'La tentation américaine d'Airbus est contestée en Europe', 3 May.
Levy, J.D. (2006) *The State after Statism: New State Activities in the Age of Liberalization*, Cambridge, MA: Harvard University Press.
Masson, H. (2003) 'La politique européenne de l'armement: la méthode des petits pas', *Annuaire stratégique et militaire*, available at http://www.frstrategie.org/barreCompetences/DEFind/politiqueeuropennne.pdf
Masson, H. and Paulin, C. (2005) 'Le marché de défense: concept et réalité', *Notes de la Fondation pour la Recherche Stratégique*, available at http://www.frstrategie.org/barreCompetences/DEFind/marche_defense.pdf
Mawdsley, J. (2000) 'The changing face of European armaments co-operation: continuity and change in British, French, and German armaments policy, 1990–2000', Ph.D. dissertation, Department of Politics, University of Newcastle upon Tyne.
Mawdsley, J. (2002) *European Defence Procurement and Industrial Policy: The Case of Germany*, Sandvika: Centre for European and Asian Studies, Norwegian School of Management.
Mawdsley, J. (2003) 'Arms, agencies and accountability: The tase of OCCAR', *European Security* 12(3–4): 95–111.
Mawdsley, J. (2004) 'The arming of the European Union: explaining the armaments dimension of European security and defence policy', *Perspectives. Central European Review of International Affairs* 22: 7–21.
Mérand, F. (2008) *European Defence Policy: Beyond the Nation State*, Oxford: Oxford University Press.
Mezzadri, S. (2000) 'L'ouverture des marchés de défense: enjeux et modalités', *EUISS Occasional Paper 12*, Paris: European Union Institute for Security Studies (EUISS), available at www.iss.europa.eu/uploads/media/occ012.pdf (accessed 19 December 2011).

Mörth, U. (2000) 'Competing frames in the European Commission – the case of the defence industry and equipment issue', *Journal of European Public Policy* 2: 173–89.
Mörth, U. (2003) *Organizing European Co-operation – The Case of Armaments*, Lanham, MD: Rowman and Littlefield.
Palier, B. (2002) *Gouverner la Sécurité sociale. Les réformes du système français de protection sociale depuis 1945*, Paris: Presses Universitaires de France.
Schmitt, B. (2000) 'From cooperation to integration: defence and aerospace industries in Europe', *EUISS Chaillot Paper 40*, Paris: European Union Institute for Security Studies (EUISS), available at oldeuiss.eu/uploads/media/cp040e.pdf (accessed 19 December 2011).
Smith, A. ([1776] 1998) *An Inquiry into the Nature and Causes of the Wealth of Nations*, Oxford: Oxford University Press.
Tilly, C. (1990) *Coercion, Capital and European States, AD 990–1990*, Oxford: Blackwell.
Von Tlesenhausen, F. (2006) 'Abschied von Prinzipien', *Financial Times Deutschland*, 13 October.
Walker, W. and Gummett, P. (1993) 'Nationalism, internationalism and the European defence market', *Chaillot Paper 9*, Paris: European Union Institute for Security Studies (EUISS), available at http://www.iss.europa.eu/publications/detail/article/nationalism-internationalism-and-the-european-defence-market/ (accessed 19 December 2011).
Weber, M. ([1922] 2002) *Wirtschaft und Gesellschaft: Grundriss der verstehenden Soziologie*, Tübingen: Mohr.

Index